BUILDING
SENTENCES

THIRD EDITION

BUILDING SENTENCES

Benita Mackie
Professor Emeritus , Catonsville Community College

Shirley Johnsen Rompf
Professor, Catonsville Community College

 Prentice Hall, Englewood Cliffs, New Jersey 07632

Library of Congress Cataloging-in-Publication Data

MACKIE, BENITA, [date]
   Building sentences / BENITA MACKIE, SHIRLEY JOHNSEN ROMPF.—3rd ed.
     p. cm.
   Includes index.
   ISBN 0-13-150138-0
    1. English language—Sentences.   2. English language—Rhetoric.
  3. English language—Grammar. I. Rompf, Shirley Johnsen, [date].
  II. Title.
PE1441.M27   1995
428.8—dc20   94-16909

Acquisitions editor: *Phil Miller*
Project manager: *Edie Riker*
Cover design: *Tom Nery*
Production coordinator: *Robert Anderson*
Editorial assistant: *Joan Polk*

© 1995, 1990, 1985 by Prentice-Hall, Inc.
A Paramount Communications Company
Englewood Cliffs, NJ 07632

Printed in the United States of America

10 9 8 7 6 5 4 3 2 1

ISBN   0-13-150138-0

Prentice-Hall International (UK) Limited, *London*
Prentice-Hall of Australia Pty. Limited, *Sydney*
Prentice-Hall Canada Inc., *Toronto*
Prentice-Hall Hispanoamericana, S.A., *Mexico*
Prentice-Hall of India Private Limited, *New Delhi*
Prentice-Hall of Japan, Inc., *Tokyo*
Simon & Schuster Asia Pte. Ltd., *Singapore*
Editora Prentice-Hall do Brasil, Ltda., *Rio de Janeiro*

Contents

Exercises

6   USING THE VERB *BE*   *87*

Recognizing Forms of the Verb *Be*, **87**
Using the Word *Be*, **87**
Forming the Future Tense, **88**
Forming the Present and Past Tenses, **88**
Forming the Present Perfect and Past Perfect Tenses, **89**
Using the Forms of the Verb *Be* as Helpers, **90**
Suggestions for Writing, **94**

Exercises

7   USING THE PRINCIPAL PARTS OF IRREGULAR VERBS   *105*

Recognizing the Principal Parts of Irregular Verbs, **105**
Using the Principal Parts of Irregular Verbs, **107**
Suggestions for Writing, **108**

Exercises

8   UNDERSTANDING COORDINATION AND SUBORDINATION   *117*

Coordinating and Subordinating within a Sentence, **117**
Coordinating and Subordinating within a Paragraph, **118**
Planning, Writing, and Editing a Paragraph, **119**
Suggestions for Writing, **119**

12 USING SUBORDINATION
Adjective Clauses

13 USING SUBORDINATION
Participial Phrases and Appositive Phrases

14 USING SUBORDINATION
Noun Clauses and Verbal Phrases as Nouns

15 MAINTAINING CONTINUITY
Verbs in Sequence

16 MAINTAINING CONTINUITY
Pronoun Reference and Agreement

17 AVOIDING COMMON SENTENCE ERRORS
Fragments, Comma Splices, and Run-On Sentences

To the Teacher

Building Sentences was written for students who require regular practice to develop and improve writing skills. The text evolved from two assumptions: first, that these students need to acquire a basic sentence sense and, second, that they can do so only by constructing sentences, not by analyzing them or by correcting errors in usage. Thus the text stresses, step by step, how to build a sentence. It does not emphasize analysis, fine points of usage, or grammatical terms although, out of necessity, it does use some grammatical terminology. Instead, the text presents manageable units of language that the students learn to synthesize into increasingly complex sentences. Each of the eighteen chapters, except the last, which is a review of punctuation, consists of explanation and examples accompanied by numerous exercises designed to move students from recognizing to combining to creating.

The order of the chapters was dictated by our experience with the capabilities and needs of students as they begin to build sentences. It does not follow a grammatical sequence of word to phrase to clause. Easier material comes early; structures that have similar uses in a sentence are in the same or adjacent chapters. Thus the more familiar prepositional phrase is presented early and the more difficult noun clause very late; a chapter on the participial phrase and the appositive phrase follows one on the adjective clause, offering similar means of adding information about nouns.

In the third edition of *Building Sentences*, we have continued the revisions of the second edition: retaining the emphasis on writing practice, we eliminated explanatory material and exercises unnecessary to the beginning writer and simplified explanations wherever we could. Exercises and chapters—most extensively, Chapters 3 and 13—are markedly revised. We rewrote and augmented the "Suggestions for Writing" given at the end of each chapter to encourage students to write and to introduce them to writing as a process. The instructor's manual will again contain sample responses to all the exercises, pretests and posttests, and quizzes.

For the third edition, we created a new Chapter 8 to serve as an introduction to the concepts of subordination and coordination within the paragraph as well as within the sentence. Following Chapter 8, the explanatory material within chapters, the revised and rewritten sentence-combining exercises, and the expanded "Suggestions for Writing"—all encourage students to compose paragraphs that are unified, organized, and coherent, appropriately developed, and carefully edited. However, the book remains, as it began, a primer for building sentences.

To the Student

Writing is a skill. Like any other skill, it requires practice. If you want to improve your tennis game, you must play regularly. If you want to improve your piano playing, you must practice the piano regularly. Similarly, if you want to improve your writing, you must write regularly.

As you work through this book, you will be completing many exercises and building sentences of many types. At first you will complete exercises using separate sentences, each unrelated to those that precede and follow. Later you will also be correcting, rewriting, and combining related sentences that form an orderly sequence. These sentences will be connected so that they state an idea and develop it in various ways such as by comparisons, examples, facts, descriptions, or explanations of events. Communicating what you think on a topic usually requires more than one sentence. When several sentences are organized in a connected sequence to develop one topic, the sentences are called a *paragraph* and set off as a unit on the page. (Notice the indentations on this page that mark off the paragraphs.) In Chapter 8, half-way through this workbook, you will be asked to focus directly on building sentences that relate to each other to form a paragraph.

To improve your skills, you will, however, need additional practice in writing about your own experiences. In this book, we suggest that you begin a journal in which you write about what you do or think from day to day. You may want to develop the habit of sitting down at the same place once a day and writing for five or ten minutes about anything that comes into your head. During such free-writing time, do not worry about grammar or spelling—just write. With daily practice, you will find writing easier, and you will probably find yourself thinking of more and more topics to write about.

The "Suggestions for Writing" at the end of the chapters offer you ideas for journal entries and, in the second half of the book, for collecting ideas or information, organizing them, and presenting them in clear paragraphs. First exploring your ideas in a journal will help you in gathering material for any writing assignment.

Write whatever you can. Only by practicing can you improve your writing.

BUILDING
SENTENCES

Building the Sentence Base 1
Subjects, Verbs, and Complements

A sentence is a group of words that expresses a complete thought. It is set off from other sentences by a capital letter at the beginning of the first word and end punctuation—usually a period (.) or a question mark (?)—after the last word.

In this chapter, you will learn that a sentence always has a subject and a verb and sometimes a third element called a **complement**. These two or three elements form the sentence **base**, or foundation. As you work through this chapter, you will learn how to recognize subjects, verbs, and complements and how to combine them to create a base for the simple sentence.

RECOGNIZING NOUNS

When we speak or write, we name persons, places, things, and ideas. The words in a sentence that name persons, places, things, and ideas are called **nouns**.

Singular and Plural Nouns

A noun can name one or more than one person, place, thing, or idea. A noun that names **one** is called a **singular** noun, and a noun that names **more than one** is called a **plural** noun.

We usually change a singular noun to a plural noun by changing its spelling. We form the plural of most nouns by adding an -s or -es at the end of the word. Some nouns, however, require different spelling changes, and a few nouns do not change at all. If you are not sure of the rules for changing nouns from singular to plural, see Appendix A.

The following chart presents examples of singular and plural nouns. Practice pronouncing these nouns. Be sure to pronounce the -s and to add a syllable for words ending in -es. Learn to spell any nouns you do not know.

In the chart, the words *a, an,* and *the,* called articles, are used before the nouns. If you are not sure of the rules for using these three articles, see Appendix B.

PEOPLE		PLACES	
Singular	*Plural*	*Singular*	*Plural*
an artist	the artists	a camp	the camps
a student	the students	a field	the fields
a waitress	the waitresses	an alley	the alleys
a boy	the boys	a dairy	the dairies
a lady	the ladies	a campus	the campuses
a man	the men	a street	the streets
a woman	the women	a building	the buildings

	LIVING THINGS			NONLIVING THINGS	
Singular	*Plural*		*Singular*	*Plural*	
a cat	the cats		a day	the days	
an apple	the apples		an answer	the answers	
a fox	the foxes		an address	the addresses	
a rose	the roses		a tax	the taxes	
a fly	the flies		a knife	the knives	
a puppy	the puppies		a step	the steps	
a sheep	the sheep		an eraser	the erasers	

IDEAS

Singular	*Plural*
an amount	the amounts
an argument	the arguments
a desire	the desires
a feeling	the feelings
an obstacle	the obstacles
a decision	the decisions
a joy	the joys

We can express the idea of more than one by using a plural noun or by naming two or more specifics that form a group. Study the following examples:

		General	*Specific*
1.	*Singular*:	boy	Paul
	Plural:	boys	Paul and Fred
2.	*Singular*:	girl	Thelma
	Plural:	girls	Thelma, Mary, and Gwen
3.	*Singular*:	month	March
	Plural:	months	March and April

As we write sentences, we decide whether to use a plural form or to name specifics.

Examples

1. The *boys* are arriving.
   Paul and *Fred* are arriving.
2. The *judges* selected three *winners*.
   Judge Stone and *Judge Wisdom* selected *Thelma, Mary,* and *Gwen.*
3. My accountant works seven days a week during two *months*.
   My accountant works seven days a week during *March* and *April.*

Nouns that name specifics are called *proper nouns.* Proper nouns begin with a capital letter. If you need a review of the difference between proper nouns and common nouns, see Appendix C.

SHOWING POSSESSION OF NOUNS

Often we need to specify to whom something or someone belongs. That is, we need to use a noun to show **whose**. Nouns that tell whose are called **possessives**.

2

a father	Whose father?	Jack's father
a coat	Whose coat?	Jack's father's coat
the hats	Whose hats?	the cowboys' hats

In these examples, the words *Jack's*, *father's*, and *cowboys'* are possessives. Notice the use of the apostrophe (') and of the letter *s* to show possession:

Jack possesses the father	Jack's father
Jack's father possesses the coat	Jack's father's coat
the cowboys possess the hats	the cowboys' hats

We follow two rules to show possession:

1. If a noun does not end in *s*, we add an apostrophe and an *s* (*Jack's, father's*).
2. If a noun ends in *s*, as most plurals do, we add only an apostrophe (*cowboys'*).

If you need practice in forming or using possessives, turn to Appendix D.

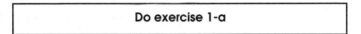

Do exercise 1-a

RECOGNIZING VERBS

In sentences, we use nouns to name subjects or objects—the persons, places, things, or ideas that we are talking or writing about. We use **verbs** to describe actions or to state existence. **Action verbs** such as *grow, learned*, and *will write* tell what someone or something does, did, or will do. **Nonaction verbs** state existence. The most commonly used nonaction verb is *be*. Other nonaction verbs include *appear, become, seem*, and *sound*.

A verb may consist of one word or more than one word. When more than one word is used, the word that pictures the action or states existence is called the **main verb**, and the other words are called **helping verbs** or **helpers**. In the following examples, the whole verbs—main verbs and their helpers—are printed in italics.

1. David *has worked* at his parents' restaurant since 1989.
2. Leslie's brother *can swim* forty laps in twenty minutes.
3. Karen *will be* a senior at Eastern High School next fall.

In these three sentences, the **main** verbs are *worked, swim*, and *be*. The helpers are *has, can*, and *will*.

The following list includes some common helping verbs:

COMMON HELPING VERBS

am	do	has	may
is	does	have	might
are	did	had	must
was	can	shall	will
were	could	should	would

Like nouns, verbs can change their spelling or form. Changes in verb form show that actions take place at different times or under different conditions or that they are performed by different persons or things. Changes of time can be indicated by verb **tenses**. In the following examples, the present, future, and past are indicated by different forms of the verb *celebrate*:

1. Today, Ted *celebrates* his thirtieth birthday.
2. Next week, Ted and his wife *will celebrate* their tenth anniversary.
3. Last year, they *celebrated* their anniversary in New York City.

The spelling of the verb can also change when the performer of the action changes:

1. I *work* in the skills center three days a week.
2. Gary *works* in the skills center three days a week.

ASSEMBLING THE PARTS OF THE BASE

Just as builders construct buildings upon a solid **base**, or foundation, so writers build sentences upon the foundation of a subject and verb. As we build a sentence base, we start with the *subject*. The subject is the person, place, thing, or idea that the sentence is about. To form a complete thought, the subject needs a **verb** to tell what action the subject carries out or to state something about the subject's condition. The subject and the verb are the base of the sentence.

Recognizing Subjects and Action Verbs

The base of many simple sentences consists of a subject (a person, place, thing, or idea) and an action verb.

Examples

1. The Smiths' <u>baby</u> <u>is sleeping</u>.

2. The <u>kitten</u> <u>played</u>.

3. The <u>athlete</u> <u>will exercise</u>.

In the three sentences above, the **subjects**—*baby, kitten,* and *athlete*—are underlined once. The **action verbs**—*is sleeping, played,* and *will exercise*—are underlined twice. In these sentences the subjects are the actors; they perform, performed, or will perform the action. If we ask **who** or **what does, did,** or **will do** the action in each sentence, the answer is the subject of the sentence:

1. Who or what is sleeping?   baby
2. Who or what played?   kitten
3. Who or what will exercise?   athlete

Recognizing Subjects, Action Verbs, and Complements

As we have seen, the bases of some sentences are made up of a subject and an action verb. Some action verbs, however, may require another word to complete the meaning of the verb. For example, consider the following sentences:

1.   The <u>man</u> <u>hit</u>.

2.   <u>Larry</u> <u>ruined</u>.

You probably feel that both thoughts are incomplete. You may be asking yourself **what** the man hit or, "The man hit what?" Similarly, you may be wondering **what** Larry ruined or "Larry ruined what?" Both of these verbs require a word to complete their meaning. We call such a word a **complement**. The complement of an action verb is called an **object**. The subject is the **doer** of the action, and the object is the **receiver** of the action. By adding an object to each of the incomplete foundations, we build a meaningful (complete) base:

1. The man hit the *jackpot*.

2. Larry ruined the *party*.

The nouns *jackpot* and *party* are the objects; they are the receivers of the action.

Study the three sentences that follow. Each sentence has a base with three elements:

Subject	+	Verb	+	Complement
(noun—doer)		(action performed)		(object—receiver)

In the sample sentences, the subjects are underlined once and the action verbs twice; the complements (objects) are circled.

1. The police officer arrested (Jack.)   Police officer arrested whom?   Jack

2. Laura finished the (assignment.)   Laura finished what?   assignment

3. Richard's mother found a (job.)   Mother found what?   job

Sometimes action verbs have two objects. The thought of the sentence is not complete unless two words receive the action of the verb. Here is an example of a verb with one object to which we may wish to add a second:

Louis gave a (necklace.)

Clearly, the necklace receives the action of the verb. When we ask the question "Louis gave what?" we find that *necklace* is the direct object of the action. However, we may wish to make the meaning more complete by explaining who received the necklace. We can add the name of the receiver, the person to whom the necklace was given. This second receiver of the action is called the **indirect object**.

Louis gave (Sybil) a (necklace.)

Both *Sybil* and *necklace* receive the action and complete the meaning of the verb. Other verbs that often take two objects are *send, tell, ask, lend,* and *promise*.

Examples

1. Ann sent (Martin) a (valentine.)

2. Joan told (Harvey) a (secret.)

3. The instructor asked the (students) a (question.)

Do exercise 1-b and 1-c

5

Recognizing Subjects, Nonaction Verbs, and Complements

We do not always build sentences by saying that a subject **does** or **did** something. As we write, we frequently want to say something about the condition or the state of the subject. By using nonaction verbs, we can add complements (1) to describe the subject or (2) to rename the subject with a different noun.

Examples

1. Henry was friendly.

   As the arrow indicates, the word *friendly* describes Henry.

2. Henry was the winner.

   As the arrow indicates, the noun *winner* renames Henry. Of course, by renaming Henry, it adds information.

Notice in sentence 2 that the subject and the noun that renames it can be reversed because they mean the same person:

The winner was Henry.

Words—such as *friendly* and *winner*—that come after nonaction verbs and describe or rename the subject are **complements**. Like objects, they complete the meaning of the sentence base. Without *friendly* and *winner* in the two examples, the subject and verb would not form a complete thought. If we wrote only

Henry was

the reader would be left wondering **what** Henry was.

Complements that rename the subject can come after the forms of the verbs **be** (such as **is, was, will be**) and **become (became)**:

1. Mary was the lead singer.

2. The friends became enemies.

Notice that *singer* and *enemies*—the words that rename—are both nouns.

Complements that describe the subject can come after many nonaction verbs.

Examples

1. Sally felt happy.

2. Grant appeared dizzy.

3. The student's speech seemed long.

Words that describe nouns are called **adjectives**. The words *happy, dizzy,* and *long* are adjectives describing the subjects.

Do exercise 1-d

6

BEGINNING SENTENCES WITH *THERE* OR *HERE*

In all the examples you have studied in this chapter, the subjects have come before the verbs. However, sentences can be constructed so that the verb comes before the subject. One way to make such a sentence is to begin a sentence with *there* or *here*. Notice the placement of the subjects in the following examples. The subjects are underlined once and the verbs twice.

Examples

1. There is a stray dog in the park.

2. There were fifteen students in my swimming class.

3. There will be a quiz on Monday.

4. Here is the receipt.

5. Here are the keys.

In sentences like these, the verb comes before the subject. Nevertheless, the subject is still easy to locate. It is the person(s), place(s), thing(s), or idea(s) that the sentence is about. In each example, when we ask **who** or **what** of the verb, the answer is the subject:

1. Who or what is in the park?	dog
2. Who or what were in my swimming class?	students
3. Who or what will be on Monday?	quiz
4. Who or what is?	receipt
5. Who or what are?	keys

Action verbs also can precede the subjects when the sentence begins with *there* or *here*. In the following examples, the subject is underlined once and the verb twice.

Examples

1. There goes Ted.

2. There go the children.

3. Here comes the bus.

4. Here come the students.

GIVING COMMANDS

Verbs that give orders or commands need no stated subject. The word *you* is understood. The word *you* means the person (subject) being ordered or commanded.

Examples of Commands (With You Understood)

1. Leave now.

2. Bring the paper.

3. Come home.

ASKING QUESTIONS

Sentences do not always make statements; some sentences ask questions. When you build questions, you usually place a verb, often a helper, first; the subject appears next, often followed by a main verb. The question ends with a question mark.

1. Is your mother working today?

2. Has Mary applied for a new job?

If the verb does not have a helper, the **base** consists only of a verb and a subject, and the verb comes first:

1. Is David at home?

2. Was Jonathan in the parade?

Do exercise 1-e

SUGGESTIONS FOR WRITING

In your journal, describe an evening you spent recently at a party, a restaurant, a tavern, or a nightclub. Use your journal writing as a way to remember and record freely everything that happened.

Once you have finished describing the experience for yourself, describe the evening for your best friend. Then describe the same evening for an older relative or an older friend. Include as many specific details as you can in both accounts.

Now read over your descriptions. How are they different? In what important ways did your reader influence your writing.

Remember that your journal is not simply a place to complete these suggested assignments; it is also a place to record any experiences that you find interesting or puzzling.

NAME _____ **DATE** _____

Correct any mistakes in the following sentences. Look for four kinds of errors:

- Errors in the spelling of plural nouns

- Errors in the use of *a, an,* and *the*

- Errors in the use of capital letters

- Errors in possessive nouns

Draw a line through each incorrect word and write your correction neatly above it. If the sentence is correct, write a *C* by its number. Sentences may contain more than one error.

EXAMPLES

_____ *Karen's*
      ~~Karens~~ camera needs new batteries.

_____ Sonny made the ~~sandwichs~~ *sandwiches* for the picnic.

_*C*_ Mr. Tucker applied for a job in Denver.

---

1. _____ Bill practiced the piano for a hour this morning.

2. _____ I have an appointment with my advisor on friday morning.

3. _____ All the radioes in the catalog are on sale.

4. _____ My children attend a elementary school near my office.

5. _____ My six cousins' will come to the reunion at Aunt Esther's house.

6. _____ My mothers instructions are always very clear.

7. _____ My father wants me to take a History course next semester.

8. _____ Lenny will be walking on crutchs for two months.

9. _____ The firefighters saved the lifes of all the people in the burning building.

10. _____ I do not like my landladys' attitude toward pets.

11. _____ Mr. and Mrs. Cox bought a antique desk for their anniversary.

12. _____ Jessica spent all weekend building shelfs in the basement.

13. _____ The new player can pick up an uniform on Saturday morning.

14. _____ Many families vacation plans were upset by the airline strike.

15. _____ My cousins from Germany will visit the capitol building next week.

16. _____ My grandmother was exhausted after the Christmas holidaies.

17. _____ The two customers complained to the waiter's boss.

18. _____ Carole plays violin with a orchestra in Miami.

19. _____ An honest person returned my uncle's car keys.

20. _____ Norma Tucker, the Mayor of my hometown, will meet the governor this afternoon.

21. _____ Three of the downtown churches are collecting toys for children in the hospital.

22. _____ The student gave a incorrect answer to the instructor's question.

23. _____ Frank's two brothers' left the party early.

24. _____ Every student in my english class passed the test yesterday.

25. _____ Ben's heros are all on the football team.

26. _____ My aunt sells real estate in New mexico.

27. _____ The childrens' toys covered the living room carpet.

28. _____ The teacher always gives his son a books for Christmas.

29. _____ Gwen borrowed Williams' car to drive to the airport.

30. _____ My mother cannot find an use for the table from her grandmother.

31. _____ Sarah and Andrew plan to spend their easter vacation in Florida.

32. _____ My sister plans to attend the university of Maryland next year.

33. _____ Dan and Wendy visited six countrys in Europe last spring.

34. _____ The young mans application impressed the employer.

35. _____ Clint has to retake chemistry 102 next summer.

36. _____ The seven men and five woman on the jury agreed on the verdict.

If you had trouble with this exercise, you need to learn some rules and practice proofreading. Explanations and practice are provided in Appendix A, Appendix B, Appendix C, and Appendix D.

Circle the numbers of the sentences you missed on the chart below so that you can see which appendix to study. You should study any appendix for which you missed more than two sentences.

Problem Sentences	Appendix Section
3, 8, 9, 12, 16, 21, 25, 33, 36	A: Plural nouns
1, 4, 11, 13, 18, 19, 22, 28, 30	B: *a, an, the*
2, 7, 15, 20, 24, 26, 31, 32, 35	C: Capital letters
5, 6, 10, 14, 17, 23, 27, 29, 34	D: Possessive nouns

NAME _____ **DATE** _____

     The action verbs in the following sentences are underlined twice. Identify the subjects and, if there are any, the objects. Underline the subjects once and circle the objects.

EXAMPLES

The girl on the bike threw the (newspaper) in the mud.

The instructor gave the (students) an (assignment.)

My little cousin giggled.

---

1. The students wrote their answers.

2. Terry will bring her camera.

3. The secretary typed the memo.

4. The mouse frightened the children.

5. The crowd cheered.

6. My cousins enjoyed the movie.

7. Beth brought Brad some flowers for his birthday.

8. Jeff's sister told Connie a secret.

9. Paul lent Gene his car.

10. The Stony Brook School had won the championship.

11. My best friend will soon move to California.

12. Pat had left Libby's umbrella in the restaurant.

13. The students passed the quiz.

14. Carly left her sweater on the bus.

15. Mr. Thom's brother wrote a book about bees.

16. Kim wept.

17. Nelson promised his employees a raise.

18. The professor explained the assignment.

19. My father invited the minister to dinner.

20. The coach cancelled the practice.

NAME _____ **DATE** _____

In each blank line, fill in an appropriate noun as the subject of the sentence. In each circle, fill in an appropriate noun as an object. Be sure that the completed sentence makes sense.

EXAMPLE

_____*Corinne*_____ found a (*wallet*) on the bus.

1. _____ will drive Kim's ( ) to school on Friday.

2. _____ borrowed my ( ) yesterday.

3. _____ calls her ( ) once a week.

4. Clarence's_____ won the ( ).

5. _____ will watch a ( ) tonight.

6. _____ sent ( ) a ( ) .

7. _____ bought a ( ) at the mall.

8. _____ will wash the ( ) by hand.

9. Cindy's_____ built a ( ) for her sister.

10. _____ plays in the park on Saturday.

11. _____ cooks ( ) every night.

12. _____ told ( ) a ( ) .

13. The boys'_____ found the ( ) .

14. _____ wrote ( ) a ( ) .

15. _____ sold a ( ) at the garage sale.

16. _____ lost a ( ) .

17. _____ will wear a red ( ) to the dance.

18. Emily's _____ broke the ( ) .

19. _____ left a ( ) in the library.

20. _____ frightened the ( ) .

NAME _____ DATE _____

     In the following sentences, the verb is underlined twice. Underline the subject once, and circle the complement.

EXAMPLES

Don's sister is a (photographer.)

The kittens were (playful.)

1. Denise's present was a surprise.

2. The baby seems tired.

3. My personal banker is Clara's mother.

4. The cabinets are beautiful.

5. Dr. Bodnar's suggestion was excellent.

6. Nick's brother is a painter.

7. Maria's letters are very long.

8. Mark's brother became a nurse.

9. Kevin will be the captain.

10. Levon's answer is correct.

11. The children appeared nervous at the end of the day.

12. The twins seem very ill.

13. Lisa's uncle is a pilot.

14. The tour through the laboratory was informative.

15. Henry's new job is boring.

16. Gloria's daughter is very studious.

17. The math problems are difficult.

18. Ali's jacket is new.

19. Dr. Thomas's students were restless.

20. Wayne is the president's new secretary.

NAME _____ **DATE** _____

In each of the following sentences, underline the subject once and the verb twice. If a verb has one or more complements, draw a circle around them.

EXAMPLES

Grandfather's newspaper arrives at five A.M.

Has the committee scheduled its final (meeting)?

1. Janet's husband refused a raise.

2. Janet's husband's grandmother is rich.

3. David missed Meredina's recital.

4. Has Mother left the gym?

5. There go the joggers.

6. Here come the winners.

7. Was Kaitlin born on September 9?

8. Jesse brought Emily's mother a dozen roses.

9. Dr. Colletti's class seemed nervous.

10. Brent's brother is a dentist.

11. My mother's behavior seemed strange.

12. Patrick ignored the customers' questions.

13. Stephanie became a veterinarian.

14. The dentist sent my father two bills.

15. Brian's business is a success.

16. Have you received the bill?

17. There are five possibilities.

18. Paul rewrote the report.

19. The supervisor rejected the employees' petition.

20. The saleswomen have elected a representative.

Using Pronouns

2

When we speak or write, we often refer to the same person, place, thing, or idea more than once. To avoid repeating the same names over and over, we use **pronouns** to replace nouns. Here are two sentences that repeat nouns instead of replacing them with pronouns:

> *Mary Beth* brought *Mary Beth's* car to Bill's garage. *Mary Beth* said *Mary Beth's car* needed an oil change and new spark plugs.

Now look at the same sentences with appropriate pronouns replacing nouns:

> Mary Beth brought *her* car to Bill's garage. *She* said *it* needed an oil change and new spark plugs.

The pronouns in this second version make repetition of the nouns unnecessary.

UNDERSTANDING PERSON

Some pronouns have three forms, called **first person, second person**, and **third person**. Before you learn the forms of these pronouns, you should understand what each **person** means.

Understanding the First Person

The term **first person** means the person or persons who are speaking. When you are speaking or writing about yourself, you use the first person singular forms of the personal pronouns. If, for example, your name is *Jane*, you would not write or say:

> Jane passed Jane's driver's test.

You would substitute pronouns (*I*, *my*) for your own name and would write or say:

> *I* passed *my* driver's test.

When you are speaking or writing about yourself and another person or persons, you often use the first person plural. For example, if you wished to comment on a report that you prepared with another person, you would begin by identifying the other person and yourself:

> Last week, Jack and I prepared a report on Frederick Douglass.

However, you would not continue to use *Jack and I* every time you wished to explain what you both did. Instead, you would use the first person plural pronoun (*we*) to stand for you and your partner, Jack:

> First, *we* located several good books in the library.

Understanding the Second Person

The term **second person** means the person or persons **to whom** you are speaking or writing. When you are speaking or writing to particular persons, you do not call them by their names every time you refer to them. For example, if you were writing a letter to your cousin Sally, you would not write

> Sally and Sally's husband should spend the Memorial Day weekend in the mountains.

Instead, you would use the second person of the personal pronouns (*you, your*):

> *You* and *your* husband should spend Memorial Day weekend in the mountains.

Similarly, when you are speaking or writing to more than one person, you use the second person plural. If you were writing to Sally and her husband, Dan, you would not use their names in your invitation:

> Sally and Dan are welcome to use the Crandalls' cabin.

Again, you would use a personal pronoun (*you*):

> *You* are welcome to use the Crandalls' cabin.

Understanding the Third Person

The term **third person** means the person(s), place(s), idea(s), or thing(s) **about whom** or **about which** you are writing or speaking. When you first mention the person or thing about whom or about which you are writing, you need to identify the person or thing by name. For example, you might begin a discussion of your friend Jean with this sentence:

> *Jean* hired an assistant manager this week.

However, as you continue to talk or write about Jean, you would not continue to mention her name every time you referred to her. Instead, you would use a singular pronoun in the third person (*she*) to stand for *Jean*:

> *She* needed help on weekends.

After you identify a person or thing, you should use pronouns as long as the meaning is clear. For instance, you would introduce discussions of your brother-in-law or of your umbrella by identifying each by name; then you would use singular third person pronouns to stand for *brother-in-law* (*he*) and the *umbrella* (*it*):

1. My *brother-in-law* has gone to New Orleans. *He* will return next Wednesday.
2. My *umbrella* broke yesterday. *It* will not open.

The third person **plural** is used to refer to more than one person or thing. Again, as you write, you must first identify the persons or things; then you can use a plural third person pronoun (*they*):

1. My two *brothers-in-law* have gone to New Orleans. *They* will return next Wednesday.
2. Both my *umbrellas* broke yesterday. *They* will not open.

USING THE PERSONAL PRONOUNS

Each of the three persons has different forms for use as **subjects, objects**, or **possessives**. Let's look first at the personal pronouns used as subjects and objects. Study this chart carefully.

	SUBJECTS		OBJECTS	
	Singular	Plural	Singular	Plural
First person:	I	we	me	us
Second person:	you	you	you	you
Third person:	he	they	him	them
	she	they	her	them
	it	they	it	them

Notice that the subject and object pronouns have three forms in the third person **singular**: masculine (*he, him*), feminine (*she, her*), and neuter (*it, it*). We substitute *he* or *him* for words like *man*: *he* if the pronoun is used as a subject and *him* if it is used as an object. We substitute *she* or *her* for words like *woman*, and we substitute *it* for words like *tree*. The third person **plural**, however, does not have different forms for masculine, feminine, or neuter. Thus, we substitute *they* or *them* for all persons or things about which we are writing—*men, women, girls, boys, trees, answers*.

Other forms of the personal pronouns are used to show **possession**. The following chart presents two types of possessives. The **possessive pronouns** on the right substitute for nouns and are used alone. The possessive **adjectives** on the left must be used in front of a noun to tell **whose**. For example, in the sentence "A page was torn from my book," the possessive adjective *my* tells **whose book** it is. Fill in an appropriate noun for each possessive adjective in the chart.

	POSSESSIVE ADJECTIVES		POSSESSIVE PRONOUNS	
	Singular	Plural	Singular	Plural
First person:	my _____	our _____	mine	ours
Second person:	your _____	your _____	yours	yours
Third person:	his _____	their _____	his	theirs
	her _____	their _____	hers	theirs
	its _____	their _____	its	theirs

Notice that, once again, the third person singular has masculine forms (*his, his*), feminine forms (*her, hers*), and neuter forms (*its, its*). However, the third person plural is the same (*their, theirs*) for masculine, feminine, and neuter nouns.

Look at the spelling of the word *their*. Do not confuse it with the word *there* meaning "in that place" or with the contraction *they're* (*they are*). Study these examples:

They brought *their* own chairs. [They possess the chairs.]
There are the papers you wanted. [The papers are "in that place."]
The clerk held up two packages and said, "*They're* already wrapped."
[The words *they are* are contracted, and the apostrophe marks the missing letter *a*.]

Using Subject Pronouns

The most common use of **subject pronouns** is as subjects of sentences. In each of the following sentences, the pronoun is a subject.

First person singular:	*I* will pick up the children.
First person plural:	*We* have a date for lunch on Wednesday.
Second person singular:	*You* have a dentist appointment on Saturday morning.
Second person plural:	*You* will all have a quiz tomorrow.
Third person singular:	Ron came early. *He* worked until five.
	Suzanne called. *She* asked for Ted.
	The car is in the shop. *It* needs a new transmission.
Third person plural:	The twins are not home. *They* went roller skating.
	The forsythia bushes bloomed in February. *They* were fooled by the warm weather.

Subject pronouns are also used as subject complements after nonaction verbs. As you learned in Chapter 1, a subject complement means the same person or thing as the subject. Thus a personal pronoun used as a subject complement renames the subject. We could exchange them. We might write:

She is the young *woman* in the navy blue suit.

Or we might write:

The young *woman* in the navy blue suit is *she*.

In both of these sentences, *she* and *woman* mean the same person. In the first sentence, *she* is a subject; in the second sentence, *she* is a complement. In both sentences, the subject form of the pronoun is correct.

Do exercise 2-a

Using Object Pronouns

Object pronouns are often used as objects of action verbs. In each of the examples that follow, the pronoun object has been circled.

First person singular:	The instructions confuse (me.)
First person plural:	Grandmother invited (us) for the weekend.
Second person singular:	Don will call (you) in the morning.
Second person plural:	The registrar sent (you) applicants the forms.
Third person singular:	My brother fell on a nail. The doctor gave (him) a tetanus shot.
	Ned challenged Cheryl to a game of chess. He beat (her) easily.
	My aunt baked an apple cake for the party. Unfortunately, the puppy ate (it.)
Third person plural:	Mary and Jill arrived at the movies early. Sue met (them) at intermission.
	My sister washed the curtains. My brother hung (them) on the line.

Using Possessive Adjectives

Look back at the chart of possessive adjectives and possessive pronouns. Like possessive nouns used as adjectives to tell **whose**, possessive adjectives precede the nouns they modify. In each of the sentences that follow, an arrow is drawn from the possessive adjective to the noun it modifies.

First person singular:	My paper is two days late.
First person plural:	Our exercises were incomplete.
Second person singular:	Frank borrowed your umbrella.
Second person plural:	Your exams have not been graded yet.
Third person singular:	Arnold drove his car to the game.
	Dana carefully repeated her answer.
	The cat ate its dinner.
Third person plural:	The Joncses took their cat to the veterinarian.
	These tennis balls have lost their bounce.

Using Possessive Pronouns

Possessive pronouns replace a noun plus a possessive adjective. For example, if you were speaking about a particular book on a shelf, you might use a possessive adjective with *book*:

1. That is *my* book.

Or you might replace the two words *my book* with the possessive pronoun:

2. That book is *mine*.

In the second example, *mine* means *my book*.

Study the following examples, in which the possessive pronouns are circled. As pronouns, these possessives can be used as subjects or as complements. Notice that the **possessive pronouns do not have apostrophes**.

First person singular:	The salad in the refrigerator is (mine.)
First person plural:	The orange camper in front of the library is (ours.)
Second person singular:	The sandwich on the dining room table is (yours,) Bob.
Second person plural:	Those two seats at the end of the aisle must be (yours.)
Third person singular:	That kitten is Danny's. That puppy is (his) also.
	Those textbooks are Laura's. The notebooks are not (hers.)
	[**Note**: We rarely use *its* as a possessive pronoun.]
Third person plural:	The coats on the sofa are Nick's and Ed's. The umbrellas are also (theirs.)

19

USING PRONOUNS ENDING IN *-SELF* OR *-SELVES*

We add *-self* or *-selves* to some of the forms of the personal pronouns to make another kind of pronoun. Study the spelling of these forms carefully.

	Singular	Plural
First person:	myself	ourselves
Second person:	yourself	yourselves
Third person:	himself	themselves
	herself	themselves
	itself	themselves

Practice

Circle the numbers of the correctly spelled pronouns in the following list:

1. themselves	3. themself	5. itsself	7. thereselves	9. ourselves
2. theirself	4. hisself	6. himself	8. ourselfs	10. themselfs

If you circled numbers 1, 6, and 9, you identified the correctly spelled pronouns.

The forms ending in *-self* and *-selves* are used only to rename a noun or another pronoun already mentioned in the same sentence.

Correct: Mr. Peterson himself gave us permission.

Correct: Margaret embarrassed herself.

The double-headed arrows show that the word being renamed by the pronoun is in the same sentence. Thus each pronoun is correct.

In the following examples, the *-self* and *-selves* forms are incorrect because they do not stand for a noun previously mentioned in the sentence:

Incorrect: Bill and *myself* will bring the cider.
Incorrect: Frank thanked the boys and *myself*.

In the first incorrect sentence, *myself* should be *I*. In the second, *myself* should be *me*.

Do exercises 2-b and 2-c

USING INDEFINITE PRONOUNS

Sometimes we must use pronouns because we have no definite persons or things in mind. The pronouns we use are called *indefinite pronouns*. Some indefinite pronouns may be **plural**:

few   many   any   some   most

These plurals are usually easy to identify and use:

A *few* of the students lost *some* of their books.

The indefinite pronouns that seem to cause problems are the **singular** ones:

FORMS OF THE SINGULAR
INDEFINITE PRONOUNS

one	everyone	each	everybody
no one	someone	nobody	somebody
anyone	either	anybody	neither

As you write, remember that these singular indefinite pronouns stand for only **one**.

1. *Someone* has lost the answer sheet. [*Someone* is singular; one person lost the answer sheet.]
2. *Everybody* has received a bill. [*Everybody* is singular; each person received a bill.]
3. *Each* of the girls has a key. [*Each* is singular; each girl has a key.]

We use the indefinite pronouns when we cannot identify or do not wish to identify a particular person or persons:

Anyone may apply for admission.
Everyone in the room has a calculator.

The indefinite pronouns should not be confused with the personal pronouns. Remember that we use the indefinite pronouns when we do not wish to or need to specify the person or persons we mean. We use the personal pronouns—*he, she,* or *you*—when we have a specific person in mind.

- Use *he* or *she* when you are speaking or writing about a specific person.
- Use *you* when you are directly speaking or writing to someone.
- Use an **indefinite pronoun** when you do **not** have a specific person in mind.

Here are some examples of correct and incorrect use of indefinite pronouns and personal pronouns:

Correct: *Most* of the visitors found a restaurant they enjoyed. [*Most* is indefinite; the writer of the sentence did not wish to specify who they were.]

Incorrect: In a city as large as Chicago, *you* can usually find the kind of restaurant *you* enjoy. [Here the writer also is making a statement about **most** or **some** or **many** of the **visitors** or **people**; the writer of the sentence does not mean only the persons (*you*) to whom he or she is speaking. Thus the word *you* is incorrect.]

Correct: This chemistry course makes large demands on *each* of the students' time.

Incorrect: This chemistry course makes large demands on *your* time.

Compare the meaning of the previous second incorrect sentence with the meaning of the following sentence, in which the speaker is directly addressing the students and uses *you* correctly:

Students, this chemistry course will make large demands on your time.

Do exercises 2-d, 2-e, and 2-f

SUGGESTIONS FOR WRITING

Are you using your journal regularly to record your thoughts, activities, and ideas? Such a journal is a valuable resource; it can help you think about the meaning of what happens to you every day. Also, making regular journal entries can help you improve your writing skills.

Write about an experience you had recently with another person or a group of people. For example, you may have gone to a movie, stopped after school for a pizza, or just taken a walk with a friend or several friends. Include as many details as you can in your account; for example, tell who went with you, where you went, when the experience occurred, how people behaved, and why the experience was enjoyable or unpleasant.

Identify the other person or persons in the first sentence. Then try to use pronouns to refer to yourself and to the other people.

NAME _____ **DATE** _____

After each of the following nouns, write the subject pronoun that can be used in its place. Then give the pronoun's person (first, second, or third) and its number (singular or plural).

EXAMPLES

the quiz   ___*it*___ ,   *third person singular*_____

the suitcases   ___*they*___ , *third person plural*_____

1. the man   _____ , _____

2. a refrigerator   _____ , _____

3. an uncle   _____ , _____

4. the decision   _____ , _____

5. the actors   _____ , _____

6. Jan, Al, and I   _____ , _____

7. the typewriters _____ , _____

8. an eraser   _____ , _____

9. a car and truck _____ , _____

10. Kurt and Lisa   _____ , _____

11. My friend and I _____ , _____

12. Tom and Jerry   _____ , _____

13. the swimmers   _____ , _____

14. the problem   _____ , _____

15. Cathy and Ted   _____ , _____

16. a woman   _____ , _____

17. the contract   _____ , _____

18. a knife and fork _____ , _____

19. the workers   _____ , _____

20. my uncles and I _____ , _____

NAME _____ DATE _____

The sentences in *a* below use personal pronouns or *-self* or *-selves* forms correctly. Use the sentences in *a* as models to fill in the blanks of the sentences in *b* with a pronoun—a personal pronoun, a possessive adjective, or a pronoun that ends in *-self* or *-selves*.

EXAMPLES

(a) Sarah did not complete her assignment.
(b) Ned did not like_____*his*_____new job.
(a) Kristy and I baked the cake ourselves.
(b) Dan and Dave planted the tomatoes ____*themselves*____.

1. (a) Yesterday, Wendy asked her mother for a new coat.

   (b) Last night, Teresa and Tynetta visited _____ aunt in the hospital.

2. (a) The children will need their umbrellas today.

   (b) My brother left _____ homework in school.

3. (a) On Saturday, Laura bought herself a new car.

   (b) Walter blamed _____ for the team's low score.

4. (a) The textbook is Dwight's, but the notebook is not his.

   (b) The truck belongs to Dee and Mike, but the camper is not _____ .

5. (a) Lee and I treated ourselves to dinner and a movie.

   (b) My grandparents drove to California by _____ .

6. (a) Julia wants to go to the party, but she has to work on Saturday night.

   (b) Bob took five courses last semester, and _____ plans to go to summer school.

7. (a) Aunt Madeline wrote to Linda and invited her for the weekend.

   (b) My husband refinished the kitchen cabinets. He also waxed _____ .

8. (a) Bill packed the clothes, but he forgot his bathing suit.

   (b) Mary lost the address, but _____ remembered the telephone number.

9. (a) The students have completed their homework.

   (b) Jeanne and I have not written _____ report.

10. (a) I tuned up the car by myself.

    (b) My brother and I cooked the dinner by _____ .

NAME _____ DATE _____

Write an appropriate pronoun or possessive adjective in each of the blank spaces. In each sentence, the verb is printed in italics.

EXAMPLE

_____*My*_____ brother *lent* _____*me*_____ fifty dollars.

1. _____ *made* an appointment with _____ instructor.

2. _____ behavior *confuses* _____ .

3. Kenneth and _____ *drove* _____ to the bus station.

4. Benita and _____ *type* the exercises on _____ computers.

5. _____ *helped* _____ study math last night.

6. _____ *met* Peggy for lunch.

7. The cabinets *have* stains on _____ drawers.

8. Gabe and Shannon *must clean* the house by _____ .

9. _____ new lamp *has* a tear in _____ shade.

10. _____ and _____ *can write* the invitations.

11. Gail *sent* _____ photographs of the wedding.

12. Alane's mother *taught* _____ to organize _____ time.

13. Nancy's mother *gave* _____ a beautiful blouse.

14. _____ boss *did* not *attend* _____ Christmas party.

15. Martha *told* _____ about _____ interview.

16. Mr. Gibbons and _____ *delivered* the prizes.

17. The other students and _____ *need* to review _____ notes for the

    test.

18. _____ and _____ *will plant* the trees by _____ .

19. _____ cat *scratched* _____ last night.

20. *Put* the picture back in _____ frame.

NAME _____ DATE _____

    Most of the following sentences contain one error in the use of pronouns or possessive adjectives. Draw a line through the error and write your correction neatly above it. If the sentence is correct, write a *C* in the space.

EXAMPLES

_____ Hal and ~~myself~~ were late for class yesterday.

_*C*_ Angela and I left our notes in the car.

═══

1. _____ Last week, Dr. Rosenberg gave myself and my classmates an assignment.

2. _____ Everyone had to write a report and present a summary of his or her report to the class.

3. _____ Each of the students had to choose their topic for the report from sixteenth-century British history.

4. _____ The instructor hisself was surprised by the many interesting subjects.

5. _____ At first, five students wanted to write they're papers on Henry VIII.

6. _____ Later, four students changed there minds.

7. _____ Tina and myself were very interested in Anne Boleyn.

8. _____ Unfortunately, their were not enough books in the library for the two of us.

9. _____ The library needs to expand it's British history collection.

10. _____ I changed my topic to Jane Seymour.

11. _____ Vance and Mike both decided to write their reports on Catherine of Aragon.

12. _____ One week later, each student had to turn in their written report.

13. _____ Each of the students had to select a day to present they're oral report to the class.

14. _____ Tina and myself chose Tuesday for our presentations.

15. _____ We surprised ourselfs by receiving A's for both the oral and the written reports.

NAME _____ DATE _____

     In this exercise, each group of scrambled words can be rearranged to build a simple sentence. Each sentence contains pronouns or possessive adjectives. Rearrange each group of words into a sentence. Add no words except *a, an,* and *the*.

EXAMPLES

lent   keys   her   she   me

She lent me her keys. _____

boss   inventory   herself   finished   my

My boss finished the inventory herself. _____

---

1. lunch   our   he   brought   us

   _____

2. textbook   you   need   will   your

   _____

3. car   there   their   is

   _____

4. doubted   story   everyone   her

   _____

5. typed   teacher   herself   exam

   _____

6. checkbook   my   is   here

   _____

7. uncle   piano   himself   bought   my

   _____

8. goggles   those   mine   are

   _____

9. coach   himself   tickets   purchased

   _____

NAME _____ **DATE** _____

Use each of the pronouns or possessive adjectives in the left margin in a sentence of your own. Choose a verb for each of your sentences from the list at the top of the exercise. Use each verb at least once.

EXAMPLES

he   *He arrived an hour late for the exam.* _____

himself *The instructor typed the quiz by himself.* _____

Verbs: lost worked arrived typed planned sold played remembered

him   1. _____

_____

their   2. _____

_____

herself 3. _____

_____

me   4. _____

_____

she   5. _____

_____

yours   6. _____

_____

ourselves 7. _____

_____

I   8. _____

_____

your   9. _____

_____

mine   10. _____

_____

Using Adjectives and Adverbs   **3**

Adjectives and **adverbs** are words in a sentence that **modify**; that is, they affect meaning by adding information to the base of a sentence. **Adjectives** modify nouns and pronouns. **Adverbs** modify verbs, adjectives, or other adverbs.

RECOGNIZING AND USING ADJECTIVES

Recognizing Single-Word Adjectives

Adjectives can be recognized by their use within a sentence. They answer any of four questions about nouns and pronouns. (In the examples that follow, arrows point from adjectives to the nouns they modify.)

Whose?

In Chapters 1 and 2, you studied the ways nouns and pronouns are made into possessives to tell to whom something or someone belongs. When these possessives describe nouns, they are adjectives. Here are two examples as reminders:

1. *Mrs. Brown's* face does not reveal *her* feelings. [The words *Mrs. Brown's* and *her* are adjectives that identify **whose** face and **whose** feelings.]

2. The *general's* aide completed *his* assignment. [The adjectives *general's* and *his* identify **whose** aide and **whose** assignment.]

Which one?

1. *This* house has been sold.

2. *These* houses have been sold. [In sentence 1, the adjective *this* tells **which** house; in sentence 2, *these* tells **which** houses. The adjectives *this* and *that* must modify a singular noun. The adjectives *these* and *those* must modify a plural noun.]

3. The *first* question has not been answered. [*First* identifies **which** question.]

4. The *last* comment startled the audience. [*Last* identifies **which** comment.]

How Many? How Much?

1. The children took *few* chances. [The adjective *few* tells **how many** chances.]

2. A *few* children drank *some* juice. [The adjective *few* indicates **how many** children; the adjective *some* indicates **how much** juice.]

3. Connie needs *six* textbooks and *several* notebooks. [The adjective *six* tells **how many** textbooks, and the adjective *several* indicates **how many** notebooks.]

What Kind of?

1. The *new* student bought the *wrong* textbook. [The adjective *new* describes **what kind of** student, and the adjective *wrong* describes **what kind of** textbook.]

2. Remember to serve the *strawberry* shortcake on *paper* plates. [The words *strawberry* and *paper* tell **what kind of** in this sentence, so they are adjectives. They modify the nouns *shortcake* and *plates*. *Strawberry* and *paper* might be used as nouns in another sentence, that is, to name a *strawberry* or a *piece of paper*.]

3. I cannot fix the *cracked* plate. [The adjective *cracked* describes **what kind of** plate.]

4. The *barking* dog awakened the *sleeping* children. [The adjective *barking* describes **what kind of** dog; the adjective *sleeping* describes **what kind of** children.]

Notice in examples 3 and 4 that verb forms are used as adjective modifiers. When verb forms are used as modifiers, they are called **verbals**. Both the *-ing* form and the *-ed* form can modify nouns:

–ing *form*	–ed *form*
a damaging remark	a damaged fender
a finishing tool	a finished product
an exciting game	an excited child

The *–ing* form (called a present participle) is used to describe a noun in terms of something the noun does: *the remark damages*; *the tool finishes; the game excites*. In contrast, the *-ed* form (called a past participle) usually describes the noun in terms of some action that has been performed on it: *the fender has been damaged*; *the product has been finished*; *the child has been excited*.

A, An, and The

The words *a*, *an*, and *the* are also adjectives. They are called **articles**. If you need explanation and practice in the use of the three articles, see Appendix B.

Placing Single-Word Adjectives

In Chapter 1, you learned a sentence pattern that places an adjective after a **nonaction** verb. An adjective in this position is called a **complement**; it **completes** the meaning of the sentence by describing the subject:

1. The signal was late.

2. The child seemed intelligent.

3. The answer sounded unrehearsed.

Other single-word adjectives are placed **in front of** the nouns or pronouns they modify. Several adjectives, each giving a different kind of information, can be used to modify the same noun. Look at the following examples. (Each arrow points from an adjective to the noun it modifies.)

1. Uncle Fred bought me *my first new* car. [Each of the three adjectives gives a different kind of information about the car: *my* tells **whose**; *first* tells **which one**; and *new* tells **what kind of**.]

2. *Harry's three history* assignments had been returned. [Each adjective gives a different kind of information about the assignments: *Harry's* tells **whose**; *three* tells **how many**; and *history* tells **what kind**.]

> **Do exercises 3-a and 3-b**

COMBINING SENTENCES BY USING ADJECTIVES

When we use adjectives, we are combining several pieces of information into one sentence. For instance, in the example about Uncle Fred in the preceding section is a combination of the information in these four simple sentences:

(S)   (V) (IO) (DO)

1. Uncle Fred bought (me) a (car.)

2. The car was new.

3. The car was mine.

4. It was the first car I had owned.

Using sentence 1 as the base, we can add the other information as adjectives modifying the direct object (DO), *car*:

Uncle Fred bought me *my first new* car.

The information in example 2—about Harry's history assignment—might also be presented in four separate sentences:

(S)   (V)

1. Assignments had been returned.

2. The assignments belonged to Harry.

3. There were three assignments.

4. The assignments were in history.

Using sentence 1 as the base, we can add the other information as adjectives modifying the subject, *assignments*:

Harry's three history assignments had been returned.

Combining simple sentences, such as those used in the preceding examples, makes writing more economical and more interesting to read. Practice in combining sentences teaches you how to emphasize one important idea and use less important information to develop it.

31

Adding Information to the Sentence Base

Sometimes we can combine sentences by simply cutting out repeated information and adding the remaining adjectives to a subject–verb **base**. Consider the relationship among the ideas in the following sentences. (Arrows point from adjectives to the nouns they modify.)

(S)   (V)   (DO)   (DO)

1. The campers packed the tent and clothes.

2. The campers were weary.

3. The tent was muddy.

4. The clothes were wet.

The first sentence contains the action, so we would probably choose to emphasize it by making it the base of the combination. In sentences 2, 3, and 4, the three adjectives—*weary*, *muddy*, and *wet*—provide the only new information. By placing each adjective in front of the noun it modifies in the base, we can write one sentence instead of four:

Combination: The *weary* campers packed the *muddy* tent and *wet* clothes.

Practice

Combine each of the following groups of sentences.

- First, put a check (√) by the sentence that you want to emphasize.
- Then circle each adjective in the other sentences.
- Cut out the repeated information and combine the sentences.

In your combination, underline the verb twice and the subject once; draw an arrow from each adjective to the word it modifies.

Group 1

1. Harriet sent Bob a basket of fruits and jellies.
2. The basket was large.
3. The fruits were fresh.
4. The jellies were fancy.

Your combination: _____

_____

_____

Group 2

1. There were three students.
2. The students seemed embarrassed.
3. The students were new.

Your combination: _____

_____

Now analyze your combinations:

Group 1: Sentence 1 has the main action; the three other sentences add descriptive details. The sentences can be combined by using the first as the base and adding the other adjectives:

Harriet sent Bob a large basket of fresh fruit and fancy jellies.

Group 2: Using sentence 2 as the base, we can reduce the other two sentences to the adjectives *three* and *new* and place them before the noun *students*:

The three new students seemed embarrassed.

> **Do exercise 3-b**

We can also combine sentences by turning a verb into a single-word adjective modifier. Study the following example of sentences combined by changing the verb to an *-ing* adjective.

Betty's parrot screams.
The parrot disturbs Betty's mother.

Combination: Betty's *screaming* parrot disturbs her mother.

The second sentence is emphasized as the base of the combination. The verb *screams* is changed to the verbal adjective *screaming*. We use the *-ing* form because the adjective describes the noun in terms of something it does. The adjective is placed before *parrot,* the noun it modifies.
Here is another example:

I burned the steak.
No one would eat the steak.

Combination: No one would eat the burned steak. [The verb *burned* is used as a verbal adjective. We use the *-ed* form because *burned* describes the noun *steak* in terms of an action performed on it.]

Practice

Use a verbal adjective to combine the following pairs of sentences:

1. The windshield shattered.
   Bill replaced the windshield.

   Combination: _____

2. My little brother cried when he saw a mouse in the closet.
   The mouse frightened my little brother.

   Combination: _____

   _____

Now check your combinations against these:

1. Bill replaced the shattered windshield.
2. My frightened little brother cried when he saw a mouse in the closet.

> **Do exercises 3-c and 3-d**

RECOGNIZING AND USING ADVERBS

Recognizing Single-Word Adverbs

Adverbs can be recognized by their use within a sentence. Adverbs answer any of four questions to add information about verbs, adjectives, or other adverbs. (In the examples, arrows are drawn from the adverbs to the words they modify.)

When?

1. The mail will arrive *soon*. [The word *soon* is an adverb telling **when** and modifying the verb *arrive*.]

2. Fred wrote his essay *yesterday*. [The adverb *yesterday* tells **when** and modifies the verb *wrote*.]

Where?

1. The puppy ran *away*. [*Away* is an adverb telling **where** and modifying the verb *ran*.]

2. Karen walked *home*. [The word *home* tells **where** Karen walked; therefore, it is an adverb. Remember that the same word can have different uses. In another sentence *home* could be used as a noun, but here it is used to provide information about the verb.]

How? (In what manner?)

1. The bus driver stopped *suddenly*. [The adverb *suddenly* tells **how** the driver stopped.]

2. *Carefully*, she climbed the ladder. [*Carefully* is an adverb telling **how** and modifying the verb *climbed*.]

How much? How little? (To what degree?)

1. The new secretary types *very* fast. [The word *very* is an adverb modifying the adverb *fast*. It tells **how** fast.]

2. It was *extremely* hot in Kansas last week. [The word *extremely* is an adverb modifying the adjective *hot* by indicating **to what degree**.]

3. Their new Volkswagen Rabbit is *very* economical. [The adverb *very* modifies the adjective *economical* by indicating **to what degree**.]

4. The student finished her lab exercises *quite* rapidly. [The adverb *quite* indicates **to what degree** the exercises were rapidly finished; it modifies the adverb *rapidly*.]

Negatives—Not and Never

The words *not* and *never* are always adverbs. They modify by cancelling the meaning of a verb or adjective:

1. He was *not* sleepy.

2. He *never* tries.

Do exercise 3-e

Placing Single-Word Adverbs

Adverbs, like adjectives, can be added to a subject–verb base. We can take pieces of adverbial information and place them to modify verbs, adjectives, or other adverbs. However, adverbs offer more placement choices than do adjectives. Frequently, adverbs can be placed in any of four positions:

- At the beginning of a sentence.
- In front of a verb or between a main verb and one of its helpers.
- Immediately after the verb.
- At the end of the sentence.

Look at the following examples:

1. *Quietly*, the boy's mother left the room.
2. The boy's mother *quietly* left the room.
3. The boy's mother left *quietly*.
4. The boy's mother left the room *quietly*.

How does sentence 3 differ in content from the other three examples? What would have happened if the direct object, *room*, had not been dropped from the sentence? Could we still place the adverb immediately after the verb, that is, between the verb and its object?

The boy's mother left *quietly* the room.

No, an adverb in that position sounds very awkward. As you combine sentences or write your own, be careful not to place an adverb between a verb and its object.

COMBINING SENTENCES BY USING ADVERBS

Sometimes we can combine sentences by cutting out information that has been repeated. Look at the following example:

1. The five-year-old child waited for a turn on the diving board.
2. She waited nervously.

In sentence 2, the adverb *nervously* is the only new information: *she* is the same person as *child*, and the verb (*waited*) is the same. We can combine the two sentences by placing the adverb in any of the four positions except at the end of the sentence. At the end of the sentence, it would be too far away from the word it modifies, *waited*. Thus, there are the following three possibilities:

Combinations

1. *Nervously*, the five-year-old child waited for a turn on the diving board.
2. The five-year-old child *nervously* waited for a turn on the diving board.
3. The five-year-old child waited *nervously* for a turn on the diving board.

- Look back at the punctuation of the three combinations.
- Notice that a comma (,) is used only when the adverb is placed at **the beginning of the sentence**.
- When an adverb comes immediately before or any place after a verb, it is not set off with a comma.

35

Here is an example of two sentences that can be combined with the adverb in all four positions:

1. The joggers paused at the traffic light.
2. They paused briefly.

Combinations

1. *Briefly*, the joggers paused at the traffic light.
2. The joggers *briefly* paused at the traffic light.
3. The joggers paused *briefly* at the traffic light.
4. The joggers paused at the traffic light *briefly*.

As you combine sentences or place adverbs in your own sentences, pay close attention to their placement and their punctuation. Sometimes placing an adverb in one of the four positions creates an awkward sentence.

Simple sentences

1. The children slept for three hours.
2. They slept soundly.

Awkward Combinations: *Soundly*, the children slept for three hours.
The children *soundly* slept for three hours.
The children slept for three hours *soundly*.

Best Combination: The children slept *soundly* for three hours.

- When the verb in a sentence has an object, the adverb usually cannot be placed between the verb and its object:

$$(S) \quad (V) \quad (DO)$$

1. <u>Karen</u> <u>removed</u> the (mirror.)

2. Karen removed it carefully.

Incorrect Placement: Karen removed *carefully* the mirror.
Correct Placements: *Carefully*, Karen removed the mirror.
Karen *carefully* removed the mirror.
Karen removed the mirror *carefully*.

FORMING ADVERBS FROM ADJECTIVES

Many adverbs are formed by simply adding *-ly* to an adjective:

Adjective	Adverb
beautiful	beautifully
careless	carelessly
cautious	cautiously
courteous	courteously
joyous	joyously
quick	quickly

If an adjective ends in -y, the -y is often changed to i before the -ly is added:

Adjective	Adverb
angry	angrily
easy	easily
guilty	guiltily
happy	happily
hasty	hastily
shabby	shabbily

If an adjective ends in -le, the -le is dropped before -ly is added:

Adjective	Adverb
capable	capably
comfortable	comfortably
miserable	miserably
simple	simply

You will often be able to combine information by changing an adjective to an adverb. For instance, consider the information given in the following two sentences:

1. The waitress dropped the tray.
2. Her manner was careless.

In the second sentence, the adjective *careless* modifies the *manner*, that is, the **way** she dropped it. We can add the idea of *careless* to the first sentence by changing the adjective to the adverb *carelessly*:

Combinations

1. The waitress dropped the tray *carelessly*.
2. *Carelessly*, the waitress dropped the tray.
3. The waitress *carelessly* dropped the tray.

Practice

Here are two more groups of sentences that can be combined by changing an adjective to an adverb. Study each sentence group, and then combine the sentences by changing an adjective to an adverb.

Group 1

1. The guests waited for the homemade ice cream.
2. Their waiting was impatient.

Your combination: _____

_____

Group 2

1. I read the instructions.
2. My reading was careful.

Your combination: _____

_____

Now check your combinations with these:

Combinations of Group 1

Impatiently, the guests waited for the homemade ice cream.
The guests impatiently waited for the homemade ice cream.
The guests waited impatiently for the homemade ice cream.
The guests waited for the homemade ice cream impatiently.

Combinations of Group 2

I carefully read the instructions.
Carefully, I read the instructions.
I read the instructions carefully.

Do exercises 3-f, 3-g, and 3-h

USING ADJECTIVES AND ADVERBS IN COMPARISONS

Single-word adjectives and adverbs can be used to state comparisons by adding a suffix (*-er* or *-est*) or by placing the adverbs *less* or *least* or *more* or *most* in front of them.

The words *less* and *more* and the *-er* ending are used to compare one with another. The words *least* and *most* and the *-est* ending are used to compare one with two or more.

USING -ER AND -EST

Adjectives	Adverbs
Mary received a *low* score on the test.	Francine drives *fast*.
Jack's score was *lower*.	Her brother drives *faster* than Francine.
Beth Anne's score was the *lowest* in the class.	Her mother drives *fastest*.

USING MORE AND MOST

Adjectives	Adverbs
Jason's apology was *sincere*.	Jason apologized *sincerely*.
Mary's apology was *more sincere*.	Mary apologized *more sincerely*.
Henrietta's apology was the *most sincere* of all.	Henrietta apologized *most sincerely* of all.

Choosing between adding the suffixes (*-er* and *-est*) or the adverbs depends on ease of pronunciation.

- Some adjectives of two syllables and all adjectives of three or more syllables add the adverbs instead of the suffixes:

  Esther is my *most* generous relative.
  Frank was the *least* ambitious of the Joneses.

- When adverbs end in *-ly*, we never add *-er* or *-est* to show comparisons. Instead, in front of the adverb, we add the appropriate adverb:

  Gertrude works *less* regularly than her sister.
  Of all my friends, Madge lives *most* luxuriously.

- Be careful not to use both a suffix and an adverbial modifier to create a comparison:

Incorrect:	Betty works *more* hard*er* than Fran.
	Jack's brother is *more* handsom*er* than mine.

CONFUSING ADJECTIVES AND ADVERBS

Sometimes, especially in conversation, people confuse adjectives and adverbs. For instance, they may use an adjective to do an adverb's job—to modify a verb. Such confusions have become so common in spoken English that we often do not notice them. However, in writing they are distracting and should be avoided.

Study the following examples of the correct use of some commonly confused adjectives and adverbs. Draw an arrow from each italicized **adjective** to the **noun** it modifies; draw an arrow from each italicized **adverb** to the **verb** it modifies.

Sentences with Adjectives	*Sentences with Adverbs*
1. Grandmother's health is a *real* worry to her.	Grandmother is *really* [or *very*] worried about her health.
2. It was a *sudden* storm.	The storm arose *suddenly*.
3. The decline of his health was *rapid*.	His health declined *rapidly*.
4. Delbert is an *awkward* dancer.	Delbert dances *awkwardly*.
5. His answer was *satisfactory*.	He answered *satisfactorily*.
6. My horse is a *sure* winner.	My horse will *surely* win.
7. The weather showed *some* improvement.	The weather improved *somewhat*.
8. The referee made a *quick* decision.	The referee decided *quickly*.
9. The roof had a *bad* leak.	The roof leaked *badly*.
10. Mr. Holland was a *good* teacher.	Mr. Holland taught *well*.

In your writing do not confuse these pairs:

Adjective	*Adverb*
1. real	really [*or* very]
2. most	almost
3. sure	surely
4. right	very
5. some	somewhat

Study the following examples of the correct use of these pairs. Draw an arrow from the italicized adjective or adverb to the word it modifies.

Sentences with Adjectives	*Sentences with Adverbs*
1. My *real* feelings were ignored.	I feel *really* [or *very*] confident.
2. *Most* children enjoy parties.	*Almost* all children enjoy parties.
3. I am *sure*.	I *surely* hope so.
4. Father was *right*.	Father looked *very* worried.
5. *Some* dancers were graceful.	Others were *somewhat* awkward.

Remember, too, that adjectives, not adverbs, are used as complements after non-action (linking) verbs such as *be, appear, seem, become, look, sound*. (The use of complements after linking verbs is explained in Chapter 1.) Adjective complements modify the subject, as in the following examples:

1. General Washington seemed *confident*.

2. The coach became *angry*.

3. The players were *eager*.

Adverbs telling how an action is done are used with action verbs, as in these examples:

1. George Washington spoke *confidently*.

2. The coach screamed *angrily*.

3. The players *eagerly* ran toward the field.

Do exercises 3-i, 3-j, and 3-k

SUGGESTIONS FOR WRITING

In your journal, describe a person whom you know well—a relative, a friend, an employer. Include as many details as you can in your description.

When you have finished your description, look back at your sentences. Have you told what the person looks like? Have you explained how the person acts? If not, try to add specific information to your sentences. Use adjectives and adverbs that describe and inform.

NAME _____ **DATE** _____

Underline each adjective in the following sentences. (Do not mark the articles *a, an,* and *the*.) Draw an arrow from the underlined adjective to the noun or pronoun it modifies.

EXAMPLES

My new kitten will not eat that cat food.

My mother hid three birthday presents in Jack's closet.

1. The hungry child ate three sandwiches.

2. My father replaced the old kitchen counter.

3. Ali wanted to buy the expensive shoes.

4. The ten new senators met in the governor's office.

5. Fred wrote two wrong answers on his exam paper.

6. The last patient is sitting in the waiting room.

7. Alan's elderly mother lives in her own home.

8. His excellent sales record pleased the boss.

9. Steve baked two chocolate cakes with vanilla icing for the bake sale.

10. The rolls in the bread box are stale.

11. Debbie's camera needs a new flash attachment.

12. The first customer will receive a gift certificate.

13. Several discs are missing from the computer lab.

14. Althea borrowed ten dollars from Mickey's brother.

15. The proud student accepted the typing award.

NAME _____ DATE _____

I. Underline the participial modifier used as an adjective in each sentence.

EXAMPLE

Ned's brother is an <u>experienced</u> mechanic.

1. The old woman frowned at the broken window.

2. The barking dog was running from room to room.

3. The two aging brothers had not seen each other for five years.

4. The teacher returned the plagiarized report.

5. The neglected plant hung in the corner.

6. The screaming love birds were disturbing Denise.

II. Use the *-ed* or the *-ing* form of the given verb to form an appropriate adjective. Write the adjective on the blank line.

EXAMPLES

frighten

The children cried at the ___*frightening*___ masks.

The ___*frightening*___ child left the party early.

1. iron

   Bob's freshly _____ shirt was draped over the kitchen chair.

   The _____ board leaned against the wall on the back porch.

2. excite

   Only one reporter heard the _____ announcement.

   The _____ reporter ran from the courtroom.

3. exhaust

   The coach had set up an _____ practice schedule.

   The _____ wrestlers were stumbling on the mats.

4. confuse

   The _____ road signs offered the driver no help.

   The _____ driver was going the wrong way on a one-way street.

NAME _____ **DATE** _____

Combine each group of sentences into one simple sentence.

- Identify and place a check (÷) by the most important sentence. Use this sentence as the base of your combination.
- Cut the other sentences to the new information (adjectives) they contain. Place the adjectives in front of the nouns and pronouns they modify in the base sentences.

EXAMPLE

✓ Ray hid the ring in a trunk.
The ring was expensive.
The trunk was old.

Combination: ___*Ray hid the expensive ring in an old trunk.*___

_____

_____

1. Sharon covered the table with a tablecloth.
The table was scratched.
The tablecloth was made of lace.

Combination: _____

_____

2. In 1983, Nick bought an orchard and a cider press.
The orchard was for apples.
The cider press was old.

Combination: _____

_____

3. The puppy and the kitten share the same toys.
The puppy is frisky.
The kitten is mischievous.

Combination: _____

_____

4. The dancer wore a costume.
The dancer danced tap.
The costume was for a bathing beauty.

Combination: _____

_____

NAME _____ DATE _____

Combine each pair of sentences by turning a verb into an *-ing* or an *-ed* adjective.
- Consider the relationship between the two sentences.
- Decide which sentence will be the subject–verb base of your combination, and place a check by it.
- Change a verb in the other sentence to an –ing or –ed form that can be used to modify a noun in the sentence that contains the base.

EXAMPLE

The weatherman repeated his warnings about the hurricane.
The weatherman's warnings about the hurricane frightened the vacationers.

Combination: *The weatherman's repeated warnings about the*

hurricane frightened the vacationers.

1. My brother was struggling.
   My brother was a portrait painter.

   Combination: _____

2. The window was shattered.
   The boy had to fix the window.

   Combination: _____

3. The interview disappointed the candidate.
   The candidate quickly left the interview.

   Combination: _____

4. The audience cheered.
   The audience stood up to honor the young violinist.

   Combination: _____

5. Jason sprained his ankle.
   Jason could not use his ankle.

   Combination: _____

6. The owl screeched.
   The owl awoke all the campers.

   Combination: _____

NAME _____ **DATE** _____

Underline each adverb in the following sentences. Draw an arrow from the adverb to the verb, adjective, or other adverb it modifies.

EXAMPLES

The bus driver stopped very suddenly.

Bill never leaves his keys here.

1. Andrea answered the questions honestly.

2. I did not finish the inventory yesterday.

3. Phil walked home very slowly.

4. Claire skates extremely well.

5. Thoughtlessly, my sister ate all the cookies.

6. I will arrive home very late today.

7. The dinner is almost ready.

8. Cautiously, the forest ranger approached the seriously injured raccoon.

9. Leave your suitcases here tonight.

10. Jody foolishly threw the receipt away.

11. The most difficult question is not on the quiz.

12. The new secretary works slowly and carelessly.

13. My office is extremely cold today.

14. Francine generously offered her ticket to her sister.

15. The feverish boy jealously watched the skiers.

NAME _____ **DATE** _____

Combine each group of sentences into one simple sentence.

- Place a check (√) by the sentence that contains the main idea. Use this sentence as the subject–verb base of your combination.
- Change an adjective in the other sentence to an adverb that can modify a verb, an adjective, or another adverb in the sentence you selected to be the base.
- Place the adverb in the base sentence and punctuate if necessary.

EXAMPLE

√ Lauren and Larry refinished the antique piano.
Their work was neat.

Combination: _____*Lauren and Larry neatly refinished the*_____
_____*antique piano.*_____

Combination: _____*Neatly, Lauren and Larry refinished the*_____
_____*antique piano.*_____

Combination: _____*Laren and Larry refinished the*_____
_____*antique piano neatly.*_____

---

1. The waitress greeted the customers.
   Her greeting was polite.

   Combination: _____

   _____

2. The children complete their chores on Saturday morning.
   Their work is routine.

   Combination: _____

   _____

3. The contestant answered the final question.
   Her answer was incorrect.

   Combination: _____

   _____

4. Shannon's grandmother is ill.
   Her illness is serious.

   Combination: _____

   _____

5. The instructor reviewed the chapter.
   The review was thorough.

   Combination: _____

   _____

6. Leslie chose a very difficult topic for her report.
   Her choice was ambitious.

   Combination: _____

   _____

7. Bill applied for a promotion.
   His application was recent.

   Combination: _____

   _____

8. My parents were angry about the accident.
   Their anger was extreme.

   Combination: _____

   _____

9. My manager decided to fire three salespeople.
   The decision was sudden.

   Combination: _____

   _____

10. The class ended.
    The ending was abrupt.

    Combination: _____

    _____

NAME _____ **DATE** _____

Each sentence has an underlined adjective. Write a related sentence using the corresponding adverb form.

EXAMPLES

Carol's apology was <u>sincere</u>.

Carol apologized sincerely. _____

The <u>cautious</u> detective examined the evidence.

The detective cautiously examined the evidence. _____

1. The <u>impatient</u> shopper rang the bell five times.

    _____

2. The <u>playful</u> dachshund chased the German shepherd.

    _____

3. Tina's smile was <u>proud</u>.

    _____

4. Jim's reply was <u>enthusiastic</u>.

    _____

5. The <u>nervous</u> students waited for their instructor.

    _____

6. Kevin's resignation was <u>bitter</u>.

    _____

7. The <u>angry</u> customers complained to the manager.

    _____

8. Jan's teaching is <u>competent</u>.

    _____

9. The <u>brave</u> soldier volunteered for an extra mission.

    _____

10. Walter is a <u>good</u> swimmer.

    _____

NAME _____ **DATE** _____

I. Make the following sentences more descriptive (that is, more informative and specific) by adding adjectives. Draw an arrow from each adjective you add to the noun or pronoun that it modifies.

EXAMPLE

Our _____*new*_____ car is in _____*Evan's*_____ driveway.

1. The _____ runner won the _____ race.

2. His _____ brother appeared _____ .

3. I brought my _____ notes to the _____ meeting.

4. My friend left _____ raincoat in _____ car.

5. The _____ schools were closed because of the _____ storm.

6. Our _____ dog spent the night in the _____ kennel.

7. The _____ man felt _____ .

II. Make the following sentences more descriptive by adding adverbs. Draw an arrow from each adverb you add to the verb, adjective, or other adverb that it modifies.

EXAMPLE

• _____*Usually*_____ , Fran's answers are _____*extremely*_____ courteous.

1. _____ , Betty completes her assignments _____ .

2. _____ , Dan quit his job.

3. I _____ make spaghetti sauce on Saturday afternoon.

4. The child stared _____ at the chocolate cake.

5. The dogs barked _____ at the mail carrier.

6. Gary danced _____ for the audition.

7. _____ , the thief ran into the alley.

8. It is _____ hot in the classroom.

NAME _____ **DATE** _____

In each sentence underline the correct word, either the adjective or the adverb.

EXAMPLE

These days, Kurt's family and friends are (real, <u>very</u>) surprised by his academic achievements.

1. Kurt had never done (good, well) in high school.

2. He had never been (real, very) interested in his subjects.

3. He had not attended classes (regular, regularly).

4. His one (real, really) interest then was cars.

5. After high school, he had (absolute, absolutely) no interest in college.

6. Kurt's only ambition was to be a (successful, successfully) mechanic.

7. He (easy, easily) found a job in a gas station.

8. But he was qualified to do only (simple, simply) repair jobs.

9. He became bored with the work (quick, quickly).

10. (Fortunate, Fortunately), his friend Tom made an excellent suggestion.

11. An extension center of the state university was (convenient, conveniently) located near Kurt's home and job.

12. Kurt could further develop his (mechanical, mechanically) skills by taking college courses.

13. At the extension center, he (wise, wisely) took a variety of courses.

14. He became (real, very) interested in history.

15. After four years of night classes, he (proud, proudly) received an A.A. degree.

16. Then he made a (brave, bravely) decision.

17. He was (apprehensive, apprehensively) about getting a B.A. degree, so he decided to go to school full-time for two years.

18. He quit his (routine, routinely) job at the gas station.

19. He (ambitious, ambitiously) registered for five courses his first semester.

20. He did very (good, well) in all his courses, particularly in history.

21. Now he is (eager, eagerly) applying to graduate schools.

22. He is (confident, confidently) that he will be accepted.

23. He (enthusiastic, enthusiastically) looks forward to becoming a history teacher.

24. (Occasional, Occasionally), his family and friends remind him of his high school days.

25. But they are (real, very) happy about his success.

NAME _____ **DATE** _____

Rearrange each group of scrambled words into one sentence. Add no words except *a, an*, and *the*.

EXAMPLES

was   advice   helpful   Terry's   extremely

Terry's advice was extremely helpful. _____

asked   question   student   hesitantly

The student asked the question hesitantly. _____

1. aunt   youngest   her   is   favorite   Olga's

_____

2. became   cold   increasingly   his   feet

_____

3. early   Grethchen's   sent   home   employer   her

_____

4. loudly   fans   angry   yelled

_____

5. all   were   there   their   movies   favorite

_____

6. Shelly   diamond   brother   gave   my   oldest   real

_____

7. complain   never   customers   some

_____

8. steadily   Clint's   improved   grades   math

_____

9. always   Barry's   generous   is   grandfather   very

_____

10. obviously   answer   incorrect   Chris's   was

_____

NAME _____ DATE _____

I. Write a sentence using each adjective given at the left of the sentence number. Draw an arrow from the adjective to the noun or pronoun it modifies.

EXAMPLES

kind ____*Gail is very kind to her younger brother.*_____

easy ____*My math teacher gives easy quizzes.*_____

good   1. _____

_____

real   2. _____

_____

careless   3. _____

_____

quiet   4. _____

_____

sure   5. _____

_____

wise   6. _____

_____

thoughtful 7. _____

_____

generous   8. _____

_____

angry   9. _____

_____

neat   10. _____

_____

II. Write a sentence using each adverb given by the sentence number. Draw an arrow from the adverb to the word it modifies.

EXAMPLES

kindly *The nurses treated the patient kindly.*

easily *I easily completed my homework.*

well   1. _____

_____

really   2. _____

_____

carelessly   3. _____

_____

quietly   4. _____

_____

surely   5. _____

_____

wisely   6. _____

_____

thoughtfully   7. _____

_____

generously   8. _____

_____

angrily   9. _____

_____

neatly   10. _____

_____

Using Prepositional Phrases

4

As we write, we often group words together to form a **phrase**. The words in the phrase work together to state one kind of information. A phrase has a single use in a sentence—as an adjective, an adverb, or a noun. Like the single-word modifiers you studied in Chapter 3, phrases allow you to place describing or identifying information in a sentence.

In this chapter, you will study one of the most frequently used phrases, the **prepositional phrase**.

BUILDING A PREPOSITIONAL PHRASE

A prepositional phrase begins with a **preposition** and ends with a noun or pronoun. This noun or pronoun is the **object of the preposition**. A phrase may also include words modifying the object. Look at these two prepositional phrases:

> in my history class
> about the new assignment

The words of each phrase work together to convey one kind of information. We might add these two phrases to a subject–verb base:

> The students *in my history class* seem upset *about the new assignment*.

In this sentence, the phrase *in my history class* identifies **which** students are meant; therefore, the phrase functions as an adjective. The phrase *about the new assignment* modifies the adjective *upset* by telling **in what manner** or **how**; therefore, the phrase functions as an adverb.

Using the Right Prepositions

A preposition is a **connector**. It connects its object to the word the phrase modifies. A preposition can make this connection because of its meaning. It indicates a particular meaningful relationship between its object and the word the phrase modifies.

The following sections indicate the most common kinds of relationships. As you proceed through these sections, you may need to look in a dictionary for definitions and examples of prepositions.

Prepositions Showing Space Relationships

Many prepositions indicate relationships in **space**; they tell **where**. Consider the spatial meaning of the following prepositions:

> on   in   inside   under   behind   near

Now read each of those six spatial prepositions into the blank space in the following sentence. In your mind, picture where the calculator is as you use each preposition.

> The calculator _____ the desk is mine.

The following list contains additional prepositions that can show spatial relationships. On the blank line after each preposition create a prepositional phrase by adding a noun object and its modifiers.

above _____

across _____

among _____

around _____

at _____

below _____

beneath _____

between _____ and _____

from _____

into _____

off [**never** off of] _____

onto _____

over _____

through _____

throughout _____

to _____

toward _____

up _____

upon _____

The prepositional phrases you created could be placed in sentences to add information about **where** something occurred or **where** someone was.

Be sure not to confuse the word *to* with the words *two* and *too*. Use *to* as a preposition; the word *two* indicates number, and *too* is an adverb indicating addition or excess:

Preposition:	to	James went *to* the dance.
Adjective:	two	James has *two* girlfriends.
Adverb:	too	James has *too* many girlfriends.
		James, *too*, has several girlfriends.

Prepositions Showing time Relationships

Many prepositions indicate relationships in **time**. Consider the time meanings of the following prepositions:

after   before   during   throughout   until   till

Read each preposition into the blank space of the following sentence and notice the relationship each establishes between *movie* (the object) and *whispered* (the word the phrase modifies).

The children whispered _____ the last movie.

The following prepositions can also show time relationships. On the blank line, create a phrase by adding a noun object and its modifiers.

about _____ in _____

around _____ since _____

at _____ for _____

by _____

Note that many prepositions have many different meanings. Some of the prepositions listed can show time or space:

Space: My boss walked *into the room*.
Time: Your mother will be home *in an hour*.

Space: The cat chased the dog *around the house*.
Time: We will arrive *around noon*.

Prepositions Showing Possession or Accompaniment

We often use the preposition *of* to state that one person or thing is possessed by or is part of another:

1. the roof *of* the house
2. the end *of* the show
3. the leaves *of* the tree

Possession might also be shown with *in, to*, or *for*:

1. the answer *to* his question
2. the last chapter *in* [or *of*] the book
3. the lawyer *for* the defense

The prepositions *in addition to, along with*, or *with* indicate that the object accompanies or contains someone or something:

1. the report *with* the fewest errors
2. the child, *along with* his parents,
3. your interpretation, *in addition to* other meanings,

The preposition *without*, of course, states the negative:

1. the only paper *without* errors
2. a child *without* parents

Prepositions Showing other Relationships

In addition to space, time, and possession, prepositions can indicate other meanings:

1. *Cause*: because of, on account of
2. *Comparison*: as, like, similar to
3. *Contrast*: unlike, except, but, in spite of
4. *Manner*: as, with, without
5. *Means*: by, through
6. *Support*: for, in favor of
7. *Opposition*: against

(Notice that some prepositions consist of more than one word: *because of, on account of, in spite of, in favor of*.)

The following examples illustrate the seven meanings. (The prepositions are in italics, and the prepositional phrases are enclosed in parentheses.)

1. We left (*because of* his rude behavior).
2. Henry looked (*like* his father).
3. Everyone (*except* Mary Anne) ate the rice pudding.
4. Henry left (*without* a smile).
5. (*By* sheer will power), Paul stopped smoking.
6. We argued (*for* a lower tax).
7. They fought (*against* my father).

As you use prepositions, be sure you select the one that establishes the meaning you intend. Remember that prepositions often have many different meanings, and you may wish to look in a dictionary for definitions and examples.

Do exercises 4-a and 4-b

Using Personal Pronouns as Objects

When personal pronouns are objects of prepositions, they should be in the **object** forms that you studied in Chapter 2.

OBJECT FORMS OF
PERSONAL PRONOUNS

Singular	*Plural*
me	us
you	you
him	them
her	them
it	them

Study the following examples. (The prepositional phrases are enclosed in parentheses, and the objects are printed in italics.)

1. (Just between *you* and *me*), Fred is wrong.

   (Just between *us*), Fred is wrong.

2. He divided the money (among my *brothers* and *me*).

   He divided the money (among *us*).

3. Sadie returned the money (to *Frank* and *me*).

   Sadie returned the money (to *us*).

USING PREPOSITIONAL PHRASES AS ADJECTIVES

Prepositional phrases often modify nouns or pronouns. Such phrases are **adjectives**. They should be placed right **after** the noun or pronoun they modify. In the following examples, the prepositional phrases are enclosed in parentheses, and an arrow connects each phrase and the noun or pronoun it modifies.

1. One (of the men) has no tools.

2. They gave me no promise (of a reward).

3. Some shingles (on the roof) (of the house) blew away.

One of the most common uses of the prepositional phrase is to modify the subject of a sentence.

- Do not confuse the subject of the sentence with the object in a prepositional phrase. Remember that the subject is **never** located inside a prepositional phrase.

Study the following sentences in which the subjects are underlined once, the verbs are underlined twice, and the prepositional phrases are enclosed in parentheses.

1. Several (of the men) worked late.

2. Each man (in the room) looked surprised.

3. Every line (of his notes) was neat.

4. Each picture (on the walls) seemed important.

USING PREPOSITIONAL PHRASES AS ADVERBS

Prepositional phrases can be used as adverbs to modify adjectives, adverbs, or verbs:

1. Francine was kind (to her parents). [The prepositional phrase *to her parents* is an adverb modifying the adjective *kind*.]

2. Leslie lives far (from her parents). [The prepositional phrase *from her parents* is an adverb modifying the adverb *far*.]

3. Harry traveled (to the convention) (in his car). [The prepositional phrases *to the convention* and *in his car* are adverbs modifying the verb *traveled*.]

Prepositional phrases used as adverbs most frequently modify verbs.

Placing Prepositional Phrases

Like the single-word adverbs, phrases used as adverbs can be positioned in several places. Their normal position is at the end of the sentence. Adverbial phrases placed at the beginning of a sentence are called *introductory* modifiers.

- Introductory modifiers are usually set off by a comma.

1. Because of his illness, Barry sometimes arrived late.
2. Barry sometimes arrived late because of his illness.

Notice that in the two examples the subjects and verbs are in their normal order.

Changing Order of Subject and Verb

When some prepositional phrases telling **where** (place) appear at the beginning of a sentence, the subject and verb pattern can be reversed to

    prepositional phrase   +   verb   +   subject

In such sentences, no comma is used to set off the prepositional phrase. Look at the following examples:

1. Through the door came the old fisherman.

2. From the lion's cave came a loud roar.

3. Between the car and the fence stood two police officers.

These sentences can, of course, be written in the normal subject–verb order by placing the phrase at the end of the sentence:

1. The old fisherman came through the open door.

2. A loud roar came from the lion's cave.

3. Two police officers stood between the car and the fence.

Using Several Modifiers

In sentences that have several phrases and single–word adjectives or adverbs, you must place the modifiers carefully. Here are some guidelines:

- Place each adjective phrase immediately after the word it modifies.

    Correct: The messenger knocked rapidly on the door *of the house.*

    Incorrect: The messenger knocked on the door rapidly *of the house.*
    [The adjective phrase *of the house* is incorrectly separated from the noun it modifies, *door.*]

- Do not place an adverb between a verb and its objects. (In the following sentences, the direct object is in italics.)

    Correct: He managed the *store* alone.
    He managed the *store* by himself.

    Incorrect: He managed alone the *store.*
    He managed by himself the *store.*
    [The adverbial modifiers—the word *alone* and the phrase *by himself*—are incorrectly placed between the verb *managed* and the direct object *store.*]

- Place single-word adverbs at the beginning of the sentence only if they modify the whole sense of the verb's action.

The following example illustrates the three rules:

Suddenly, the manager of the restaurant pushed the cashier away from the thief.

Note the placement of the adjective and the three adverbs:

The adjective phrase *of the restaurant* is placed immediately after *manager,* the noun it modifies.
The adverb *suddenly,* which modifies the whole action, may be placed at the beginning.
The adverb *away* is placed after the direct object *cashier.*
The adverb phrase *from the thief* is placed after *away,* the adverb it modifies.

Compare the placement of adjectives and adverbs in the following sentences. Why are the placements clear in the first two examples but not in the third?

Clear: During intermission, he reluctantly met his sister's friends at the refreshment booth.

Reluctantly, he met his sister's friends at the refreshment booth during intermission.

Awkward: He met his sister's friends at the refreshment booth during intermission reluctantly.

[*Reluctantly* is unnecessarily far from the verb it modifies, and the pileup of adverbs at the end sounds awkward.]

COMBINING SENTENCES BY USING PREPOSITIONAL PHRASES

Adding Prepositional Phrases to a Sentence Base

Like single-word adjectives and adverbs, prepositional phrases can be added to a subject–verb base. We can often eliminate unnecessary repetition by combining sentences in this way. Sometimes we can simply select the most important of the sentences to be the sentence base and then cut the new information in the other sentences to a prepositional phrase, discarding the words that were repeated.

Look at the following pair of sentences. The first sentence is obviously the more important, and the second adds only the information in the prepositional phrase.

The lamp needs a new light bulb.
The lamp is on the night table.

Combination: The lamp on the night table needs a new light bulb.

Since the phrase *on the night table* modifies the noun *lamp*, it functions as an adjective and must be placed immediately after the noun.

Look at the following group of sentences. Again, the first is the important one; the second and third add only the information in the prepositional phrases.

Karen washed the sweaters.
Karen washed them by hand.
Karen washed them in cold water.

Combination: Karen washed the sweaters by hand in cold water.

The two phrases read smoothly at the end of the sentence after the direct object.

Changing a Sentence into a Prepositional Phrase

In combining the information in several sentences, you can sometimes change a sentence into a prepositional phrase and then add it onto a base. Here are examples of sentences that can be combined in that way.

61

Group 1

The time was 3:00 P.M. [This sentence can be changed to a prepositional phrase, *at 3:00 P.M.*]
The history class was over.

Combinations: The history class was over at 3:00 P.M.
     At 3:00 P.M., the history class was over.

Group 2

The movie was over. [This sentence can be changed to a prepositional phrase, *after the movie.*]
We drove back to Ocean City.

Combinations: We drove back to Ocean City after the movie.
     After the movie, we drove back to Ocean City.

Both *at 3:00 P.M.* in group 1 and *after the movie* in group 2 modify the verb in the combinations. Thus, they are adverbs. Like other adverbs that modify verbs, prepositional phrases can be placed at the beginning or at the end of a sentence. Remember that an adverbial phrase at the beginning of a sentence is set off by a comma. A phrase at the end of the sentence should not be set off by a comma.

Do exercise 4-c

Reducing a Prepositional Phrase to a Single-Word Possessive

A prepositional phrase formed by the prepositions *in, of, to,* or *for* can sometimes be changed into a possessive noun (see Chapter 1). The possessive noun can then be added to a sentence base. Combining such information in this way is often more economical and thus more effective than using a whole phrase (or sentence) to convey the adjective information, **whose** or **which**.

Group 1

The whistle had fallen in the sand.
The whistle belonged *to the lifeguard.*

Combination: The *lifeguard's* whistle had fallen in the sand.

Group 2

He broke two of the windows.
The windows were *in the car.*

Combination: He broke two of the *car's* windows.

Practice

Now practice changing a phrase to a possessive:

Group 3

Coffee and doughnuts will be served in the lounge.
The lounge is for the teachers.

Combination: _____

_____

In your combination, you should have changed *for the teachers* to the plural possessive *teachers'* to create this sentence:

Coffee and doughnuts will be served in the *teachers'* lounge.

Reducing a Prepositional Phrase to a Single-Word Adjective or Adverb

Sometimes a prepositional phrase can be reduced to a single-word adjective or adverb without changing the meaning of the sentence. Again, such changes can often make writing more economical and more effective. Here are three examples:

1. Her ability *in the area of athletics* surprised her friends.
   Reduced: Her *athletic* ability surprised her friends.
2. Lee always spoke *in a loud voice*.
   Reduced: Lee always spoke *loudly*.
3. The garage *of our new neighbors* is full of boxes.
   Reduced: *Our new neighbors'* garage is full of boxes.

In the first sentence, the phrase *in the area of athletics* can easily be reduced to the adjective *athletic*. In the second sentence, *in a loud voice* can be changed to the adverb *loudly*. In sentence 3, the phrase *of our new neighbors* can be changed to the possessive *our new neighbors'*, keeping the modifiers *our* and *new*. In each example, the reduction of a phrase to a single-word modifier makes the sentence more economical without changing the meaning of the original sentence.

Practice

Reduce the prepositional phrases italicized in the following sentences to single-word modifiers—possessive adjectives, other adjectives, or adverbs.

1. Tom performs his duties as a stock boy *in a satisfactory manner*.

   Reduced: _____

   _____

2. Students *in nursing* must register early.

   Reduced: _____

   _____

3. The kitchen *of my son* is always *without a spot*.

Reduced: _____

_____

Check your reduced sentences against the following examples:

1. **Correct:**   Tom *satisfactorily* performs his duties as a stock boy.
                  Tom performs his duties as a stock boy *satisfactorily*.
   Incorrect: Tom performs *satisfactorily* his duties as a stock boy.
                  Tom performs his duties *satisfactorily* as a stock boy.
                  [You should not separate the verb *performs* from its object, *duties*, or separate the noun *duties* from the adjective phrase that modifies it, *as a stock boy*.]
2. **Correct:**   *Nursing* students must register early.
3. **Correct:**   My *son's* kitchen is always *spotless*.

Do exercises 4-d, 4-e, and 4-f

SUGGESTIONS FOR WRITING

Explain the route you follow to walk, ride, or drive from one place to another. For example, you might give directions from your apartment to your bus stop, or you might write about your route from your house to a shopping mall. Try to use prepositional phrases to help make your route clear.

Now look back over your sentences. Have you given specific and correct information at the right times: for instance, have you given specifics such as "Make a right turn at the third light after the Shell station"?

After you have made your directions as clear as you can, ask a friend or a relative to read your directions to see if he or she can follow them. If your reader has trouble understanding your directions, make any necessary changes.

NAME _____ **DATE** _____

Place parentheses around the prepositional phrase in each of the following sentences. (Some sentences may have more than one phrase.) Then underline the subject once and the verb twice.

EXAMPLE

Many (of the players) are practicing (in the gym.)

===

1. We searched for the earring in the car.

2. Bob went to the movies with my sister.

3. Several of my friends work at the mall on weekends.

4. The answer to the problem is in the back of the book.

5. After the accident, the money was divided between Owen and Roy.

6. Because of the snowstorm, the meeting was postponed until Friday.

7. Each of Jim's daughters has a phone in her room.

8. Since 1987, the elementary school has been overcrowded.

9. I will meet you in the cafeteria at 7:30.

10. Four of Eleanor's friends have moved to Georgia within the past two months.

11. The table on the porch has been covered with newspapers for a week.

12. The student aide helped the students with their assignments during the teacher's absence.

13. Linda, unlike her sister, is never late for choir rehearsal.

14. Two of the students in my Spanish class have been to Spain.

15. Each of the band members needs a music stand.

16. The dog chased the cat around the tree.

17. Among my old letters, I found a picture of my grandmother.

18. The principal has received many phone calls about the math teacher.

19. All of the basketball players except James attended the practice on Saturday.

20. Alice went to Jennifer's party without Ronald.

NAME _____ **DATE** _____

Select a preposition that fits each of the blank spaces in the following sentences. If you have any doubts about the meaning of a preposition, check it in a dictionary.

EXAMPLE

Max left for the movies ____*without*____ me.

1. We will leave for school _____ 7:30.

2. Nina planted the lilac bushes _____ the garage.

3. The two-year-old stood _____ his two older brothers.

4. The bowler _____ the highest score will win the trophy.

5. All the student aides _____ Marlene use the word processor.

6. Lenny went _____ his first sign language class _____ Saturday.

7. Anne sent Virginia a box of oranges _____ Florida.

8. My father always falls asleep _____ his favorite chair _____ the news.

9. George walked _____ the room proudly.

10. Rose divided the homemade chocolates _____ the six guests.

11. I have not visited my hometown _____ 1988.

12. Phillip will pick you up _____ the concert.

13. My daughter refused to sit _____ me _____ the movie theater.

14. My boss borrowed a book _____ herbs _____ me.

15. Jenny can't leave work _____ 7:00.

16. The young man walked _____ us angrily.

17. Eric jogs _____ the track twenty times every morning.

18. You will find the answers to the math questions _____ the back

    _____ the textbook.

19. The puppy hid _____ the bed.

20. Edith has to finish her studying _____ 11:30.

NAME _____ **DATE** _____

     Read through each group of sentences, paying close attention to the relation of one thought to another. Then combine each group into one sentence with only one subject and verb.

- Select the main sentence in the group to use as the base of your combination, and put a check beside it.
- Use the information in the other sentences to create prepositional phrases.
- Place the prepositional phrases in the main sentence.
- Set off introductory phrases with commas.

EXAMPLE

    Jill started taking piano lessons in March.   The lessons are at the university.
✓ Since then, Jill has been taking lessons.   The lessons are from Mrs. Hughes.

Combination: *Since March, Jill has been taking piano lessons at the university from Mrs. Hughes.*

---

1. I met my old friend.   We met at a quiet cafe.
   My old friend was from high school.   We met after work.

   Combination: _____

   _____

2. The sweaters should be put away.   The sweaters should be put in the trunk.
   The sweaters are in the hall closet.   Moth balls should be put with the sweaters.

   Combination: _____

   _____

3. Keith unexpectedly arrived.   Four friends were with him.
   Keith arrived during dinner.   They were from his old high school.

   Combination: _____

   _____

4. The union meeting was over.   We started at the union headquarters.
   We walked.   We finished walking at City Hall.

   Combination: _____

   _____

5. Wilma visited her sister in 1988.   Her sister lives in Oregon.
   Since then, Wilma has not visited her sister.

   Combination: _____

   _____

6. Palmer takes photographs.
   One photograph was printed
   in the magazine section

   The magazine section was in the newspaper.
   The newspaper came out on Sunday.

   Combination: _____

   _____

NAME _____ **DATE** _____

    Reduce each italicized prepositional phrase in the following sentences to a possessive noun, an adjective, or an adverb.

EXAMPLE

The children left the house *in a quick manner.*

Reduced: *The children left the house quickly.* _____

---

1. The guests approached the dinner table *in an eager manner.*

   Reduced: _____

2. All students *of nursing* must register on December 8.

   Reduced: _____

3. The choir sang the anthem *without joy.*

   Reduced: _____

4. The assignment *for the students* was written on the board.

   Reduced: _____

5. The minister listened to the woman's story *with sympathy.*

   Reduced: _____

6. The costume *of the dancer* needs to be altered.

   Reduced: _____

7. The baby *with dimples* smiled at the toddlers.

   Reduced: _____

8. The new chairs *for my brother* are in the car.

   Reduced: _____

9. Syd waited for the bus *with impatience.*

   Reduced: _____

10. Nathan entered the abandoned warehouse *with fear.*

    Reduced: _____

NAME _____ DATE _____

Write a sentence using the preposition that is given in front of each number and any one of the verbs that follow. (You will, of course, use some of the verbs more than once.) In your sentence enclose the prepositional phrase in parentheses, and underline the subject of the verb once and the verb twice.

read   worked   stayed   told   received   sent   walked   lived

EXAMPLE

during *(During the winter,) my mother worked in Washington.* _____

until   1. _____

          _____

from   2. _____

          _____

of   3. _____

          _____

to   4. _____

          _____

with   5. _____

          _____

at   6. _____

          _____

near   7. _____

          _____

in   8. _____

          _____

about   9. _____

          _____

except   10. _____

          _____

NAME _____ **DATE** _____

Using the principles you have learned in the first four chapters of this book, combine each group of sentences into one simple sentence with only one subject and one verb.

- Select one sentence in each group to be the base of your combination, and put a check beside it.
- Identify the new information added by each of the other sentences.
- When possible, reduce prepositional phrases to single-word modifiers—possessive nouns, adjectives, or adverbs.
- Set off introductory modifiers with a comma.

Check to be sure your combination has only one subject and one verb. Underline the subject once and the verb twice in your combination.

EXAMPLE

Americans have become interested.
The interest began in the 1980s.
Their interest increased.
Their interest was in using chili peppers.
They used the peppers in cooking.

Combination: *Since the 1980s, Americans have become increasingly interested*

in using chili peppers in cooking.

---

1. Grocery stores stock a variety of chilies.
   The stores are across the United States.
   The variety is wide.
   The variety ranges from the red habenero.
   It ranges to the yellow bell pepper.
   The habenero is hot.
   The heat is fiery.
   The bell pepper is mild.

   Combination: _____

   _____

   _____

2. Chefs work in their backyards.
   The chefs live in the suburbs.
   Chefs have learned to sear poblano peppers.
   The poblanos are large.
   The poblanos are green.
   They sear the poblanos on hot coals.

   Combination: _____

   _____

   _____

3. The cooks peel the poblanos.
   The poblanos are charred.
   Then, the cooks stuff the peppers.
   The peppers are thick.
   The peppers are soft.
   The stuffing is cheese.

   Combination: _____

   _____

   _____

4. Wreaths decorate the walls.
   The wreaths are made of Anaheim chilies.
   The chilies are dried.
   The walls belong to suburban kitchens.

   Combination: _____

   _____

   _____

5. Most people enjoy eating chilies.
   They enjoy the variety or the heat.
   The variety is of their flavors.
   The heat is spicy.

   Combination: _____

   _____

   _____

6. However, some people seem addicted.
   The addiction is to the sharper chilies.
   Examples of the sharper chilies are the hot jalapeno and the New Mexico red.

   Combination: _____

   _____

   _____

7. Hot chilies trigger hormones.
   The hormones are called endorphins.
   Hot chilies are like opiates.
   They produce a feeling.
   The feeling is joyful.
   The feeling is of well-being.

   Combination: _____

   _____

   _____

8. Chili peppers have all these qualities.
   Consequently, chili peppers have found a place.
   The place is prominent.
   The place is in cooking.
   The cooking is in North America.

   Combination: _____

   _____

   _____

Using the Principal Parts of Verbs

5

RECOGNIZING THE PRINCIPAL PARTS OF REGULAR VERBS

Verbs have many kinds of uses and are written in different forms to fit these uses. The different forms of a verb are created by changes in spelling and pronunciation. Verbs are called **regular** if they change in the same (regular) way by additions at the end of the main form. The **irregular** verbs, which you will study in Chapter 7, change in many different ways.

Four important forms of verbs are called the **principal parts**. A regular verb has only three forms for its principal parts because two of the parts, the **past** and **past participle**, are the same. However, since these parts have different uses, they are listed separately. (In Chapter 6, you will see that the irregular verbs have different forms for the past and past participle.) In the following examples, notice how the ending *-ed* creates the **past** and **past participle** and the *-ing* creates the **present participle**.

PRINCIPAL PARTS OF REGULAR VERBS

Main	Past	Past Participle	Present Participle
ask	asked	asked	asking
use	used	used	using
drop	dropped	dropped	dropping
try	tried	tried	trying

Notice that the spelling changes as the *-ed* and *-ing* are added to the main part of *drop* and as the *-ed* is added to *try*. If these changes are not familiar to you, you may need to study the spelling rules and do the exercises in Appendix E.

CREATING VERB TENSES

The principal parts of all verbs, regular or irregular, have many uses within sentences. As you learned in Chapter 1, we can use verbs alone or with **helpers** that show condition or time. We call the **time** of a verb its **tense**. In this chapter, you will study ways of indicating various tenses by using three of the principal parts—the main, the past, and the past participle—both alone and with helpers. (The uses of the present participle, the *-ing* form, are explained in Chapter 6.)

USING THE MAIN VERB

Singular and Plural in the Simple Present Tense

The **simple present tense** is formed from the **main** verb. In a dictionary, the main verb is the form under which the definitions will be given. In all verbs except the verb *be*, the present tense has only two forms—one with an *-s* or *-es* ending for the **third person singular**, and one without the -s or -es for **all the other persons**, singular or plural. (The verb *be* is explained in Chapter 6; in the present tense, its forms are *am*, *is*, and *are*.)

In the present tense, then, a verb that ends in -s is in the third person singular. Look at this example of the verb *ask* in the present tense:

	Singular	Plural
First person:	I ask	we ask
Second person:	you ask	you ask
Third person:	she asks	they ask
	he asks	they ask
	it asks	they ask

As with nouns, there are spelling rules for adding -s or -es at the end of verbs. Look at the following examples. (You will find further explanation and exercises in Appendix E.)

Main Verb	Third Person Singular
confess	he confesses
push	it pushes
study	she studies
try	he tries

Making Verbs Agree with the Subject

The subject and verb in a sentence must be in the same **number** and **person**. When they are in the same number and person, they **agree**. If a subject is in the third person singular—that is, if it is a *he*, a *she*, or an *it*—the present tense verb must end in -s or -es.

Note that nouns and verbs are opposite in this use of the -s ending. The third person singular verb has an -s, but the third person singular noun does not. The third person plural noun has an -s, but the plural verb does not. (Remember, however, that not all plural nouns end in -s. See Appendix A.)

THIRD PERSON

Singular Nouns (No -s)	Singular Verbs (With -s)
boy	walks
friend	helps
student	learns

Plural Nouns (With -s)	Plural Verbs (No -s)
boys	walk
friends	help
students	learn

In the following examples, the subjects are underlined once and the verbs twice.

1. (a) You drive well.

   (b) Mary Anne drives fast.

2. (a) My parents often bring a gift for my daughter.

   (b) My father often brings us ice cream for dinner.

3. (a) The <u>women</u> in our neighborhood <u>have</u> little time for gossip.

   (b) The <u>woman</u> in the last seat <u>has</u> a dog on her lap.

Be particularly careful when an **indefinite pronoun** (see Chapter 2) is the subject of a sentence. The following indefinite pronouns are third person **singular**; they require a present tense verb that ends in *-s*:

one	nobody	each
anyone	anybody	either
everyone	everybody	neither
someone	somebody	

The following are examples with subjects underlined once and verbs twice:

1. <u>Each</u> of the students <u>reports</u> to an advisor.

2. <u>Neither</u> of the twins <u>works</u> at Penney's.

3. <u>One</u> of the houses <u>has</u> a new roof.

4. <u>Everyone</u> <u>needs</u> a flu shot.

Look at examples 1, 2, and 3 again. Remember that no part of a prepositional phrase can be the subject. The first example is about *each*, not students. The second is about *neither*, meaning *not one*; it is not about twins, meaning the plural two. Example 3 is about *one*, not all of the houses. Place parentheses around the prepositional phrases in sentences 1, 2, and 3 to remind yourself not to confuse the object of a preposition with the subject of a verb.

Do exercises 5-a, 5-b, and 5-c

Using the Simple Present Tense

The simple present tense has two frequently used meanings. We can use the simple present tense for an action going on in the present:

Her head *rests* on his shoulder.

This means that **right now** her head rests there. However, we most often use the simple present tense to state that something happens **routinely** or **habitually**.

Harry *studies* the guitar at the Ragtime School of Music.
The rain *falls* heavily in March.

The simple present tense *studies* does **not** mean that Harry is studying right this minute; it indicates that Harry studies from time to time as part of his routine.

As we create the time of the action in sentences, we often use adverbs (single words or phrases) along with the verb tense. Notice in the following examples how the adverbs indicate that an action is routine or habitual.

1. Harry studies *every night*.
2. Maggie goes to bed *at 11:30* on week nights.

3. Bill drinks two cups of coffee *with every meal*.
4. The tulips in Dan's garden bloom *in April*.
5. Blake's attitude changes *weekly*.

Do exercise 5-d

Using the Future Tense

The future tense is formed by placing *shall* or *will* in front of the main verb. (*Shall* may be used with the first person.)

	Singular	Plural
First person:	I shall ask	we shall ask
	I will ask	we will ask
Second person:	you will ask	you will ask
Third person:	she will ask	they will ask
	he will ask	they will ask
	it will ask	they will ask

The future tense is used for actions that **will occur** at some future time. (In the following examples, subjects are underlined once and verbs twice.)

Paula will leave for graduate school in September.

By 1999, our school will have 4,000 students.

USING THE PAST

The past (*-ed*) form of the principal parts is used alone to create the past tense.

	Singular	Plural
First person:	I asked	we asked
Second person:	you asked	you asked
Third person:	she asked	they asked
	he asked	they asked
	it asked	they asked

The past tense explains actions that happened in the past and are all over:

Last night, they searched the yard for the missing pearls.

We frequently use the past tense to narrate happenings in time (chronological) order. In such a sequence of happenings, all the verbs should remain in the past tense. Shifts of tense can be confusing to the reader. Study the following examples of consistent tense.

Consistent Tense

Past: Jack *walked* to his car. He *jerked* the door open. He *jumped* inside.

Present: Joan *works* hard on her school assignments. She *works* hard on her part-time job. She *enjoys* her free time.

Now look at these examples of mixed tenses.

Mixed Tenses

Shifted from present to past: Jack *walks* to his car. He *jerks* the door open. He *jumped* inside.

Shifted from past to present: Joan *worked* on her school assignments. She *worked* hard on her part-time job. She *enjoys* her free time.

Be careful not to mix tenses. When you need to change from one tense to another, be sure to use adverbs to let your reader understand the change:

1. *All weekend*, Margaret worked on her car. She *always* tries to keep her possessions in good repair, and her car is no exception.
2. Tom works slowly, especially on his chemistry assignments. *Last week*, he spent six hours studying and eight hours working problems.

(Chapter 15 provides further explanation and practice in the consistent use of verb tense.)

USING THE PAST PARTICIPLE

In order for a past participle to be used as a verb (that is, with a subject to form the base of a sentence), the past participle must have a helper. Three forms of the verb *have*—the present forms *have* and *has* and the past form *had*—are used with a past participle to create the so called **perfect tenses**. (**Perfect** is a grammatical term and has nothing to do with the common meaning of the word *perfect*.)

Constructing the Past Perfect Tense

The helping verb *had* is used with a past participle to form the **past perfect tense**.

	Singular	*Plural*
First person:	I had asked	we had asked
Second person.	you had asked	you had asked
Third person:	she had asked	they had asked
	he had asked	they had asked
	it had asked	they had asked

Using the Past Perfect Tense

The past perfect tense is used for an action that **had occurred** before another past action. Study the relation of the past perfect tense to the past tense in the following pairs of sentences. (The subjects are underlined once and the verbs twice.)

1. Last week, <u>Matthew</u> <u>studied</u> in the library for ten hours.

   The week before, <u>he</u> <u>had studied</u> twenty hours at home.

2. <u>Jack</u> <u>completed</u> his term paper at midnight.

   All afternoon, <u>he</u> <u>had talked</u> with his friends.

3. My <u>friends</u> <u>arrived</u> at eleven.

   However, <u>I</u> <u>had not completed</u> my homework.

Sequence of Tenses

The following chart shows the relation of the past perfect tense to the past, present, and future. (Assume that time moves from left to right, from the past through the present into the future.)

SEQUENCE OF TENSES

Past Perfect Tense	Past Tense	Present Tense	Future Tense
(had + past participle)	(one word)	(one word)	(shall or will + main verb)
had asked	asked	ask(s)	will ask
had visited	visited	visit(s)	will visit

Starting in the future, we might use these tenses in reverse order to indicate the following range of actions:

Ask

1. Tomorrow, Todd will ask Jill to the dance.

2. Harry always asks Mary to school dances.

3. Yesterday, Martha asked Brent to the Sadie Hawkins' Day dance.

4. The week before, she had asked George.

Visit

1. Next summer, Beth will visit her sister in Canada.

2. Beth visits her sister every year.

3. Last year, Beth also visited her brother in Mexico City.

4. Until last year, she had not visited him for five years.

Constructing the Present Perfect Tense

The helpers *has* (for the third person singular) and *have* (for the others) are used with the past participle to create the **present perfect tense**:

	Singular	Plural
First person:	I have asked	we have asked
Second person:	you have asked	you have asked
Third person:	she has asked	they have asked
	he has asked	they have asked
	it has asked	they have asked

Making Subjects and Verbs Agree

The helping verb used to create the present perfect must **agree** with the subject. The third person singular helper *has* is used with a third person singular subject:

1. The student has finished the drill.

2. Each of the students has finished the drill.

The other helper, *have*, is used with all other persons, singular and plural:

1. I have finished the drill.

2. We have finished the drill.

The helpers *has* and *have* are also used to construct questions in the present perfect tense. In a question, the helping verb appears before the subject. However, the helper and the subject must agree.

1. Has each of the students finished the drill?

2. Have the students finished the drill?

Using the Present Perfect Tense

The present perfect indicates action that began in the past. The time indicated by the present perfect is less definite than that indicated by the past tense. When you need to specify a definite past time, use the past tense:

Incorrect: Yesterday, Betty has worked in her uncle's office.
Correct: Yesterday, Betty worked in her uncle's office.

The simple past tense (*worked*) must be used because *yesterday* is a definite time.
The **present perfect tense** can be used to indicate three kinds of time.

- The present perfect indicates an action that began in the past, has continued to the present, and is still going on:
  a. Harry has studied the violin for six years.
  b. The girls have waited by the telephone for two hours.
- The present perfect indicates an action that began in the past and has continued up to the present:
  a. My mother has finished the art course.
  b. Two students have not completed the lab assignment.
- The present perfect indicates a past action that occurred at no identified time:
  a. Melanie has learned the importance of education.
  b. Those five landlords have refused to cooperate with us.

> **Do exercises 5-e and 5-f**

USING MODALS

Special helpers called **modals** are used with verbs to place special conditions on the action of the verbs, such as *possibility, obligation, or emphasis*. Modals are also used to ask questions.

The following modals are used frequently:

should	would
may, might	must
do (does), did	can, could

Look at the way that modals affect the meaning of the verbs in the following sentences:

1. Why should I drive my brother to school? (The modal *should* indicates obligation.)
2. George may arrive after ten o'clock. (The modal *may* indicates possibility.)
3. Emily did finish the quiz on time. (The modal *did* indicates emphasis.)

Using Modals to Build Negatives

Modals are often used with the adverbs *not* and *never* to create negative statements. In particular, *does* and *do* are often used to create negative statements in the present tense, and *did* is often used to create negative statements in the past tense. Notice how a modal is used with the base form of the verb to change the meaning of the following sentences:

1. Ginger always plays tennis on Wednesday afternoon.
   Ginger *does* not play tennis on Wednesday afternoon.
2. Ginger and George always play tennis on Wednesday afternoon.
   Ginger and George *do* not play tennis on Wednesday afternoon.
3. Last semester, Bill and I played tennis once a week.
   Last semester, Bill and I *did* not play tennis at all.

Using Modals to Begin Questions

Modals can also be used to begin questions. In the following questions, notice that the modal is used with the base form of the verb:

1. *Does* Mike still smoke a pipe?
2. *Do* the swimmers practice on Saturday morning?
3. *Did* Helene attend the party last night?
4. How *may* I help you?

SUGGESTIONS FOR WRITING

In your journal, describe the routine that you follow on the busiest day of your week. Try to include all the activities that make the day hectic. You might begin with a sentence such as the following: *On Wednesday morning, I leave the house at 6:45 A.M. to catch the 7:00 A.M. bus to Suffolk Community College.*

Once you have written sentences about your routine, reread them carefully. Have you provided specific information about your activities? Have you told exactly what the activities are and where and when you engage in them?

Also check the verb tense. Make sure that you have written each sentence in the *present* tense, the tense used to describe routine actions. If you have made any mistakes, correct them.

NAME _____ **DATE** _____

In each sentence, identify the subject and underline it once. Then choose the verb that agrees with the subject and underline it twice. Remember that the subject of the sentence is never found within a prepositional phrase.

EXAMPLE

Each <u>swimmer</u> on the team (<u><u>swims</u></u>, swim) in three events.

===

1. Kelly (works, work) in the library two nights a week.

2. The students in Dr. Roberts 's class (studies, study) in the library.

3. Everyone in the class (borrows, borrow) Bill's notes.

4. The plants on the porch (needs, need) water.

5. The book on the dining room table (belongs, belong) to Larry.

6. Patrick and I (opens, open) the store every Saturday.

7. Each of the tutors (has, have) a schedule.

8. Kristy and Stephanie (uses, use) the computer for vocabulary work.

9. My aunt (supervises, supervise) the cooking at our house.

10. Someone in the office (smokes, smoke).

11. The clothes on the ironing board (needs, need) to be washed.

12. After class, we (meets, meet) in the cafeteria for a cup of tea.

13. Seven rolls of film (needs, need) to be developed.

14. Neither of the teams (practices, practice) on Tuesday.

15. Every afternoon, Dale (walks, walk) her two dogs around the neighborhood.

16. The players on my sister's soccer team (has, have) a practice every other morning.

17. One of the sisters (lives, live) in Connecticut.

18. You (seems, seem) tired today.

19. Suzanne and Claire (visits, visit) the art museum at least once a month.

20. Terri (sells, sell) homemade fruitcakes at Christmas.

21. Everyone in the course (attends, attend) regularly.

22. My English teacher (expects, expect) me to complete many exercises.

23. Everyone in Linda's neighborhood (stays, stay) home on Halloween.

24. The doors to the computer lab (remains, remain) locked at all times.

25. Nobody (respects, respect) Dr. Dillon.

NAME _____ DATE _____

Expand the following sentences by adding a prepositional phrase in the blank after the subject. Then underline the correct form of the verb given in parentheses.

EXAMPLES

The secretaries ___*in my office*___ (wants, <u>want</u>) a raise.

Neither _*of the swimmers*_ (<u>has</u>, have) a team suit.

1. Each _____ (appears, appear) nervous.

2. The managers _____ (leaves, leave) early.

3. Several _____ (lives, live) in the same small town.

4. Many _____ (commutes, commute) to work in Atlanta.

5. Both _____ (wants, want) to use the evening to study.

6. The men _____ (needs, need) to train.

7. Many _____ (loses, lose) sight of their goals.

8. The friendship _____ (seems, seem) to have changed.

9. Mike's answers _____ never (sounds, sound) rude.

10. The fish _____ (smells, smell) fresh.

11. The children _____ often (annoys, annoy) the bus driver.

12. All _____ (uses, use) the school computers.

13. One _____ always (misses, miss) the quiz.

14. The teenagers _____ (shovels, shovel) snow after every storm.

15. Fern's pride _____ (pleases, please) her family.

NAME _____ **DATE** _____

    Most of the sentences in this exercise have an incorrect verb. Identify the subject of the sentence and underline it. Identify the verb and underline it twice. If the verb is incorrect, cross it out and write the correct **present tense** form neatly above it. If the sentence is correct, write a *C* by its number.

EXAMPLES

_____ Rose and Laura ~~drives~~ *drive* to College Park every Tuesday morning.

__*C*__ Every Wednesday, I arrive at work at 8:00 A.M.

1._____ The aides in the learning lab helps the students use the computers.

2._____ I takes a piano lesson every Thursday afternoon.

3._____ One of the cars have a flat tire.

4._____ Beth expect her children to finish their chores on Saturday morning.

5._____ Every year, we visit my aunt in Florida.

6._____ Joellen and Jill study in the library on Thursday afternoon.

7._____ That little puppy dig in my garden.

8._____ Julia and Amy always serve their parents breakfast on Sunday.

9._____ The curtains in the downstairs bedroom needs to be hemmed.

10._____ The cake on the porch taste delicious.

11._____ All the students prepares for their final exams carefully.

12._____ Each of the twins play the flute.

13._____ Every morning, he pick up his friend on the way to school.

14._____ The counselor usually discusses Juliene's schedule with her.

15._____ Almost every evening, I see rabbits in the backyard.

NAME _____ DATE _____

Write a sentence of seven or more words using the present tense form given by each number. Be sure to use the word as a **verb**, not as a noun. Also, be sure that your sentence describes a regular action.

EXAMPLES

explain   *Every Monday, the two lab assistants explain the assignment*

for the week.

explains   *At the beginning of each session, a lab assistant explains*

the experiment.

understand   1. _____

_____

understands   2. _____

_____

walk   3. _____

_____

walks   4. _____

_____

read   5. _____

_____

reads   6. _____

_____

make   7. _____

_____

makes   8. _____

_____

bring   9. _____

_____

brings   10. _____

_____

NAME _____ **DATE** _____

Most of the sentences in this exercise have an incorrect verb—an incorrect helper, an incorrect principal part, or both.

- In each sentence underline the subject once and the verb twice.
- If a verb is incorrect, cross it out and write the correct form above it.
- Write *C* by the number of each correct sentence.

EXAMPLES

_____ Last night, my brother has taped my favorite movie.

_____ Each of the guests ~~have~~ *has* arrived.

__*C*__ Has Harry read the newspaper?

1._____ We had not open the letter from Dean Jones.

2._____ Ed tryed to fix the furnace by himself.

3._____ Everyone in the neighborhood have complained about the new highway.

4._____ Yesterday, the plumber replace the leaking faucet.

5._____ The hummingbirds has not used my new feeder all summer.

6._____ Neither of the English instructors has read the novel.

7._____ Has Garth ask his new employer about his medical insurance?

8._____ The janitors in the science building has waxed all the floors.

9._____ Many of the bus riders have request a transfer.

10._____ My friend Sue has written me three letters last month.

11._____ Blythe has not pay her telephone bill yet.

12._____ The word problems on last week's math quiz have confused some students.

13._____ Charles have refused to mow the lawn.

14._____ The icicles on the telephone lines has melted.

15._____ Yesterday, the bookstore has ordered more English workbooks.

NAME _____ DATE _____

     Write a sentence of eight or more words using the verb given by each number. Use adverbs with the verb to indicate the time of the action.

EXAMPLE

has borrowed *During the past year, my cousin Marie has borrowed*

              every hat and coat in my wardrobe.

have washed   1. _____

                   _____

has searched   2. _____

                   _____

planted   3. _____

                   _____

has allowed   4. _____

                   _____

had volunteered   5. _____

                   _____

has taken   6. _____

                   _____

invited   7. _____

                   _____

have brought   8. _____

                   _____

have voted   9. _____

                   _____

suggested   10. _____

                   _____

Using the Verb *Be*   **6**

The forms of the verb *be* are used very often in writing and in speech. They are frequently used to build sentences such as the following:

Palmer *was* busy.
Sally and Cordelia *were* the captains.
There *are* five of us on the team.

Equally as common are the uses of the verb *be* as a **helper**. In this chapter, you will study the many forms of the verb *be* and the uses of these forms as helpers to create what are called the **passive voice** and the **progressive forms** of verbs.

First, let us look at the many forms the verb *be* can take in writing.

RECOGNIZING FORMS OF THE VERB *BE*

The verb *be* is the most irregular verb in English; that is, it has more different forms than any other verb. Specifically, there are four forms of the main verb and two forms of the past:

Main	Past	Past Participle	Present Participle
be	was	been	being
am	were		
is			
are			

The several forms of the verb *be* have a variety of uses.

USING THE WORD *BE*

- The word *be* itself **must have a helper** when it is used in writing (except, of course, when it is used as a command with the subject *you* understood).
  1. Frank *can* be home by eight.
  2. Sadie *should* be at her grandmother's house.
  3. Our guests *will* be here soon.
  4. This address *must* be wrong.
  5. *Be* home by midnight. (In this command, the subject *you*, the person spoken to, is understood.)
- You must be especially careful not to use the word *be* alone to create the present tense:

Incorrect: Betty *be* home.
                  Sally *be* tired today.
Correct: Betty *is* home.
                  Sally *is* tired today.

FORMING THE FUTURE TENSE

The future tense uses *be* as the main verb with *shall* or, more frequently, with *will* as the helper. This combination is used for the singular and plural in all persons:

	Singular	Plural
First person:	I shall be	we shall be
	I will be	we will be
Second person:	you will be	you will be
Third person:	she will be	they will be
	he will be	they will be
	it will be	they will be

In the following examples, notice how the underlined adverbs work with the verb tense to indicate the time of the action:

1. I will be home <u>by six</u>.

2. We will be ready <u>soon</u>.

3. Cynthia will be in Chicago <u>next week</u>.

4. The women will be back from lunch <u>at two</u>.

FORMING THE PRESENT AND PAST TENSES

The forms *am, is,* and *are* are used for the present tense, and *was* and *were* are used for the past. Notice in the following chart how each is used to show number and person:

	PRESENT TENSE		PAST TENSE	
	Singular	Plural	Singular	Plural
First person:	I am	we are	I was	we were
Second person:	you are	you are	you were	you were
Third person:	she is	they are	she was	they were
	he is	they are	he was	they were
	it is	they are	it was	they were

As you work with subject–verb agreement, remember what you studied in the earlier chapters:

- The first person plural includes the person speaking plus another or others:

  Henry and I were = we were
  Bill, Pat, and I were = we were

- Nouns in the third person must be identified as singular or plural:

	Singular			Plural	
Noun		*Pronoun*	*Noun*		*Pronoun*
the girl was	=	she was	the girls were	=	they were
the man was	=	he was	the men were	=	they were
the book was	=	it was	the books were	=	they were

- Two or more third person singulars joined make a plural:

the teacher and the student were = they were
the pen, the ink, and the notebook were = they were

- If you place the form of the verb *be* before the subject to construct a question, you must be especially careful to make the subject and verb agree:

Are the students in the library?

Was Gabe at the mall yesterday?

Do exercise 6-a

FORMING THE PRESENT PERFECT AND PAST PERFECT TENSES

Like all past participles, the past participle *been* is used with the helpers *has*, *have*, or *had* to form the two perfect tenses:

			Singular	Plural
PRESENT PERFECT	*First person:*	I have been	we have been
	Second person:	you have been	you have been
	Third person:	she has been	they have been
		he has been	they have been
		it has been	they have been

			Singular	Plural
PAST PERFECT	*First person:*	I had been	we had been
	Second person:	you had been	they had been
	Third person:	she had been	they had been
		he had been	they had been
		it had been	they had been

Remember that in writing, **all** past participles require helpers to form the perfect tenses. The word *been* should never be used without a helper.

Incorrect:	Randy *been* here a week.
Correct:	Randy *was* here a week.
	Randy *has been* here a week.
	Randy *had been* here a week.

Incorrect:	Sue *been* at the train station for two hours.
Correct:	Sue *was* at the train station for two hours.
	Sue *has been* at the train station for two hours.
	Sue *had been* at the train station for two hours.

Do exercise 6-b, 6-c, and 6-d

USING THE FORMS OF THE VERB *BE* AS HELPERS

In all its tenses and forms, the verb *be* can be used as a helper. As a helper, it is used with the past participle of other verbs (*-ed* form of regular verbs) to create what is called the **passive voice**; it is also used with the present participle (*-ing* form) of other verbs to make **progressive forms**.

Using the Verb *Be* in the Passive Voice

Recognizing the Active and the Passive Voice

Many action verbs can have two voices, one called **active** and the other called **passive**. If the subject **does** the act stated by the verb, the verb is in the active voice. Look at the following examples in which the subject is the **actor**, the verb is in the **active voice**, and a direct object **receives the action**:

1. Jack dropped the hammer.
2. Mother mailed the letters.
3. Fred can answer your questions.

We can convey the same information by using the **passive voice**. We simply rewrite the sentence so that the direct object is the subject (and still the receiver of the action) and change the verb to the passive:

Correct tense of be	+	the past participle
1. was		dropped
2. were		mailed
3. can be		answered

1. The hammer was dropped.
2. The letters were mailed.
3. Your questions can be answered.

Notice that these passive sentences do not tell **by whom** the action wass done. We can add this information as a prepositional phrase:

1. The hammer was dropped *by Jack*.
2. The letters were mailed *by mother*.
3. Your questions can be answered *by Fred*.

Tenses of the Passive Voice

Passive verbs can be used in any tense. The tense is created by the helper, which is the appropriate tense of the verb *be*; the action of the verb is given in the past participle (*-ed* form).

Study the following charts; notice that the appropriate forms of the verb *be* create the tense.

90

		Singular	Plural
FUTURE PASSIVE	First person:	I will be asked	we will be asked
	Second person:	you will be asked	you will be asked
	Third person:	she will be asked	they will be asked
		he will be asked	they will be asked
		it will be asked	they will be asked
PRESENT PASSIVE	First Person:	I am asked	we are asked
	Second Person:	you are asked	you are asked
	Third Person:	she is asked	they are asked
		he is asked	they are asked
		it is asked	they are asked
PAST PASSIVE	First Person:	I was asked	we were asked
	Second Person:	you were asked	you were asked
	Third Person:	she was asked	they were asked
		he was asked	they were asked
		it was asked	they were asked
PRESENT PERFECT PASSIVE	First Person:	I have been asked	we have been asked
	Second Person:	you have been asked	you have been asked
	Third Person:	she has been asked	they have been asked
		he has been asked	they have been asked
		it has been asked	they have been asked
PAST PERFECT PASSIVE	First Person:	I had been asked	we had been asked
	Second person:	you had been asked	you had been asked
	Third Person:	she had been asked	they had been asked
		he had been asked	they had been asked
		it had been asked	they had been asked

Choosing Between the Active and Passive Voices

The passive voice is very helpful when we do not know or cannot name who does the action, that is, who the actor or actors are.

Mary Jane *is* rarely *asked* to sing.
Harriet *has been asked* many times.

The passive also enables us to focus on the receiver of the action when the receiver for some reason is more important than the actor.

The game *has been postponed* until Saturday afternoon.
The winner *will be announced* next week.

However, whenever possible, you should keep the verbs in your sentences in the active voice. Sentences that tell *who does what* or *who did what* are generally stronger than sentences in the passive voice.

Weak: The salad was prepared by James.
Stronger: James prepared the salad.
Weak: The speech was delivered by Margot Paulson.
Stronger: Margot Paulson delivered the speech.

Do exercise 6-e

91

Using the Verb *Be* in Progressive Forms

When we want to emphasize that an action **progresses** (continues) over time, we use a **progressive form** of a verb. The progressive form is created by adding an appropriate tense of the verb *be* in front of a present participle (*-ing* form of a verb). The *-ing* part gives the meaning, and the *be* helper gives the tense.

Remember that the *-ing* form cannot be used as a verb unless it is preceded by some form of the verb *be*. The *-ing* form alone does not make a verb:

Incorrect:	Jack *standing* behind the movie star.
Correct:	Jack *was standing* behind the movie star.

Adding *-ing* to the Main Verb

Usually, the present participle of a verb is formed simply by adding *-ing* to the main verb; however, some verbs drop a final *e* or double a final consonant. Look at the following list of main verbs and their present participles. If you need explanation or practice in spelling the *-ing* forms, turn to Appendix E.

Main Verb	Present Participle
cry	crying
smoke	smoking
fail	failing
dine	dining
drop	dropping

Creating Tenses of the Progressive

The tense of the helper *be* gives the tense of the progressive verbs. Notice the times indicated by the helping verb *be* in the following sentences:

Future:	I *will be* studying this evening.
Present:	I *am* studying for my final examinations.
	We *are* studying for our final examinations.
	Every student *is* studying for the final examination.
Past:	During the storm, Beth *was* studying for her final examination.
	Ronald and Ben also *were* studying.
Present perfect:	Beth *has been* studying for two weeks.
	Beth and Ben *have been* studying for two weeks.
Past perfect:	Beth and Ben *had been* studying for two hours.

As you use the progressive tenses, check the **agreement** of the subject with the verb. The number and gender of the helper *be* must agree with those of the subject.

You will probably use the present tense of the progressive more often than the other tenses. The present progressive is formed by the appropriate present forms of *be* plus the present participle.

Study the following chart; notice that the present forms of the verb *be* are used to create the present progressive tense.

Present Progressive

First person:	I am asking	we are asking
Second person:	you are asking	you are asking
Third person:	she is asking	they are asking
	he is asking	they are asking
	it is asking	they are asking

92

The other tenses of the progressive are created in the same way as the present progressive—by placing the appropriate tense of *be* in front of the present participle.

Future progressive:	shall be *or* will be	+	a present participle
Past progressive:	was *or* were	+	a present participle
Present perfect progressive:	have been *or* has been	+	a present participle
Past perfect progressive:	had been	+	a present participle

Using the Present Progressive Tense

Consider the differences in the meaning of the following two sentences:

Present progressive:	The instructor is explaining the new assignment.
Simple present:	The instructor explains new assignments at the end of every class.

The present progressive indicates that the instructor is explaining right now. The simple present indicates that the instructor routinely explains new assignments; it does not say that the instructor is explaining now.

For actions that **are occurring** right now, we use the present progressive forms, not the simple present:

Correct:	You *are studying* Chapter 6 right now.
Incorrect:	You *study* Chapter 6 right now.

Using Other Tenses in the Progressive

The other tenses of the progressive are used to emphasize the **duration** of an activity or condition.

1. Horace *was visiting* his grandmother at the time of her heart attack.
2. During May, we *will be driving* across Canada.
3. All semester, Alice *has been trying* to make up an incomplete in Chemistry 204.
4. Until last week, Frances *had been dating* Gerald regularly.

Do exercise 6-f

Avoiding Common Errors

As you use the verb *be* alone or as a helper, remember to follow the guidelines that have been explained in this chapter. In particular, remember the following rules of written English:

- The forms of the verb *be*—whether used alone or as helpers—must agree with the subject in person and number:
  1. Sadie *is* [not *am* or *are*] finishing her report.
  2. The girls on the team *are* [not *is* or *am*] in the locker room.

- The word *be* itself is never a verb unless it has a helper in front of it:
  1. The children *are* [not *be*] practicing.
  2. The children *will be* practicing all afternoon.

- Without a helper, the present and past participles cannot be used as verbs:

Incorrect: Sara *yelling* at the referee.
Correct: Sara *was yelling* at the referee.

Incorrect: Janice *saving* her money for a trip to Mexico next summer.
Correct: Janice *is saving* her money for a trip to Mexico next summer.

Incorrect: Last June, James *awarded* a scholarship by his father's company.
Correct: Last June, James *was awarded* a scholarship by his father's company.

Do exercises 6-g, 6-h, and 6-i

SUGGESTIONS FOR WRITING

Use your journal to take a personal inventory. List all of your strengths and accomplishments. For instance, you may wish to write about being a strong swimmer, about being the first member of your family to attend college, about learning to type forty words per minute, about passing your last math quiz.

Now look back over your sentences. Select one accomplishment and develop this idea. Explain exactly what you did and why your achievement was important to you.

When you have written your sentences, check their verb tense. Because you have already accomplished these things, all of your sentences should be in the *past* tense.

NAME _____ DATE _____

Analyze the following twelve sentences:

- Underline each subject once.
- Write on the blank line at the left whether the subject you underlined is a *he*, a *she*, an *it*, or a *they*.
- Draw a circle around any prepositional phrases that come between the subject and the verb.
- Select the correct verb given in the parentheses and underline it twice.

EXAMPLES

_____*they*_____ The grades (on the biology exam) (be, is, are) on Dr. Daihl's door.

_____*it*_____ The pen (on the desk) (am, is, are) a present from Dad.

1. _____ The two windows in the basement (am, is, are) cracked.

2. _____ The men in my father's office (be, is, are) all interested in football.

3. _____ (Be, Is, Are) the coffee hot?

4. _____ One of the tutors (was, were, is) absent yesterday.

5. _____ (Was, Were, Are) my cousins from Anchorage at Karen's party on

Saturday night?

6. _____ One of the instructors (was, were, been) in the president's office before

lunch.

7. _____ The records in the attic (is, are, be) warped.

8. _____ The patient with the three broken toes (is, are, be) in Dr. Taylor's

office.

9. _____ The knives on the kitchen counter (is, are, be) very sharp.

10. _____ Last night, each of the cars in the driveway (was, were, been) stuck in

the snow.

11. _____ The woman behind you (are, is, be) Sara's cousin.

12. _____ The cars in the back lot (was, were, am) ready for delivery.

NAME _____ DATE _____

Identify any helping verbs in each sentence and underline them twice. Then double underline the correct verb given in parentheses.

EXAMPLES

The teacher's comments on my homework papers (was, <u>were</u>, been) very helpful.

Barbara <u>has</u> never (was, were, <u>been</u>) a strong tennis player.

1. My guitar (is, am, be) out of tune.

2. Here (is, am, be) the check for the rent.

3. Laura has never (was, been, be) interested in photography.

4. I (be, were, am) the only nurse on duty tonight.

5. My nephew (be, is, are) at the mall with his friends.

6. There (be, been, is) no excuse for Lee's behavior.

7. Kraft's computer (was, were, been) broken for a month.

8. Mary's three daughters have (be, been, were) at the swimming pool all evening.

9. Ethel's flashlight has (was, been, be) on the kitchen table for a month.

10. There (been, was, were) several reasons for the delay.

11. Rick and I have never (be, been, were) interested in golf.

12. My plans for the trip (was, were, been) impractical.

13. (Are, Is, Be) the band members still in the auditorium?

14. There on the couch (be, was, were) the tickets to the concert.

15. (Be, Is, Are) Mark's car still at the body shop?

16. Cathleen's final exam (be, is, are) on Dr. Pond's desk.

17. Has Helen (be, been, was) in the hospital before?

18. There have not (be, been, was) any sales in my department this week.

19. Anna (was, were, been) home with the flu for two weeks.

20. Miss Short's students have (was, be, been) ready for the history test all week.

NAME _____ DATE _____

Most of the following sentences contain one error in the use of the verb *be*. Draw a line through the error and write your correction neatly above it. If the sentence is correct, write a *C* to the left of it.

EXAMPLES

_____ The manager's letters ~~been~~ *have been* ready for an hour.

_____ One of the contracts ~~were~~ *was* missing.

1. _____ The assistant managers was in the lounge.

2. _____ Every one of the addresses were incorrect.

3. _____ Dr. Erb will be in her office at 1:00.

4. _____ Gil's answers to the detective's questions was surprising.

5. _____ The inventory is not finished.

6. _____ The toolbox are not in the garage.

7. _____ Sam's mother will not be at work until after lunch.

8. _____ The men on the construction crew was ready to quit.

9. _____ All the children be ready for a nap.

10. _____ The cookies is all burnt.

11. _____ Each of the applicants are anxious to get the job.

12. _____ The roads are treacherous.

13. _____ The recipes is in the cabinet over the oven.

14. _____ Your application been on file for two months.

15. _____ Last week, four of the waiters was on vacation.

16. _____ Neither of the secretaries was ready to return to work.

17. _____ The bride's dress be too large.

18. _____ James been on the basketball team for two semesters.

19. _____ Either of the appointments are convenient.

20. _____ The sandwiches in the refrigerator is for the meeting.

NAME _____ DATE _____

Write a sentence of eight or more words using the verb given before each of the numbers. Use the verbs just as they are; do not add helpers or main verbs. Try to use adverbs that work with the verb tense to specify the time of the sentence.

EXAMPLES

were _____*By eight this morning, the boys were all ready.*_____

has been _*Fred's aunt has always been a very generous person.*_____

am   1. _____

            _____

was   2. _____

            _____

will be   3. _____

            _____

had been   4. _____

            _____

is   5. _____

            _____

may be   6. _____

            _____

has been   7. _____

            _____

must be   8. _____

            _____

have been   9. _____

            _____

can be   10. _____

            _____

NAME _____ **DATE** _____

Rewrite the following sentences so that they give the same information but use the active voice of the verb. Keep the active verb you use in the same tense as the original passive.

EXAMPLE

Bill is often invited to parties by his cousin Tina.

Active: *Tina often invites her cousin Bill to parties.*_____

1. The practice was cancelled by the coach.

 Active: _____

2. The reading list will be distributed by Dr. Hamilton.

 Active: _____

3. The examinations are always graded by the student aide.

 Active: _____

4. Martin was driven to the concert by his aunt.

 Active: _____

5. The editorial in the school newspaper was signed by Louis Jett.

 Active: _____

6. The application was filed by Chris O'Connelly.

 Active: _____

7. The highest score on the entrance exam was received by my sister.

 Active: _____

8. Our basement apartment was rented by two students from Wisconsin.

 Active: _____

9. The accounting error was not found by either of the two auditors. [Use the word

 neither with the active verb.]

 Active: _____

10. The math assignment was not understood by anyone in the class. [In your sentence,

 use *no one* as the subject of the active verb.]

 Active: _____

NAME _____ DATE _____

Read each sentence and decide whether the verb should be in the simple present or in the present progressive. Underline the appropriate verb twice.

EXAMPLES

Once a week, my uncle (<u><u>takes</u></u>, is taking) my two cousins to the video store.

This morning, my uncle (takes, <u><u>is taking</u></u>) my two cousins to the video store.

1. Every summer, my family (spends, is spending) a week at the beach.

2. Kevin (stays, is staying) with his friend in San Francisco this week.

3. Before every chemistry class, Sarah (reviews, is reviewing) her notes.

4. Robert's meetings always (last, are lasting) two hours.

5. Every morning, Joan (exercises, is exercising) before breakfast.

6. Chuck (paints, is painting) his apartment this morning.

7. Conscientious students usually (attend, are attending) classes regularly.

8. My supervisor (prepares, is preparing) the inventory this morning.

9. My parents always (enjoy, are enjoying) a weekend in New York.

10. Graham often (leaves, is leaving) his lacrosse stick on the bus.

11. The counselor (waits, is waiting) in his office for my schedule.

12. This month, the student aides (complain, are complaining) about the extra work.

13. Lynn (writes, is writing) to her sister once a month.

14. The electricians usually (take, are taking) their coffee break at 10:00 A.M.

15. Every summer, we (swim, are swimming) at the neighborhood swimming pool.

16. The new bookstore near the campus (has, is having) a sale all day.

17. Stan rarely (watches, is watching) television.

18. Every day after class, Dottie (meets, is meeting) her friends for a cup of coffee.

19. Dr. Rasmussen (presents, is presenting) a paper at a conference in Dallas this

    morning.

20. Gail's oldest brother never (calls, is calling) their parents before a visit.

NAME _____ **DATE** _____

Underline any helping verbs in each sentence twice. Then, in the blank space, write the correct form of the verb printed at the left of the sentence number. (See Appendix E if you have trouble spelling the verbs in their -*ed* or -*ing* endings.)

EXAMPLES

move   Sonny has _____*moved*_____ three times in the last year.

enjoy   Beth does not _____*enjoy*_____ her long swim team practices.

---

taste   1. My mother has never _____ lobster.

finish   2. In high school, I never _____ my math homework.

push   3. After the swim meet on Saturday, the losing team _____ the coach into the pool.

employ   4. The local fast food restaurants _____ many college students.

save   5. Mary and Robert have been _____ for a house for ten years.

copy   6. The class will _____ the quiz questions from the board.

crack   7. My mother's favorite vase was _____ by the movers.

wax   8. Sandra _____ her new car every week.

apply   9. Donna had not _____ for her real estate license.

repair   10. That refrigerator has been _____ three times.

shop   11. Katie and her mother had been _____ all afternoon.

paint   12. Fran _____ all the shutters on the front windows last weekend.

bless   13. At the baptism, the crying baby was _____ by the priest.

receive   14. I have not _____ my grades for last semester.

rock   15. Every night, my father _____ my baby brother in the rocking chair.

wrap   16. None of the birthday presents has been _____ yet.

surprise   17. The twins will be _____ by their grandparents' visit.

hope   18. Charlayne was _____ for a larger tax refund.

stay   19. Julia is _____ home with a cold today.

use   20. The computers in the library are _____ by many students and instructors.

Identify the subject of each sentence by underlining it once. Then fill in the blank space with one or more helping verbs. Be sure the helping verb and subject agree in person and number.

EXAMPLES

<u>Francis</u>_____*has*_____ never studied French.

Both <u>cars</u> _____*were*_____ destroyed in the accident.

1. The registrar _____ reviewed my transcript before the meeting.

2. Crystal _____ work a double shift tomorrow.

3. By noon yesterday, every student in Dr. Jordan's history class _____ completed the exam.

4. The Smiths _____ planning their summer vacation since January.

5. The basketball team _____ compete against the league champions tomorrow night.

6. A term paper_____ always required in Nursing 243.

7. The essays _____ graded before our next class.

8. The most difficult piano solo at the recital last night _____ played by my friend Linda.

9. The new truck in the driveway _____ owned by my brother's girlfriend.

10. Kurt _____ parked his new car in his neighbor's garage all week.

11. Next semester, Peggy _____ study electronics.

12. Alex _____ interview the mayoral candidates later this afternoon.

13. Mrs. Morse _____ not reviewed the chapter before the quiz.

14. My father_____ never studied Latin.

15. Messages for the doctor _____ always recorded carefully.

16. Twice before, the smokers _____ asked to put out their cigarettes.

17. Dawn _____ tutoring her cousin in chemistry all afternoon yesterday.

18. Three customers _____ complaining to my manager right now.

19. The gray coat in the front closet _____ never been cleaned.

20. By last Sunday, all the winners_____ notified.

NAME _____ **DATE** _____

Write sentences of eight or more words using the verb forms given by each number. Use the verbs as they are: do not drop any words, and do not add helpers or other verbs.

EXAMPLES

were returned *The two library books were not returned on time.*

will be attending *The band members will be attending the practice*
all afternoon.

is recovering 1. _____

_____

will be cleaned 2. _____

_____

has ordered 3. _____

_____

had been approved 4. _____

_____

will be helping 5. _____

_____

has developed 6. _____

_____

has been confused 7. _____

_____

have been polished 8. _____

_____

were arguing 9. _____

_____

had explained 10. _____

_____

Using the Principal Parts of Irregular Verbs

7

Many verbs in English are **irregular**; that is, they do not form the past and the past participle by adding *-ed* to the main verb. Irregular verbs are used in the same ways as the regular verbs you studied in the earlier chapters. However, because the past and the past participle are not the same, you must learn the two forms and be careful as you use them to form the various tenses.

RECOGNIZING THE PRINCIPAL PARTS OF IRREGULAR VERBS

The following list contains some of the most common irregular verbs. Study it carefully and refer to it as you work the exercises in this chapter. As you study the list, use this guide for using helpers with the four principal parts:

- **Main Verb** is used   without helpers as the **present tense** (adding an-*s* or -*es* in the third person singular). with the helpers *shall* or *will* to form the **future tense**. with modals such as *must, may, might, can, could, should, would, do, (does), did*.

- **Past** is used   alone (never with a helper) as the **past tense**.

- **Past participle** is used   never alone (always with a helper): with *have* or *has* to form the **present perfect tense**, with *had* to form the **past perfect tense**, and with the tenses of the verb *be* to form the **passive voice**.

- **Present participle** is used   always with a helper (some part of the verb *be*) to form a **progressive tense**.

Main Verb	Past	Past Participle	Present Participle
be (is, am, are)	was, were	been	being
beat	beat	beaten	beating
become	became	become	becoming
begin	began	begun	beginning
bite	bit	bitten	biting
break	broke	broken	breaking
bring	brought	brought	bringing
buy	bought	bought	buying
catch	caught	caught	catching
choose	chose	chosen	choosing
come	came	come	coming
cost	cost	cost	costing
cut	cut	cut	cutting

(Main Verb)	(Past)	(Past Participle)	(Present Participle)
dig	dug	dug	digging
do	did	done	doing
draw	drew	drawn	drawing
drink	drank	drunk	drinking
drive	drove	driven	driving
eat	ate	eaten	eating
fall	fell	fallen	falling
feel	felt	felt	feeling
fight	fought	fought	fighting
find	found	found	finding
fly	flew	flown	flying
forget	forgot	forgotten	forgetting
get	got	gotten	getting
give	gave	given	giving
go	went	gone	going
grow	grew	grown	growing
have	had	had	having
hear	heard	heard	hearing
hide	hid	hidden	hiding
hold	held	held	holding
keep	kept	kept	keeping
know	knew	known	knowing
lay (put down)	laid	laid	laying
lead (guide)	led	led	leading
leave	left	left	leaving
lie (recline)	lay	lain	lying
lie (tell an untruth)	lied	lied	lying
lose	lost	lost	losing
make	made	made	making
meet	met	met	meeting
pay	paid	paid	paying
put	put	put	putting
quit	quit	quit	quitting
raise (lift)	raised	raised	raising
read	read	read	reading
ride	rode	ridden	riding
ring	rang	rung	ringing
rise (go up)	rose	risen	rising
run	ran	run	running
say	said	said	saying
see	saw	seen	seeing
sell	sold	sold	selling
send	sent	sent	sending
set	set	set	setting
shake	shook	shaken	shaking
show	showed	shown, showed	showing
shut	shut	shut	shutting
sing	sang	sung	singing
sink	sank	sunk	sinking
sit	sat	sat	sitting
speak	spoke	spoken	speaking
spend	spent	spent	spending
stand	stood	stood	standing
steal	stole	stolen	stealing

(Main Verb)	(Past)	(Past Participle)	(Present Participle)
swear	swore	sworn	swearing
swim	swam	swum	swimming
swing	swung	swung	swinging
take	took	taken	taking
teach	taught	taught	teaching
tear	tore	torn	tearing
tell	told	told	telling
think	thought	thought	thinking
throw	threw	thrown	throwing
wear	wore	worn	wearing
win	won	won	winning
write	wrote	written	writing

Using a Dictionary

If you are not accustomed to using a desk-sized dictionary to check the principal parts of irregular verbs, you should take a few minutes to explore how such a dictionary presents verbs.

If a verb is regular and simply adds -ed to form the past and the past participle, the dictionary gives only the main verb. If the verb is irregular, however, the dictionary will list the principal parts. Check the principal parts of any of the following verbs you do not know:

bend	deal	hang (a person)	shine	spring
bet	feed	hang (a thing)	shoot	sting
bid	flee	hit	shrink	stink
blow	fling	hurt	slay	stride
breed	forbid	lend	sleep	strike
burst	forgive	light	spin	strive
cling	freeze	mean	split	wake
creep	grind	rid	spread	wring

USING THE PRINCIPAL PARTS OF IRREGULAR VERBS

In using the principal parts of irregular verbs, be especially careful to choose the correct part and to spell it correctly. Note that for most irregular verbs the past and the past participle are different. Remember that the **past** is always used **alone**—without a helper—and that the **past participle** is always used **with a helper**—*have, has, had* or some form of the verb *be*:

Correct: The runner *came* up to the starting gate.
The runner *had come* up to the starting gate.

Incorrect: The runner *had came* up to the starting gate.
The runner *come* up to the starting gate.

Correct: I *flew* to Chicago many times.
I *have flown* to Chicago many times.

Incorrect: I *have flew* to Chicago many times.
I *flown* to Chicago many times.

Correct: My uncle *ate* in the delicatessen on Chester Street.
My uncle *has eaten* in the delicatessen on Chester Street.
My uncle *had eaten* in the delicatessen on Chester Street.

Incorrect My uncle *had ate* in the delicatessen on Chester Street.
My uncle *eaten* in the delicatessen on Chester Street.

Correct:	Bob *went* there twice last week.
	Bob *had gone* there twice last week.
Incorrect:	Bob *has went* there twice last week.
	Bob *gone* there twice last week.

Do exercises 7-a, 7-b, 7-c, 7-d, and 7-e

SUGGESTIONS FOR WRITING

Select a project that you have been involved in for an extended period of time. For example, you may have painted your house or apartment over the past few months; you may have taken a course in Chinese cooking; you may have refinished an old piece of furniture. Make a list of all the things you did to complete this one project.

Read over your actions. Number them in the order in which you completed them.

Now write an explanation of what you did step by step. Describe each step in a clear sentence in the past tense. Try to use adverbs as time indicators.

NAME _____ **DATE** _____

Identify the subject in each sentence and underline it once. Underline any helping verbs twice. Then choose the correct verb from inside the parentheses and underline it twice. (Use the list of irregular verbs that begins on page 105 to check your answers.)

EXAMPLES

Our history <u>teacher</u> (<u>forgot</u>, forgotten) to announce our quiz.

Our English <u>teacher</u> <u>has</u> (forgot, <u>forgotten</u>) to assign homework all this week.

1. The snow (began, begun) to fall at midnight.

2. The new gymnasium was not (began, begun) until September.

3. Jason has not (spoke, spoken) to his brother for two years.

4. I (spoke, spoken) to Aunt Bess on the telephone this morning.

5. Dora has (lay, lain, laid) in bed with the flu for six days.

6. After work, Wendy (lay, lain, laid) down on the couch for fifteen minutes.

7. Max's front tooth was (broke, broken) during the soccer game.

8. The painters (broke, broken) four window panes.

9. Todd (choose, chose, chosen) the strawberry shortcake.

10. As of yesterday, Bonnie had (choose, chose, chosen) a pink dress for the wedding.

11. The combination of the safe is (knew, known) by only three people.

12. Only two students (knew, known) the answer to the fifth question.

13. Shannon had never (did, done) any cooking before.

14. Last summer, I (did, done) all the cooking for three weeks.

15. Last night, thirty people (came, come) to Robert's open house.

16. Brenda's grandparents have always (came, come) to her Christmas party.

17. Dave (became, become) nervous about his first day on the job.

18. Stan's puppy has (became, become) very difficult to control.

19. Kim has not been (saw, seen) on campus all week.

20. I (saw, seen) Bruce at the mall on Saturday.

NAME _____ DATE _____

In the blank space, write the correct form of each verb given to the left of the number. In selecting the part of the verb, pay particular attention to helpers and to adverbs that indicate time.

EXAMPLES

grow   Pete's oldest son has ____*grown*____ four inches in the last year.

steal   Eight watches were ____*stolen*____ from the jeweler's window.

---

take   1. Jenny _____ Hal to his favorite restaurant last night.

find   2. Dolores has not _____ her missing house key.

sing   3. My father has been _____ in the church choir for twenty years.

meet   4. Nan will _____ her fiance's family at the wedding.

write   5. The essay with the highest grade was _____ by the student

   with the lowest average.

cost   6. Last year, that computer_____ two thousand dollars.

bite   7. The toddler has been _____ by a raccoon.

bring   8. Last year, the secretary_____ a cake to the office on her own

   birthday.

run   9. Charlotte will be _____ in her first marathon next week.

teach   10. Mrs. Sias has been_____ second grade for ten years.

hide   11. My brother always_____his money in a coffee can in the

   kitchen cabinet.

throw   12. During the first two innings, the pitcher had been _____

   curve balls.

lay   13. The movers carefully_____the mirror on the dining room table.

send   14. All my bills have been_____to my old address.

sink   15. The sailboat had _____ in the storm.

lie   16. We all _____ down on the riverbank to rest after the swim.

draw   17. The art class was _____ a live model yesterday.

swear   18. The jury will be _____ in on Tuesday.

win   19. The mayoral election is usually _____ by a Democrat.

shake   20. The salad dressing had not been _____ enough.

NAME _____ **DATE** _____

From the list of irregular verbs given on pages 105–107, select an appropriate form to fit in each blank space. Watch for helping verbs as a clue to the right form. Do not use the past form with a helping verb.

EXAMPLES

My grandfather's ring was ____*given*____ to my cousin.

Tom _____*quit*_____ his job at the car wash last Saturday.

1. My little brother cannot _____ still in a movie theater.

2. The sleeve of Janet's favorite coat had been _____ in the fight.

3. The children next door _____ at the bus stop for an hour every school

   morning.

4. My old dog has _____ down the basement stairs many times.

5. Last winter, Mr. Marconi's farm was _____ to a real estate developer.

6. The table is _____ for ten people.

7. The exhausted child is _____ on the living room floor.

8. Paul will _____ a very frisky horse in the horse show on Saturday.

9. The theater near campus has been _____ the same movie for two weeks.

10. My grandmother_____ her first glass of champagne at my sister's wedding

11. Jim was _____ anxious about moving to Utah.

12. Henry had never _____ his father about the car accident.

13. Jane has been _____ that novel all afternoon.

14. Erin will be _____ in five events at the meet on Saturday.

15. My mother has never _____ a new car.

16. The home run ball was _____ by a five-year-old boy.

17. All of Jack's debts will be _____ by Friday.

18. The rent money has already been _____ on food.

19. Raymond will _____ fresh flowers for the church service.

20. The sun had not _____ by 7:00 A.M.

NAME _____ **DATE** _____

An irregular verb is used incorrectly in each of the following sentences. Rewrite the sentence using correct forms of the past tense or perfect tenses.

As shown in the example, some sentences can be corrected in more than one way. You need to write only one correct sentence.

EXAMPLE

Linda's godparents have never gave her a birthday gift.

Linda's godparents never gave her a birthday gift.

or _Linda's godparents have never given her a birthday gift._

or _Linda's godparents had never given her a birthday gift._

1. Brian has wrote an excellent answer to the last question.

_____

_____

2. The telephone rung five times during dinner.

_____

_____

3. My sister worn my dress to the dance last night.

_____

_____

4. Tom had drove to Washington many times.

_____

_____

5. Karen had got an overdue notice from the library.

_____

_____

6. Last week, Richard had went bowling five times.

_____

_____

7. Bart has never flew to Miami.

_____

_____

8. Lila shown the new parrot to her mother.

_____

_____

9. The librarian has took all her plants home.

_____

_____

10. Last night, John sung a solo at the winter concert.

_____

_____

11. Carlos has rode the subway to work for three years.

_____

_____

12. My little cousin was emotionally shook by the car accident.

_____

_____

13. Boris has gave Miguel at least three hundred dollars.

_____

_____

14. Francesco stolen the videotapes from our basement.

_____

_____

15. Franklin drunk all the grapefruit juice in my refrigerator.

_____

_____

NAME _____ DATE _____

Use each form given to the left of the number as the verb in a sentence of eight or more words.

In your sentence, underline the verb twice. Underline the subject once. Make helping verbs agree with the subject.

EXAMPLE

drew   *Kate's oldest brother drew a map in the sand for the children.*

drawn   *The winning sketches were drawn by my neighbor's six-year-old*

          daughter.

broke   1. _____

          _____

broken   2. _____

          _____

began   3. _____

          _____

begun   4. _____

          _____

ate   5. _____

          _____

eaten   6. _____

          _____

chose   7. _____

          _____

chosen   8. _____

          _____

wrote   9. _____

          _____

written   10. _____

          _____

Understanding Coordination and Subordination

8

In the first seven chapters of this book, you have been building simple sentences which communicate one idea. Throughout the rest of this book, you will be working on understanding relationships among ideas and kinds of information and then building sentences which communicate these relationships to the reader. In the workbook exercises and in your writing, you will be asked to indicate clear, appropriate relationships within sentences and from sentence to sentence in a paragraph.

COORDINATING AND SUBORDINATING WITHIN A SENTENCE

In Chapters 9 through 14, you will be primarily concerned with principles of **coordination** and **subordination** within a sentence. You will decide whether two words or groups of words are coordinate (equal in importance) or whether one is subordinate (not equal in importance) to another.

To determine that words are coordinate, you will decide how their meanings are equal. For example, consider the following sentences with coordinate elements:

1. Tory completed his math problems, his English exercises, and his history reading assignment.
2. Lori maintains her car by changing the oil and replacing the oil filter regularly.
3. My older brother lives in California, but my younger brother lives in Maine.

In the first sentence, *his math problems, his English exercises,* and *his history reading assignment* are equal because they are the same kinds of things: they are all types of assignments. In the second example, *changing the oil* and *replacing the oil filter* are equal because they are both subparts of the same idea—maintaining a car. In the last example, the older brother idea and the younger brother idea are of equal importance because both ideas communicate the same kind of information—information about where these family members live.

Other groups of words may have a different relationship. One idea may be **subordinate** to the other. For example, consider the following sentences, in which the more important element has been underlined:

1. Pam left the meeting early because she had a doctor's appointment.

2. The Board of Education spokesperson who announced the teacher transfers was not prepared for the student protests.

3. The manager insisted that all employees work one Saturday every month.

In each of these examples, one idea is subordinate to another less important idea. In the first example, Pam's doctor's appointment is the reason for her leaving the meeting and is therefore subordinate to her leaving. In the second example, *who announced the teacher transfers* provides additional information about the board member, information that is subordinate to the main idea of the student protests. Finally, in the last example, the manager's insistence is the main idea; what the manager insisted is the subordinate idea.

As you work through Chapters 9 through 16, you will learn to make decisions about coordinating and subordinating ideas. Your choices will be determined by the main idea which you are trying to prove with your sentences. This main idea will be developed in a series of sentences called a **paragraph**.

COORDINATING AND SUBORDINATING WITHIN A PARAGRAPH

As you expand and refine your sentences, you will be ready to give more thought to writing paragraphs. A **paragraph** is a group of sentences that develops one idea about a single topic.

In a sentence, the most important single idea is usually stated in the subject–verb core, which generally tells *who does what*. In a paragraph, the most important single idea is usually stated in one complete sentence called the **topic sentence**. All the other sentences in the paragraph contribute to the development of the topic sentence.

Consider the following paragraph:

> **My cousin Betty is a very irresponsible person**. First, she is irresponsible at work. Her boss at the local video store complains that she routinely arrives for work twenty minutes late. He also becomes impatient with her because she never puts the returned videos back on the shelves. Betty is also irresponsible with her friends. Her friends Cheryl and Ben invited her to dinner last week; Betty accepted the invitation but then forgot to show up. When she realized what she had done, she invited Cheryl and Ben to her favorite restaurant for lunch. But when the waiter brought the check, Betty had no cash and had forgotten her credit card. If Betty doesn't learn to be more responsible, she is going to lose both her job and her friends.

In this paragraph, all of the sentences prove the point stated in the topic sentence, that Betty is irresponsible. Thus, all of the sentences about work and friends are **subordinate** to the topic sentence. The two subpoints, work and friends, are **coordinate** to each other because they have the same relationship to the topic sentence. The two work examples about Betty's lateness and her failure to reshelve the videos are **coordinate** to each other but **subordinate** to the sentence *First, she is irresponsible at work*. Similarly, the two sentences about Cheryl and Ben are **coordinate** to each other but **subordinate** to the sentence *Betty is also irresponsible with her friends*.

When you write sentences developing a single topic, you must consider the coordinate and subordinate relationships among the sentences. You must also make sure that you include enough specific information and that you present this information in a logical order. In the sample paragraph, the sentences give specific information about Betty's irresponsible behavior. They are in a logical order because the two work examples immediately follow the statement about Betty's lack of responsibility at work and the two friendship examples immediately follow the statement about Betty's lack of responsibility toward her friends.

PLANNING, WRITING, AND EDITING A PARAGRAPH

As you complete this book, you will be combining sentences to form paragraphs and writing paragraphs on your own. You will need to remember that writing a paragraph involves three steps: planning, writing, and editing. The "Suggestions for Writing" and the exercises in the remaining chapters of this book will help you to learn to follow these three steps to build paragraphs.

Planning a paragraph involves choosing one main idea and writing a *topic sentence* which states the main idea. When you plan your paragraph, you also need to decide what kinds of sentences you will write to support your paragraph. For instance, the writer of the paragraph about Betty had to first decide that the main idea was Betty's irresponsibility; then the writer had to decide that the two situations in which she was irresponsible were her job and her friendships. Finally, the writer had to choose specific examples which would illustrate Betty's irresponsibility.

Writing a paragraph involves building sentences which prove the point. When you write your supporting sentences, you need to make sure that they all prove your topic sentence idea. It would have been incorrect to include a sentence about Betty's generosity in the paragraph which set out to prove that she was an irresponsible person. You also need to include as much specific information as possible; *twenty minutes late*, for example, is very specific. Finally, you need to write your sentences in a logical order: details must follow the general statements which they support.

Editing is your last step. When you edit, you check your sentences to make sure that you have maintained clear coordinate and subordinate relationships and appropriate connections. You also check the individual sentences to make sure that you have built them correctly. You will need to pay special attention to your verbs and your pronouns. (Chapters 15 and 16 will offer some special help in these areas.) Of course, you will also want to check your punctuation and spelling.

SUGGESTIONS FOR WRITING

Look back over the paragraph about Betty's irresponsible behavior on page 118. Try to plan, write, and edit a paragraph of your own about a friend of yours who is irresponsible. You may be able to find an idea for this paragraph in notes you have already made in your journal.

Be sure to **plan** your paragraph carefully before you start to write. First, write a topic sentence using the person's name: for example, *My friend Janet is a very irresponsible person.* Then decide on two places or aspects of life in which this person is irresponsible, such as school and home. These two places or aspects are called the subtopics of the paragraph because they are subordinate to the topic sentence.

Choose two specific examples, two particular occasions on which your friend has failed to be responsible, for each subtopic. Jot down all these ideas in the following form.

Topic Sentence: _____ *is a very irresponsible person.*

1. Subtopic: _____

   _____

   a. Specific Example: _____

   _____

   _____

b. Specific Example: _____

_____

_____

2. Subtopic: _____

_____

a. Specific Example: _____

_____

_____

b. Specific Example: _____

_____

_____

The plan makes it clear that the subtopics are subordinate to the topic sentence and the examples are subordinate to the subtopics.

Now **write** support sentences for each of your ideas. Make sure that you include specific information for each example. Tell exactly what happened. Also be sure that you stick to the single idea of irresponsibility; do not include any information about your friend's other qualities. At the end of your paragraph, add a closing sentence which, like the closing sentence of the paragraph about Betty, restates the topic sentence idea in different words.

Finally, **edit** your sentences. Make sure that they are correct. In particular, check your verbs to make sure that they are in the correct tense. When you write your topic sentence about a quality that the person displays regularly, you will want to use the *present tense*; however, when you discuss something that the person did in the past, you will want to use the *past* tense.

Using Coordination

9

Compound Elements of a Simple Sentence

A simple sentence states one complete thought by using a subject, a verb, and, if necessary, complements (an object or adjective or noun complement). The following simple sentence has three elements in the sentence **base**: one subject (underlined once), one verb (underlined twice), and one direct object (circled).

The boys prepared the (vegetables.)

We might, however, name specific parts or kinds of each of the three elements and join the specifics with a **coordinator**, *and*:

General		Specific
boys	=	Bob and Frank
prepared	=	washed and peeled
vegetables	=	potatoes, carrots, and onions

If we substitute the specific words for the general words, we still have a simple sentence, one that says the same thing about the same subject. However, the new sentence gives much more specific information:

Bob and Frank washed and peeled the (potatoes,) (carrots,) and (onions.)

This chapter shows how to **compound** (combine) equally important, similar information by using **coordinators** as the **connectors**. Specifically, you will work with three single-word coordinators and four paired coordinators:

Coordinator	Meaning
and	means *plus*; the elements are being added one to another
but	means *contrast*; the elements are contradictory
or	means a *choice*; one element is chosen

Paired Coordinators	Meaning
either . . . or	emphasizes the choice
neither . . . nor	emphasizes a negative choice—*not* this nor that
both . . . and	emphasizes both elements
not only . . . but also	emphasizes both elements

All the elements of the simple sentence may be compounded—two or more subjects, objects, verbs, adjectives, adverbs, or phrases. In the following sections, you will study some compound elements that create special problems.

USING COMPOUND SUBJECTS

Frequently, we want to say that several persons (subjects) are doing the same thing. We might generalize to write a simple sentence such as this:

Two students are taking the (test.)

Or we might want to name the students:

Beth Williams is taking the (test.)

Floyd Jones is taking the (test.)

However, if we wish to name the two specific subjects, we do not need a whole sentence for each. The nouns (*Beth Williams* and *Floyd Jones*) are equal in importance since both are students and both are doing the same thing—taking the test. Because they are equal, we can join them with an appropriate coordinator or, if we wish special emphasis, a pair of coordinators. Because they are doing the same thing, both nouns can be made the compound subject of the same verbs as in the following combinations:

1. Beth Williams **and** Floyd Jones are taking the (test.)

2. **Both** Beth Williams **and** Floyd Jones are taking the (test.)

When we compound two or more than two, we must be certain that they are equal in importance and that they serve identical functions in the sentence.

Pronouns in Compound Subjects

Remember that the **personal pronouns** have different forms for subjects, objects, and possessives. (See Chapter 2.)

- In compound subjects, be sure to use the correct "subject" forms of pronouns.
- Remember, too, that the first person (**I** and **we**) comes after other nouns or pronouns in the compound.

As a review, study the following examples of correct and incorrect usage for pronouns in compound subjects:

Incorrect:	**Me** and Dave are planning a trip to Alaska.
Correct:	Dave and **I** are planning a trip to Alaska.
Incorrect:	Cindy, Marie, Bill, and **me** have been close friends since grade school.
Correct:	Cindy, Marie, Bill, and **I** have been close friends since grade school.

Do not confuse the -self and -selves forms of pronouns with the personal pronouns.

- The reflexive/intensive pronouns, recognized by the *-self* or *-selves* endings, are used only to **rename** a noun or pronoun already mentioned in a sentence.
- They cannot be used as any element (subject or object, single or compound) unless they **rename** another noun or pronoun.

Study the following examples of correct usage. Draw an arrow from the *-self* or *-selves* forms to the nouns they rename.

Correct Reflexive and Intensive Pronouns

1. Mother **herself** had misplaced the keys.

2. Mother had misplaced the keys **herself**.

3. Father blamed only **himself**.

4. She spent all her money on **herself**.

5. Sally and I blamed **ourselves** for the accident.

Look at the following incorrect examples. What is wrong with each? Can you correct them?

Incorrect Reflexive and Intensive Pronouns

1. Mother and **myself** searched everywhere for her keys.

2. Frank and **yourself** are the losers.

3. **Myself** and my cousins plan to spend two days in San Diego.

Check your corrections with these:

1. Mother and **I** searched everywhere for her keys.
2. Frank and **you** are the losers, *or*, **You** and Frank are the losers.
3. My cousins and **I** plan to spend two days in San Diego.

Agreement with Compound Subjects

The coordinator *and* and the paired coordinators *both . . . and* and *not only . . . but also* are used to **add** one subject to another.

- These coordinators make a **plural** subject, and the verb must also be plural to agree.

Singular subjects and verbs:	My dog **snores**.
	My cat **snores**.
Combined in the plural:	My dog and my cat **snore**.
	Both my dog and my cat **snore**.
Singular subjects and verbs:	The teacher **was** happy.
	The student **was** happy.
Combined in the plural:	The teacher and the student **were** happy.
	Both the teacher and the student **were** happy.

Frequently, more than the verb must be brought into line with the subject. Notice in the following combinations that the **verbs**, the **possessive pronouns**, and the **objects** are changed to agree with the compound (plural) subject.

1. Jack always brings his car.
   Susan always brings her car.
   Combination: Jack and Susan always **bring their cars**.

2. Sam attends his exercise class regularly.
   I attend my exercise class regularly.
   Combination: Sam and I **attend our** exercise **classes** regularly.

Compare the combination of the next group of sentences (#3) with that in #2:

> 3. Sam attends an exercise class.
>   I attend the same exercise class.
>   *Combination*: Sam and I **attend** the same exercise **class**.

Why is the object plural (*classes*) in sentence 2 and singular (*class*) in sentence 3? Do you see the difference in meaning? As you work with coordination, always keep your attention on what you mean, not just on the mechanics of compounding two or more elements.

When we use the coordinators *or* and *nor* or the pairs *either . . . or* and *neither . . . nor*, we are not adding; we are giving alternatives, offering **one** choice or another. Look at the following examples; the verb is singular because the subject is singular—one animal **or** the other, **not** one **and** the other:

> 1. The dog or the cat snores.
> 2. Either the dog or the cat snores.
> 3. Neither the dog nor the cat snores.

Note, too, how using the pairs (*either . . . or, neither . . . nor*) emphasizes the choice between the two singular nouns, *dog, cat*. Obviously, the two nouns will not always be singular. Remember these two additional rules:

- When the two nouns (or pronouns) joined by *or* or *nor* are both plural, the verb is plural:

  Neither the dogs nor the cats **snore**.

- When the two nouns (or pronouns) are of different number or person, the verb agrees with the **nearer** one:

  Neither the teacher nor the **students were** happy.
  Neither the students nor the **teacher was** happy.

Punctuation of Compound Subjects

When we compound only **two** elements, we join them with a coordinator and **no comma**:

> **Incorrect**: Oaks, and elms grow in Maryland.
> **Correct**: Oaks and elms grow in Maryland.

Note, too, that the second subject is **not** set off from the rest of the sentence with a comma:

> **Incorrect**: Rain and hail, slashed the countryside.
> **Correct**: Rain and hail slashed the countryside.

When we compound **three or more**, we construct **a series**.

- Each item in the series is separated from the next by a comma:

  George Washington, Thomas Jefferson, and Benjamin Franklin are my father's heroes.
  The Declaration of Independence, the Constitution, and Lincoln's Gettysburg Address are often quoted by politicians.

Remember that the items are separated from each other, not from the rest of the sentence:

    Incorrect: Rain, hail, and sleet, slashed the countryside.
    Correct: Rain, hail, and sleet slashed the countryside.

Do exercises 9-a and 9-b

USING COMPOUND VERBS

Just as the subject of a sentence can be two or more coordinate nouns or pronouns, so the verb can consist of two or more coordinate verbs.

- Two coordinate verbs can be joined with a single-word or a paired coordinator.
- Three or more verbs can be written as a series, that is, as items separated by commas.

As you compound two verbs or construct a series, remember that you are still writing **a simple sentence** as long as the same subject is doing the same things:

1. I wrote him twice **but** received no answer.

2. Sadie **either** swims **or** jogs every day.

3. Charles **neither** exercises **nor** eats well-balanced meals.

4. The two students finished the experiment **and** left.

Each of the four sentences is a simple sentence with a **compound verb**. Look back at the fourth sentence; it combines the following two sentences:

1. The two students finished the experiment.

2. The two students left.

The verbs in the two sentences can be combined because they have **the same subject**, *students*. If we name the two students, we have a **simple sentence** with **both a compound subject and a compound verb**:

Combination:

Bill Rice and Pete Hendricks finished the experiment and left.

Consistent Tense for Compound Verbs

To be combined into a compound verb, **coordinate** verbs must also be in the same **tense**:

    Correct: Cheryl swims and jogs regularly.   Present Tense

    Correct: Cheryl swam and jogged regularly.   Past Tense

    Incorrect: Cheryl swims and jogged regularly.   Mixed Tenses

In the first sentence, the two verbs are in the present tense. The tense is **consistent**, and the sentence is correct. The second sentence is also correct: both verbs are in the past tense. The third sentence is not correct: the tense **shifts** from the present *swims* to the past *jogged*.

When we have coordinate verbs with helpers, we **usually do not repeat the helper**. However, be sure the action is clear when you omit a helper. If you are writing a series, either you must omit the helper for each verb after the first, or you must add the helper for each verb.

Correct: Cheryl will swim and jog this afternoon.

Correct: Cheryl can swim everyday, jog five times a week, and still enjoy dancing on Saturday night.

Correct: Cheryl must swim and jog regularly to keep fit.

Incorrect: Cheryl can swim everyday, jog five times a week, and still enjoys dancing on Saturday night.

Incorrect: In order to keep fit, Cheryl must eat well, swim regularly, and must jog five times a week.

Consistent Person and Number for Compound Verbs

As you combine verbs to make a compound verb, be sure all the verbs in the compound agree with the subject in **number** and **person**. (See Chapters 2 and 5 for a review of these terms.) Study these examples:

Correct: A good salesperson knows the merchandise and shows it willingly to customers.

Incorrect: A good supervisor understands the work of the employees and consult with them regularly. (*Consult* should be changed to *consults* to agree with the singular subject *supervisor*.)

Punctuation of Compound Verbs

When you join only **two** verbs, **no comma** separates them. No matter how many complements or modifiers come between one verb and another, if there are only two verbs in the compound, you should not separate them with a comma:

The judge turned slowly toward the defendant and began to deliver the sentence.

In a **series** (a list of **three or more**), the verbs are separated from each other by commas:

> The judge nodded to the prosecutor, turned slowly toward the defendant,
>
> and began to deliver the sentence.

Do exercises 9-c, 9-d, 9-e, and 9-f

USING COMPOUND COMPLEMENTS

In making complements **compound**, we follow the same general rules that we use with subjects and verbs:

- The complements must be equal in importance.
- The complements must be joined with coordinators.
- Complements in a series must be separated from each other with commas.

Compound complements will also have the same relationship to the subject and verb of the sentence base.

Adjective Complements

Adjective complements can be compounds as well as single words. In the following examples, the circled adjectives modify the underlined subjects.

1. The day was (hot) and (humid.)

2. The entrance exam seemed (long) and (difficult.)

3. The boys were (alert,) (happy,) and (eager) to begin.

4. My cousin is always either very (silly) or very (serious.)

Object Complements

Objects of action verbs and of prepositions may also be compounded. As you use compound objects, be especially watchful of personal pronouns (see Chapter 2). Be sure to use "object" forms. In the following examples, the objects are circled. As you study the examples, underline the verbs twice and place a check over the prepositions.

1. Fred's dog chewed his father's (slippers) and his mother's (gloves.)

2. The angry cat ran between (Jane) and (me.)

3. Just between (you) and (me,) the test was too easy.

127

4. The workers demanded a (raise,) a shorter work (week,) and dental (insurance.)

5. With his (bonus) and his mother's (gift,) he will buy either a new (CD player) or a microwave (oven.)

6. My father bought new (wristwatches) and signet (rings) for my (brother) and (me.)

7. Father brought my (sister) and (me) a (pennant) and a (program.)

8. Beverly prepared both a macaroni (salad) and a tuna fish (casserole.)

Do exercise 9-g

USING COMPOUND ADVERBS AND ADJECTIVES

Both adverbs and adjectives can be used in pairs or in series:

Compound Adverbs

1. **Quickly** and **quietly**, the little boy returned to his seat.
2. The teacher spoke **softly** but **enthusiastically**.
3. The old man approached the stranger **slowly** and **cautiously**.
4. **Tactfully** but **frankly**, the manager pointed out our errors.

Compound Adjectives

5. The nurse looked at the child's **bruised** and **twisted** knee.
6. The doctor—**embarrassed, frightened**, and **humbled**—hurried from the judge's chambers.
7. Into the room walked a **skinny, freckled** young man.
8. She gazed at the **wilted, faded** flowers.

Coordinate Adjectives

Look back at the examples of compound adjectives in the preceding section. Notice in sentences 7 and 8 that the adjectives are separated by a comma, not a co-ordinator such as *and* or *but*. **Coordinate adjectives** are punctuated differently from other compound elements.

Look at these three sentences:

1. The lake was clear.
2. The lake was cold.
3. We swam in the lake.

In a combination, we would probably want to emphasize the third sentence. The first and second sentences simply add information about the lake: both *clear* and *cold* are adjectives modifying *lake*. They both give the same kind of equally important information: they tell (**what kind of**) lake. They are **coordinate** adjectives. We could write either of the following combinations:

1. We swam in the clear and cold lake.
2. We swam in the cold and clear lake.

However, coordinate adjectives can also be written with a comma instead of a coordinator between them. Be careful to separate the adjectives from each other, not the adjectives from other words in the sentence:

Correct: We swam in the clear, cold lake.
We swam in the cold, clear lake.
Incorrect: We swam in the cold, clear, lake.

Nouns can, of course, have more than two coordinate adjectives, but the same rules apply:

- The use of a coordinator is optional.
- If no coordinator is used, adjectives are separated **from each other with commas**.

Look at the following group of four sentences:

The hikers struggled to reach the top of the mountain.
The hikers were hot.
The hikers were tired.
The hikers were hungry.

The three adjectives (*hot, tired, hungry*) describing the hikers are coordinate. They can be written in any order:

hot, tired, hungry	hungry, hot, tired
tired, hungry, hot	hot, hungry, tired
hungry, tired, hot	tired, hot, hungry

Two possible combinations of the sentences are

1. The hot, tired, hungry hikers struggled to reach the top of the mountain.
2. The hot, tired, **and** hungry hikers struggled to reach the top of the mountain.

Recognizing Coordinate Adjectives

Adjectives that modify the same noun are not always coordinate. You can check the equality of adjectives by asking two questions:

1. Can the adjectives be connected with the coordinator *and*?
2. Can the order of the adjectives be changed?

Consider the following three sentences.

The tent was beginning to mildew.
The tent was old.
The tent was canvas.

Old and *canvas* are both adjectives describing *tent*, but they are not of equal importance. *Canvas* specifies the material of the tent; it must be placed immediately in front of the word *tent*; therefore, the order of the adjectives must be

> old canvas tent
> **not**
> canvas old tent

Nor can *and* be placed between them:

> old and canvas tent

The two adjectives are not coordinate. In the combination the adjectives would not be separated by a comma:

> *Combination*: The old canvas tent was beginning to mildew.

> **Do exercises 9-h, 9-i, and 9-j**

SUGGESTIONS FOR WRITING

Take another look at the paragraph that you wrote at the end of Chapter 8. Now try to write another paragraph, this time about a different friend with a different quality. For example, you may choose to prove that your friend Bill is a very generous person. (Other adjectives would include *selfish, sympathetic, unsympathetic, honest, dishonest, hardworking, lazy, consistent,* and *inconsistent.*) Once again, if you have been using your journal to record your everyday thoughts and feelings, you may be able to use your journal entries to find a subject for this new paragraph.

Be sure that you **plan** your paragraph first. After you write your topic sentence, choose as your subtopics two places or areas of life in which your friend displays the quality you have chosen. A person, for instance, may be honest at work and at school. Once you have limited yourself to two subtopics, you will be able to choose two specific examples for each place, that is, two particular times when your friend has proved himself or herself to be honest or selfish or hardworking.

Write your sentences carefully, taking time to develop them with specific details which give exact information. You would not want to make a general statement such as *When Bill's cash register contained a lot of money that could not be accounted for, he gave the money to his boss.* Rather than use the phrase *a lot of money,* you would want to specify exactly how much money: for example, *$87.* When you have written your examples, write a closing sentence, such as *Both Bill's employers and his teachers value his honesty.*

Do not forget to **edit** your sentences. Pay special attention to your verb tense.

NAME _____ **DATE** _____

Most of the following sentences contain errors in coordination, agreement, punctuation, or pronoun forms. Correct these errors.

- Underline the subject once and the verb twice.
- Cross out each error and write your correction above it.
- Write a *C* by the number of each correct sentence.

EXAMPLES

_____ Neither my father nor I ~~knows~~ *know* how to swim.

_____ Jason and ~~myself~~ *I* will bring the refreshments.

__*C*__ The syllabus, textbook, and final exam were inside the desk.

---

1. _____ The oil and filters in Skip's car has not been checked for six months.

2. _____ Neither her checkbook nor her keys was in the purse.

3. _____ Either his cousins or his sister has lent him the money.

4. _____ Each of the children need a permission slip.

5. _____ Harry Mann, Frank Friendly, and Betty Boop, have applied to only two

   colleges.

6. _____ Mary Ellen, and her friend Francine go fishing every weekend.

7. _____ The confused student and the frustrated teacher, sat staring at each other.

8. _____ The girl in the pink dress, and the boy in the grey suit left together.

9. _____ The cashier, the assistant manager, and the little old woman chased after the thief.

10. _____ John Donne, William Shakespeare, and Emily Dickinson were my father's

    favorite poets.

11. _____ Me and my brother do not like poetry.

12. _____ Eight young men and three old women, stood at the gate.

13. _____ Both myself and Sidney knew how to repair the motor.

14. _____ Betty and myself have already saved enough money for the trip to Canada.

15. _____ Me and David decided not to go to Florida during spring break.

NAME _____ **DATE** _____

Fill in the blanks in the following sentences with appropriate subjects (nouns or pronouns) and their modifiers.

EXAMPLE

Neither __*Sidney*__ nor __*her brothers*__ have an excuse for their rudeness.

═══

1. Both _____ and _____
   were growing in Grandfather's garden.

2. The _____ and _____
   were stolen over the weekend.

3. Jerry's _____ and _____
   were lying under his pickup truck.

4. His _____, _____,
   and _____ were left on the kitchen floor.

5. _____, _____,
   and _____ have only three more days to pay their
   tuition.

6. _____ or _____
   was listening on the phone extension.

7. _____ and _____
   have lost our lunch money.

8. Neither _____ nor _____
   has asked a girl to the picnic.

9. Neither _____ nor _____
   have asked their boyfriends to the picnic.

10. Either _____ or _____
    has taken my calculator out of my locker.

11. The _____, _____,
    and _____ were missing from Pete's locker.

12. Both _____ and _____
    seemed worried about the test.

13. _____ and _____
    were eager to begin our trip.

14. _____ or _____
    has taken my surf board.

15. _____ and _____
    were the only skaters still on the ice.

Identifying and Correcting Compound Verbs

NAME _____ **DATE** _____

Most of the following sentences contain errors in the coordination, punctuation, or forms of compound verbs. Correct these errors.

- Underline the subjects once and the verbs twice.
- Draw a line through each error and write your correction above it.
- Write a *C* by the number of each correct sentence.

EXAMPLES

1. _____ He parked the car, ~~runs~~ *ran* through the rain, and then met us in the theater.

2. _C_ The children and their chaperones ate in the cafeteria and then toured the Air and Space Museum.

1. _____ Every Sunday, Ralph visited his mother, phones his sister, and wrote letters to his grandparents.

2. _____ Pete and Rick bowl on Wednesdays and play tennis on Thursdays.

3. _____ The Johnsons and the Smiths argued for several weeks and then choose not to rent a beach house together.

4. _____ The shipment was sent early Monday morning and arrives in North Platte on Thursday.

5. _____ We will leave at 8:00 A.M., arrive in Chicago at noon, and board the plane for Montreal an hour later.

6. _____ I may watch the evening news, and then go to bed.

7. _____ Diane visited Wilmington, and then went on to Philadelphia.

8. _____ The report was read by each of the commissioners and, then released to the press.

9. _____ The little boy blushed, scraped his right foot back and forth in the gravel, and hangs his head.

10. _____ Geraldine's dog can eat two cans of dog food, drinks a large bowl of milk, and still is hungry.

11. _____ My sister was listening to her stereo and, trying to study at the same time.

12. _____ Our mother comes into the room quietly, turned off the stereo, and smiles sweetly.

13. _____ William, Frank, and Bill cuts the firewood, splits it, and stacked it by the back door.

14. _____ My father wash and dried his clothes at the laundromat on M Street.

15. _____ The two men finished stacking the wood, and walked slowly toward the house.

133

NAME _____ DATE _____

Fill in the blanks with appropriate verbs and their modifiers and complements.

EXAMPLE

Jack walked to his car, *scraped the ice off the windows* _____,

put his package in the trunk _____, and _____ *drove off* _____.

1. The cab driver opened his door, eased himself out of the cab, and _____

_____ .

2. Dollie Dangerfield neither _____ nor _____

_____ hard.

3. Several trees _____ and _____

during the storm.

4. The fishermen turned to the boys on the beach and _____ .

5. My reading teacher usually _____ or _____

_____ .

6. For unknown reasons, my cousin always _____ or

_____ .

7. Each of his friends _____ or _____

_____ every week.

8. My best friend _____ , _____ ,

and _____ .

9. On our visit to New Orleans, we _____ and

_____ .

10. My aunt and uncle neither _____ nor

_____ .

11. Before noon, the students must _____ or

_____ .

12. The protestors had _____ but

_____ .

13. The little dog _____ twice and then

_____ .

14. Before tomorrow, I should _____ ,

_____ , _____ , and

_____ .

15. Each Saturday, Beverly _____ in the morning,

_____ in the afternoon, and _____

in the evening.

NAME _____ **DATE** _____

　　　Complete each of the following sentences by adding a **coordinator** and **one** coordinate verb with its complements and modifiers. Be sure that the verb you add is in the same tense as the one given. Remember that **no comma** is needed to separate **two** compound verbs. Underline each subject once and each verb twice.

EXAMPLES

Blake quit school *and began to work as a gardener on the campus*

of Arizona State University.

The Hendersons sold their house *and moved into a condominium*

in Carefree, Arizona.

1. He swims every Saturday _____

2. After work, Eric goes to the library _____

_____

3. The librarian helped us locate articles in the card catalog _____

_____

4. Bill and Diane shucked the oysters _____

_____

5. The secretary smiled _____

6. The new student walked into the cafeteria _____

_____

7. After work, we will pack our bags _____

_____

8. The new owner opened the car door _____

_____

9. Jack Smart has selected the music for tonight's concert _____

_____

10. By the end of the week, the students must complete their research _____

_____

NAME _____ **DATE** _____

    Combine the following groups of sentences into one simple sentence by using a compound subject, a compound verb, or both. Be sure to change verbs and pronouns so that **subjects, verbs**, and **pronouns** agree.

    When you finish, read through the topic sentence and your combinations. Notice how they form a paragraph, with your combinations providing examples to support the topic sentence.

Topic Sentence: My brother and sister have always given me advice and expected me to profit from their experience.

EXAMPLE

My brother told me to plan my college career carefully.
My brother insisted on my making a trip to the college and picking up a schedule of classes.
My sister told me to plan my college career carefully.
My sister insisted on my making a trip to the college and picking up a schedule of classes.

Combination: _____ *My brother and sister told me to plan my college career*

carefully and insisted on my making a trip to the college and picking up a

schedule of classes. _____

---

1. They advised me to select a specific curriculum.
   They stressed the importance of analyzing the general education courses to find the best ones for me.

   Combination: _____ _____

   _____

2. They told me to study the registration information.
   They suggested making up two or three trial schedules.

   Combination: _____

   _____

3. According to them, only the well-prepared student gets a liveable schedule.
   Only the well-prepared student completes the registration process in one day.

   Combination: _____

   _____

   _____

4. As usual, I did not follow my brother's good advice.
   I did not follow my sister's good advice.
   I chose instead to talk to a few friends about the college.

   Combination: _____

   _____

5. Following my friends' advice, I called the registrar's office.
   I was given the days and hours of registration.
   I chose a date and time convenient for me.

   Combination: _____

   _____

6. At the school, a counselor answered all my questions about courses and programs.
   The counselor enabled me to select the best curriculum for me, electronics.

   Combination: _____

   _____

7. The counselor also helped me plan a perfect schedule.
   The counselor explained the easiest way to complete my registration.

   Combination: _____

   _____

8. My class schedule fits my work schedule perfectly.
   My class schedule leaves me time each day to study in the library.

   Combination: _____

   _____

9. My brother is pleased with his role as advisor to his baby sister.
   My sister is pleased with her role as advisor to her baby sister.
   My brother plans to talk to me soon about preparing to transfer to a four-year school.
   My sister plans to talk to me soon about preparing to transfer to a four-year school.

   Combination: _____

   _____

10. As usual, I will listen carefully.
    Then I will make my own plans.

    Combination: _____

    _____

    _____

NAME _____ **DATE** _____

Combine each of the groups of sentences into one **simple sentence** by making a compound complement. Be sure to move the modifiers of complements into the combination.

Again, notice how all of your combinations develop the topic sentence idea, this time by telling the story of the writer's attempt to raise money.

Topic Sentence: At the end of my senior year in high school, I needed three hundred dollars to repair my car and four hundred dollars to pay my college tuition.

EXAMPLE

I had no money in my wallet.
I had no one to lend me seven hundred dollars.

Combination: _____ *I had no money in my wallet and no one to lend me seven*

hundred dollars.

---

1. During May, I sold my new guitar.
    I sold my old stereo.

    Combination: _____

    _____

2. However, I received only forty dollars for the guitar.
    I received only twenty-five dollars for the stereo.

    Combination: _____

    _____

3. With only sixty-five dollars, I became depressed.
    I became irritable even around my best friends.

    Combination: _____

    _____

4. It was June.
    It was time for a desperate move.

    Combination: _____

    _____

5. I gave up my plans for a summer at the beach.
    I gave up my dream of developing the world's greatest tan.

    Combination: _____

    _____

6. At this point, I could not be picky about working conditions.
   I could not be choosy about wages.

   Combination: _____

   _____

7. I became another wage-slave.
   I became another victim of America's fast-food craze.

   Combination: _____

   _____

8. My assignment was frying hamburgers on a grill.
   My assignment was frying french fries in deep fat.

   Combination: _____

   _____

9. At the end of every day, I felt worn out.
   At the end of every day, I felt greasy from head to toe.

   Combination: _____

   _____

10. My skin became red.
    My skin became blotchy.

    Combination: _____

    _____

11. By mid-July, I was deeply depressed.
    I was ready to sell my car and forget college.

    Combination: _____

    _____

NAME _____ **DATE** _____

     Combine each of the groups of sentences into one **simple sentence** by using prepositional phrases and adjectives to describe nouns. When the adjectives are coordinate, separate them with commas.

Topic Sentence: Four of the houses on my street belong to members of my family.

EXAMPLE

The house belongs to my uncle.
The house is red.
The house is made of brick.
The house has a porch.
The porch is inviting.
The porch is comfortable.

Combination: ___*The red brick house with the inviting, comfortable porch be-*___

     ___*longs to my uncle.*___

1. Aunt Lill and Uncle Herman own the bungalow.
   The bungalow is unpainted.
   The bungalow is untidy.
   The bungalow is on the corner lot.
   The corner lot is small.

   Combination: _____

   _____

2. My grandparents own a house.
   The house is a ranch.
   The house is large.
   Gardens surround the house.
   The gardens are lush.
   The gardens arc well kept.

   Combination: _____

   _____

3. My parents and I live in a house.
   The house is a split level.
   The house is small.
   The house has a lawn.
   The lawn is large.
   The lawn is hilly.

   Combination: _____

   _____

NAME _____ DATE _____

Write a simple sentence of ten or more words using the coordinator given by each number.

and

1. _____

_____

_____

_____

but

2. _____

_____

_____

_____

or

3. _____

_____

_____

_____

either . . . or

4. _____

_____

_____

_____

both . . . and

5. _____

_____

_____

_____

neither . . . nor

6. _____

_____

_____

_____

NAME _____ **DATE** _____

Combine each of the following groups of sentences into one simple sentence by writing compound subjects, verbs, complements, adjectives, or adverbs.

Notice that your combinations will develop the topic sentence idea; they will tell the story of what happened to the writer during the snowstorm.

Topic Sentence: I will always remember the winter of 1938 and the igloo my brothers and I made in the deep snow that lasted from January to February.

EXAMPLE

I watched the snow through the bay window in our living room.
The window was large.
My three brothers watched the snow through the window.

Combination: *My three brothers and I watched the snow through the large bay window in our living room.*

---

1. The snowflakes were white.
   The snowflakes were thick.
   They fell silently.
   They seemed to absorb all the noises of the street.

   Combination: _____

   _____

2. The snow formed a white blanket on the ground.
   The blanket was smooth.
   The snow formed cotton wrapping on the trees.
   The snow formed cotton wrapping on the shrubs.
   The cotton wrapping was soft.

   Combination: _____

   _____

3. On the second day of the snowfall, I was eager to go outside to play.
   My brothers were eager to go outside to play.

   Combination: _____

   _____

4. We ran into the storage room in the basement.
   We began searching through our beach toys.

   Combination: _____

   _____

5. We found our spades.
   We found our sand pails.
   Our pails were old.
   We found our shovels.
   The shovels were rusty.
   The shovels were bent.

   Combination: _____

   _____

6. Our mother helped us into our snowsuits.
   Our mother helped us into our rubber boots.
   Our snowsuits were heavy.
   Our snowsuits were wool.
   Our mother laughed us out the back door.

   Combination: _____

   _____

7. We felt like brave Arctic explorers.
   We soon looked like four snowmen.
   We looked like fat snowmen.

   Combination: _____

   _____

8. As usual, my oldest brother, Charles, took the lead.
   He soon had us organized into a team of Eskimos.

   Combination: _____

   _____

9. In single file behind Charles, we marked off a large circle in the center of our back yard.
   Then, with pounding feet, we packed the snow inside the circle to create the floor of our igloo.
   The floor was icy.
   The floor was solid.

   Combination: _____

   _____

10. We packed the soft snow into our buckets to make ice bricks.
    The bricks were hard.
    We placed the bricks on top of each other.
    We smoothed them down with our mittens to round the sides toward the center.

    Combination: _____

    _____

11. The finished igloo was four feet high.
    It was seven feet in diameter.
    It was six inches thick.

    Combination: _____

    _____

12. In the early afternoon, we came into our large kitchen.
    The kitchen was warm.
    We placed our snowsuits near the wood stove on the back porch.
    We placed our mittens near the wood stove on the back porch.
    The snowsuits were woolen. The mittens were woolen.
    The snowsuits were soggy. The mittens were soggy.
    We set our boots upside-down in the wood box.

    Combination: _____

    _____

    _____

    _____

13. We were exhausted.
    But we were proud.

    Combination: _____

    _____

14. By late February, the igloo had caved in.
    It could no longer shelter my brothers.
    It could no longer shelter me.

    Combination: _____

    _____

15. But the memory of the igloo is frozen in time.
    It returns with the white whirl of a January blizzard.
    Or it slips into a room with the smell of wet wool drying.

    Combination: _____

    _____

Using Coordination

Building Compound Sentences

10

In Chapter 9, you studied ways of compounding (combining) coordinate elements within a simple sentence. You practiced using compound subjects, verbs, complements, prepositional phrases, and single-word modifiers. In this chapter, you will learn ways of compounding (joining) two or more simple sentences to make a **compound sentence**.

IDENTIFYING COORDINATE SIMPLE SENTENCES

Simple sentences can be combined into one sentence only if they are coordinate, that is, if the ideas of the simple sentences are **of equal importance and closely related**. Here are two simple sentences that can be joined to form one compound sentence:

Simple sentence: Theresa works the night shift at the admissions desk at Mercy Hospital.

Simple sentence: Her brother Tony works the day shift at a gas station around the corner.

Each sentence is of equal importance. Each sentence is about a family member and his or her job. Because the two ideas are coordinate and related, the sentences can be combined into one compound sentence:

Compound sentence: Theresa works the night shift at the admissions desk at Mercy Hospital, and her brother Tony works the day shift at a gas station around the corner.

Sentences that are not coordinate should not be combined into a compound sentence. If the ideas do not make sense together, if they are not related and of equal importance, the simple sentences should not be compounded. Look at the following simple sentences:

Simple sentence: Theresa works the night shift at the admissions desk at Mercy Hospital.

Simple sentence: Her cousin Joe lives in Oklahoma City.

The ideas of the two sentences are not coordinate: the first explains where Theresa works and the second where her cousin lives. They should not be compounded:

Incorrect: Theresa works the night shift at the admissions desk at Mercy Hospital, and her cousin Joe lives in Oklahoma City.

CHOICES IN COMPOUNDING

When two closely related simple sentences have the same subject or the same verb, they often can be combined either as a compound sentence or as a simple sentence with compound elements, such as subjects or verbs. Here are two sentences with the same subject:

Simple sentence:	Brian dieted for three weeks.
Simple sentence:	He lost ten pounds.

They can be joined to make a compound sentence with two subject–verb bases and two equal ideas:

Compound sentence:	Brian dieted for three weeks, and he lost ten pounds.

Or, because the two subjects (*Brian* and *he*) are the same person, they can also be combined into a simple sentence with a compound verb:

Simple sentence:	Brian dieted for three weeks and lost ten pounds.

This sentence is **simple** because the coordinator *and* joins only two verbs with the same subject, *Brian*.

Both combinations are correct. The choice depends on how much emphasis we want to place on Brian as the **doer of the action**. If we want to emphasize him as the doer, we use the compound sentence, which renames the doer (*he*).

However, you must be aware of the differences in the two kinds of sentences so that you can punctuate them correctly. Remember that, within a simple sentence, **two** verbs (or subjects or complements) joined by a coordinator such as *and* are not separated by a comma (see Chapter 9). In the next section, you will study ways of punctuating compound sentences.

WRITING AND PUNCTUATING COMPOUND SENTENCES

There are several ways to combine simple sentences to form a compound sentence.

Using a Comma with a Coordinator

Two simple sentences can be combined by one of the coordinators—*and, but, or, for, so, yet, nor*—and a **comma**, which is placed before the coordinator. The three most commonly used coordinators are *and, but*, and *or*.

Each of the coordinators shows a different relationship between the two ideas it joins. In each of the following examples, note the relationship established by the coordinator and the placement of the comma in front of the coordinator.

1. *And* shows **addition**:

Simple sentences:	Marta painted the shutters.
	Joe stained the shingles.
Compound sentence:	Marta painted the shutters, *and* Joe stained the shingles.

Simple sentences:	My sister arrived early this morning.
	My brother arrived at noon.
Compound sentence:	My sister arrived early this morning, *and* my brother arrived at noon.

2. *But* shows **contrast**:

Simple sentences:	Nancy wants to go to the party. Her husband wants to stay home.
Compound sentence:	Nancy wants to go to the party, *but* her husband wants to stay home.
Simple sentences:	Ed planned to go shopping. His parents expected him to stay with his little brother.
Compound sentence:	Ed planned to go shopping, *but* his parents expected him to stay with his little brother.

3. *Or* shows **choice**:

Simple sentences:	Harvey may spend the summer on his sister's ranch in Texas. Harvey may live at home and take two summer school courses at the local community college.
Compound sentence:	Harvey may spend the summer on his sister's ranch in Texas, *or* he may live at home and take two summer school courses at the local community college.
Simple sentences:	Nora may buy a new car. Nora may have her old car repaired.
Compound sentence:	Nora may buy a new car, *or* she may have her old car repaired.

4. *For* indicates that the second clause **explains the reason for** the first:

Simple sentences:	Larry was ready for the test. Larry had studied all night.
Compound sentence:	Larry was ready for the test, *for* he had studied all night.
Simple sentences:	My uncle did not retire until his seventy-fifth birthday. My uncle loved teaching.
Compound sentence:	My uncle did not retire until his seventy-fifth birthday, *for* he loved teaching.

5. *So* indicates that the second event happened **as a result of** the action or condition described first:

Simple sentences:	I was having trouble paying my rent. I started looking for a roommate.
Compound sentence:	I was having trouble paying my rent, *so* I started looking for a roommate.
Simple sentences:	William hated the cold Connecticut winters. William moved to Key West.
Compound sentence:	William hated the cold Connecticut winters, *so* he moved to Key West.

6. *Yet* indicates **a change** in behavior, in attitude, or in the way something is perceived:

Simple sentences:	Sandy had seemed willing to help clean up. Sandy left immediately after dinner.

Compound sentence:	Sandy had seemed willing to help clean up, *yet* she left immediately after dinner.
Simple sentences:	Nick wanted to find a more challenging job. Nick hated to leave his friends at the office.
Compound sentence:	Nick wanted to find a more challenging job, *yet* he hated to leave his friends at the office.

7. *Nor* indicates that the second statement presents **another negative idea**:

Simple sentences:	The travelers were not prepared for the cold weather. The travelers were not prepared for the heavy rain.
Compound sentence:	The travelers were not prepared for the cold weather, *nor* were they prepared for the heavy rain. [Note that the subject–verb order in the second statement is reversed: *were they*.]
Simple sentences:	I have not completed my application. I have not had my transcripts sent.
Compound sentence:	I have not completed my application, *nor* have I had my transcripts sent. [Note again the reversal of subject and verb after "nor."]

> **Do exercises 10-a and 10-b**

Using the Semicolon

Another way to combine simple sentences into a compound sentence is by using the semicolon (;). The semicolon signals to the reader that the statement following it is equal in importance and related to the whole statement that precedes it. As you read through the following examples of sentence combinations, notice the equal relationships of the two clauses joined by the semicolon.

Simple sentences:	My sister-in-law sent her resume to eighty-five law firms. Seventeen of the firms have asked her to schedule an interview.
Compound sentence:	My sister-in-law sent her resume to eighty-five law firms; seventeen of the firms have asked her to schedule an interview.
Simple sentences:	My brother's Mustang needs a new transmission. My sister's Audi needs a new clutch.
Compound sentence:	My brother's Mustang needs a new transmission; my sister's Audi needs a new clutch.

Adding Conjunctive Adverbs

The semicolon used to join two statements in a compound sentence indicates that they are related. It does not, however, let the reader know **what** the relationship is: it does not tell **how** they are related. By using a **conjunctive adverb**, you can indicate the relationship between the statements.

as a result	moreover
consequently	nevertheless
furthermore	otherwise
however	therefore
in addition	thus

Frequently, the conjunctive adverb comes immediately after the semicolon, at the beginning of the statement it is connecting to the preceding one. However, like other adverbs, it may also be placed by the verb or at the very end of the sentence. Look carefully at the various placements of *however* in the following sentences:

1. The conjunctive adverb may be placed by the verb or at the end of the sentence; *however*, it usually comes at the beginning of the statement it is connecting.
2. The conjunctive adverb usually comes at the beginning of the statement it is connecting; it may, *however*, be placed by the verb.
3. The conjunctive adverb usually comes at the beginning of the statement it is connecting; it may be placed at the end of the sentence, *however*.

Note that in all its positions, the conjunctive adverb is set off by commas.

Using Appropriate Conjunctive Adverbs

As you combine statements into compound sentences, pay close attention to the relationships between the ideas. Then, if you wish, signal this relationship by an appropriate conjunctive adverb.

1. *However* and *nevertheless* indicate **contrast**:

Simple sentences:	Pat wanted to register for data processing on Saturday morning. The class was already filled.
Compound sentence:	Pat wanted to register for data processing on Saturday morning; *however*, the class was already filled.

Simple sentences:	Chester had failed physics twice. He decided to take it again in summer school.
Compound sentence:	Chester had failed physics twice; *nevertheless*, he decided to take it again in summer school.

2. *Consequently, as a result, therefore,* and *thus* indicate that the event or condition explained in the second statement was **caused by** the event or condition in the first:

Simple sentences:	Craig spent his entire paycheck on clothes. Craig had to cancel his vacation.
Compound sentence:	Craig spent his entire paycheck on clothes; *consequently*, he had to cancel his vacation.

Simple sentences:	Gabe lost fifteen pounds last month. His clothes do not fit.
Compound sentence:	Gabe lost fifteen pounds last month; *as a result*, his clothes do not fit.

Simple sentences:	Only ten students registered for the drawing class. The class was cancelled.
Compound sentence:	Only ten students registered for the drawing class; *therefore*, it was cancelled.
Simple sentences:	The union leaders angrily rejected management's offer. A strike seemed inevitable.
Compound sentence:	The union leaders angrily rejected management's offer; *thus*, a strike seemed inevitable.

3. *Furthermore, moreover,* and *in addition* indicate **addition**:

Simple sentences:	The new downtown shopping mall will create over three hundred permanent jobs. The new downtown shopping mall will provide temporary work for hundreds of construction workers.
Compound sentence:	The new downtown shopping mall will create over three hundred permanent jobs; *furthermore*, it will provide temporary work for hundreds of construction workers.
Simple sentences:	The city tax rate has doubled during the past ten years. City assessments have risen dramatically.
Compound sentence:	The city tax rate has doubled during the past ten years; *moreover*, city assessments have risen dramatically.
Simple sentences:	My English instructor expects us to keep a daily journal. My English instructor requires us to submit two paragraphs every week.
Compound sentence:	My English instructor expects us to keep a daily journal; *in addition*, he requires us to submit two paragraphs every week.

4. *Otherwise* indicates that the event in the second statement **will happen** if the event in the first does not occur:

Simple sentences:	Paula must pay her parking tickets by Friday. Paula will not be able to renew the registration of her car.
Compound sentence:	Paula must pay her parking tickets by Friday; *otherwise*, she will not be able to renew the registration of her car.

Do exercises 10-c, 10-d, 10-e, and 10-f

AVOIDING COMMA SPLICES AND RUN-ON SENTENCES

In the previous sections of this chapter, you saw several ways by which closely related simple sentences can be joined either by a comma and a coordinator or by a semicolon. You should be careful to use one of these two connectors and avoid joining two statements (1) with just a comma or (2) with nothing to connect them. These two incorrect ways of joining simple sentences are called the **comma splice** and the **run-on sentence**.

Study the following examples. In the sentences containing **comma splices**, no coordinator is used with the comma; the comma alone **splices** (connects) the two statements. In the **run-on sentences**, there is no signal that one statement has ended and a second is to begin.

Simple sentences:	I had two flat tires. I still arrived in time for the wedding.

Incorrect Combinations

Comma splice:	I had two flat tires, I still arrived in time for the wedding.
Run-on sentence:	I had two flat tires I still arrived in time for the wedding.

Correct Combinations

Comma with coordinator:	I had two flat tires, *but* I still arrived in time for the wedding.
Semicolon:	I had two flat tires; *however*, I still arrived in time for the wedding.

> **Do exercise 10-g**

SUGGESTIONS FOR WRITING

Your journal has been helping you to develop many skills. It has been helping you to record important experiences and events, to practice your sentence writing skills, and to develop your ability to build paragraphs.

Chapters 8 and 9 suggested that you build paragraphs about two of your friends. Now try to build a paragraph about two different ways in which your studies are regularly interrupted. You might start the **planning** process by writing a topic sentence like the following: *Every time I try to study at home, I am interrupted.* You would then need to decide on two types of interruptions, such as phone calls and visitors, or two types of people who interrupt you, such as family and friends. These types become your subtopics. The next step would be to choose two specific interruptions for each type.

Write the sentences for the paragraph carefully, concentrating on developing your idea with specific details. For example, if one of your interruptions is phone calls, you might write about last Wednesday night, when your cousin Howard called you just as you had begun to understand a particular physics problem. Make sure that you stick to your main idea, follow your plan as you write, and add a closing sentence.

Do not forget to **edit** your sentences. Check to make sure that you have followed the new punctuation rules that you learned in Chapters 9 and 10.

154

NAME _____ DATE _____

Rewrite each pair of simple sentences as one **compound sentence**. To join the two statements, use a **comma** and one of these coordinators: *and, but, or*.

Some sentences might be combined by using an *and* or by using one of the other two coordinators. Notice how the choice of coordinator shifts the meaning in some combinations.

EXAMPLES

Ken bought a new three-speed bicycle.
His sister bought a fifteen-speed racing bike.

Compound sentence: *Ken bought a new three-speed bicycle, and his sister*

bought a fifteen-speed racing bike.

Sammy invited twenty of his relatives and friends to the track meet.
Only his mother and father came.

Compound sentence: *Sammy invited twenty of his relatives and friends to the*

track meet, but only his mother and father came.

---

1. Janice was weeding the kitchen garden.
   Her mother was planting rose bushes.

   Compound sentence: _____

   _____

2. The children went swimming.
   Their parents went water skiing.

   Compound sentence: _____

   _____

3. For weeks, Tim had looked forward to playing goalie in the game.
   The coach suspended him for missing practice.

   Compound sentence: _____

   _____

4. Parents may send for tickets in advance.
   Children may purchase tickets at the door.

   Compound sentence: _____

   _____

5. The three girls were not running very fast.
   The security guard was not able to catch them.

   Compound sentence: _____

   _____

6. The men went for a stroll through the park.
   Their wives began a game of softball.

   Compound sentence: _____

   _____

7. The pie is on the table.
   The coffee will not be ready for another five minutes.

   Compound sentence: _____

   _____

8. My youngest brother may rent an apartment in Sacramento.
   My sister may buy a house in Fresno.

   Compound sentence: _____

   _____

9. The daffodils are blooming.
   The magnolia buds have not begun to open.

   Compound sentence: _____

   _____

10. The Boy Scouts walked bravely back to their tents.
    The counselor knew they had been frightened by the story.

    Compound sentence: _____

    _____

NAME _____ **DATE** _____

Look back at the pairs of simple sentences you were given in exercise 10-a. In each pair, the subject in the first sentence is different from the subject in the second. The combinations of such sentences become compound sentences; each half has a separate subject and verb.

The pairs of sentences in the following exercise all have the same subject. Each pair may be combined as a compound sentence **or** as a simple sentence with compound elements such as verbs or objects. Remember that the compound sentence emphasizes the subject by repeating it.

Combine each of the following pairs (1) as a compound sentence with a comma and a coordinator and (2) as a simple sentence with compound elements.

EXAMPLE

Brenda bought a new fifteen-speed bicycle.
Brenda started riding it an hour every day.

Compound sentence: _____*Brenda bought a new fifteen-speed bicycle, and she*

*started riding an hour every day.*_____

Simple sentence: _*Brenda bought a new fifteen-speed bicycle and started riding*

*an hour every day.*_____

---

1. We may take a grill for steaks to the picnic.
   We may simply serve cold sandwiches.

   Compound sentence: _____

   _____

   Simple sentence: _____

   _____

2. The class must apologize to the janitor.
   If not, the class must serve detention.

   Compound sentence: _____

   _____

   Simple sentence: _____

   _____

3. The Smiths needed a new washing machine.
   The Smiths spent all their money on a stereo set.

   Compound sentence: _____

   _____

   Simple sentence: _____

   _____

4. I may spend the day at the museum.
   I may take my daughter to the zoo.

   Compound sentence: _____

   _____

   Simple sentence: _____

   _____

5. Laura needs a job.
   Laura has not filled out any applications.

   Compound sentence: _____

   _____

   Simple sentence: _____

   _____

6. Kathleen and Joe needed a larger apartment.
   Kathleen and Joe could not afford a higher rent.

   Compound sentence: _____

   _____

   Simple sentence: _____

   _____

7. I will knit a sweater for the baby.
   I will crochet an afghan for the baby.

   Compound sentence: _____

   _____

   Simple sentence: _____

   _____

NAME _____ **DATE** _____

Combine each pair of simple sentences into one **compound sentence**:

- Consider the relationship between the two simple sentences.
- Signal this relationship by joining them with a **semicolon** alone or a **semicolon with an appropriate conjunctive adverb**.

EXAMPLE

Sharon's boss is delighted with her work.
Sharon's boss refuses to give her a raise.

Compound sentence: *Sharon's boss is delighted with her work; however, he*

refuses to give her a raise.

1. The children were bored by the bus trip to Philadelphia.
   The children became excited when they saw the Liberty Bell.

   Compound sentence: _____

   _____

   _____

2. Franklin is attending the community college.
   Franklin's two sisters are attending the state university.

   Compound sentence: _____

   _____

   _____

3. Cindy gains twenty pounds one month and loses fifteen the next.
   Cindy is constantly buying new clothes.

   Compound sentence: _____

   _____

   _____

4. Five students did not attend Professor Goodwill's review session.
   The five students failed Professor Goodwill's midterm exam.

   Compound sentence: _____

   _____

   _____

5. Jane must pass her final examination in chemistry.
   Jane will have to repeat the course.

   Compound sentence: _____

   _____

   _____

6. The Reynolds family bought a house at the beach last year.
   The Reynolds family spent the summer touring the United States.

   Compound sentence: _____

   _____

   _____

7. Only three journalism students applied for positions on the school newspaper.
   The faculty advisor extended the deadline for applications.

   Compound sentence: _____

   _____

   _____

8. Millie majored in biology in college.
   Millie now works for the Utah Historical Society.

   Compound sentence: _____

   _____

   _____

9. Erin must return to Japan before May 30.
   Erin may have to pay income tax to the United States.

   Compound sentence: _____

   _____

   _____

10. My sister is failing her statistics class.
    My sister is getting A's in all her other classes.

    Compound sentence: _____

    _____

    _____

NAME _____ **DATE** _____

     Combine each pair of simple sentences into one **compound sentence**. Use whichever connector you prefer:

- a comma with a coordinator,
- a semicolon, or
- a semicolon with a conjunctive adverb.

EXAMPLE

Mary Anne has the entire summer off.
Her husband has only a two-week vacation in July.

Compound sentence: _Mary Anne has the entire summer off, but her husband_

has only a two-week vacation in July.

or

Compound sentence: _Mary Anne has the entire summer off; however, her_

husband has only a two-week vacation in July.

---

1. The store manager asked all the clerks to work overtime to take inventory.
   The store manager also asked all the clerks to spend one Sunday each month cleaning the store.

   Compound sentence: _____

   _____

   _____

2. Ruth finished studying at 10:00 P.M. the night before her history exam.
   Ruth was prepared and well rested in the morning.

   Compound sentence: _____

   _____

   _____

3. Marilyn is taking six courses this semester.
   Her husband is taking two courses, working part-time, and writing for the school newspaper.

   Compound Sentence: _____

   _____

   _____

4. The lawn had not been mowed.
   The shrubs had not been trimmed.

   Compound sentence: _____

   _____

   _____

5. In the next three weeks, Harriet must write a lab report every day.
   In the next three weeks, Harriet's daughter must work all the problems in three
   chapters of her algebra book.

   Compound sentence: _____

   _____

   _____

6. My cousin Harold had always wanted to be a dentist.
   My cousin Harold accepted a scholarship to law school.

   Compound sentence: _____

   _____

   _____

7. Next summer, I may work on my uncle's farm in Iowa.
   Next summer, I may work in a cannery in Oregon.

   Compound sentence: _____

   _____

   _____

8. The Burtons' accountant promised them a huge income tax refund.
   The Burtons have spent the last three evenings planning their summer vacation.

   Compound sentence: _____

   _____

   _____

9. The summer had been very hot and dry.
   The fall was cold and wet.

   Compound sentence: _____

   _____

   _____

NAME _____ **DATE** _____

Turn each of the following simple sentences into **compound sentences** by adding a second statement.

- Be sure you write a compound sentence, one that has two separate subjects and verbs.
- Check your punctuation carefully.
- Use appropriate coordinators and conjunctive adverbs.

EXAMPLE

Sybil took a yoga class, *but she still needed an aerobic exercise to lower her* _____

cholesterol level. _____

1. My cousin lives only one mile from the college _____

_____

2. Swimming is an excellent exercise _____

_____

_____

3. The assistant manager had not filled in our time cards _____

_____

4. My family has never taken a long vacation _____

_____

_____

5. My favorite food is lobster _____

_____

6. He was too late to see the news _____

_____

7. In Arizona, the temperatures rose to 102° Fahrenheit _____

_____

8. The semester was almost over _____

_____

9. Frank and I may go to see our grandparents _____

_____

10. I was nervous my first day in English class _____

_____

11. Last night, I tried to call my friend Louise _____

_____

12. Bobby did not take good care of his horse _____

_____

13. My friends no longer share my interests _____

_____

14. Martha prepared a delicious fruit salad _____

_____

15. The morning was foggy and damp _____

_____

16. The class began at 8:00 A.M. _____

_____

17. The tall woman hurried down the hall _____

_____

18. Brad selected two colorful prints for his office _____

_____

19. The little dog was deaf and blind _____

_____

20. By 1988, Americans owned more cats than dogs _____

_____

NAME _____ **DATE** _____

     Use each of the words given by the numbers to write an original **compound sentence** about your experiences at school or at work.

EXAMPLES

1. nor

    The students in my geography class had not read the assignment, nor had

    they prepared to answer the questions distributed by the teacher's aide.

2. moreover

    Everyone in my biology class had written a lab report; moreover, each student

    had studied an additional chapter and was prepared to answer questions.

1. and

    _____

    _____

2. but

    _____

    _____

3. or

    _____

    _____

4. nor

    _____

    _____

5. so

    _____

    _____

6. yet

    _____

    _____

7. for

    _____

    _____

8. as a result

9. however

10. consequently

11. in addition

12. otherwise

NAME _____ **DATE** _____

Identify and correct the errors in each of the following sentences:

- Underline each subject once and each verb twice.
- Label each incorrect sentence as
  CS for comma splice or
  RO for run on.
- Rewrite each as a correct sentence with
  a comma and a coordinator,
  a semicolon, or
  a semicolon and a conjunctive adverb.

EXAMPLES

RO During the storm, the telephone wires blew down the electricity went off.
  During the storm, the telephone wires blew down, and the electricity

  went off.

CS I want to take three courses this semester, I have time for only one.
  I want to take three courses this semester; however, I have time for only

  one.

_____ 1. My sister is having a garage sale, she has collected all my mother's and
aunt's old jewelry.

_____

_____

_____ 2. Sharon missed the first hour of the exam, the instructor would not let her
stay to finish.

_____

_____

_____ 3. The supervisor did not wish to argue her decision to suspend Jim was
final.

_____

_____

_____ 4. The little pup was running all around its mother stood quietly in the
doorway.

_____

_____

_____ 5. Jody left work two hours early this afternoon, her parents have not heard from her.

_____

_____

_____ 6. Mark lives forty miles from the university he spends two hours commuting every school day.

_____

_____

_____ 7. Kevin's parents were proud of him, he was the first member of his family to graduate from college.

_____

_____

_____ 8. The dishes had not been washed, the laundry had not been folded.

_____

_____

_____ 9. Sidney had lived in Wyoming for four years he had never visited Yellowstone National Park.

_____

_____

_____ 10. The breathing exercises seemed easy in our practice sessions, however, they were much more difficult in the water.

_____

_____

_____ 11. Helga had not been in the little town long, she was not used to strangers greeting her on the streets.

_____

_____

Using Subordination

Adverb Clauses

11

UNDERSTANDING SUBORDINATE CLAUSES

A **clause** is a group of related words that has a subject and verb and expresses one idea. The **simple sentence** you studied in the first nine chapters of *Building Sentences* is a clause that states a single **complete idea**. In your writing, you use a capital letter at the beginning and a period (or question mark) at the end of each simple sentence because each is a complete unit of thought; it is not dependent for its sense on words outside the sentence. Look at this simple sentence:

> Carla is commuting forty miles to the state university.

It is one **clause**: it has one **base**—subject (*Carla*) and verb (*is commuting*). The meaning of the clause is complete; it can be set off as a simple sentence.

In Chapter 10, you learned to combine two closely related simple sentences into a **compound sentence**, one that joins two equally important, closely related ideas. We might, for instance, combine the complete clause used as a simple sentence with a second, closely related (**coordinate**) clause:

> Her brother Wilbert is taking courses at the community college in town.

The combination makes **a compound sentence**:

> Carla is commuting forty miles to the state university, and her brother Wilbert is taking courses at the community college in town.

These two **equal** clauses have been joined by a comma and a coordinator (*and*).

In this chapter, you will again be building sentences that contain two related clauses, but the clauses will be different from each other in function and in importance. You will be constructing **complex sentences**.

As you read, think through the following points carefully. They will help you understand this chapter and the two that follow.

- The word *complex* indicates that, though the clauses in the sentence are related, they have **different functions**.
- In a **complex sentence**, one idea is presented as the *main clause*; a second idea, an idea that depends upon the main clause to make its meaning and function clear, is stated in a **subordinate clause**.
- Subordinate clauses are of three types: adverb clauses, adjective clauses, and noun clauses.

In this chapter, you will work on **adverb clauses**.

RECOGNIZING ADVERB CLAUSES

Adverb clauses function in a sentence in the same ways as single-word adverbs and prepositional phrases used as adverbs. (See Chapters 3 and 4.)

- Adverb clauses tell **when**, **where**, **why**, **how**, or **to what degree** (how much or how little).
- They modify verbs, adjectives, or other adverbs.
- When they modify verbs, they can often be placed at the beginning or at the end of a sentence.

Consider the following two simple sentences:

1. Carla is commuting forty miles to the state university.
2. The state university offers a degree program in forestry.

Placed together, these two sentences seem to be related in a special way. The second sentence seems to provide a reason for Carla's commuting to the university. In other words, the second sentence tells **why**. Since information that tells **why** is one of the functions of an **adverb clause**, the second sentence can be rewritten as an **adverb clause** and combined with the first to build a complex sentence:

Combination: Carla is commuting forty miles to the state university **because it offers a degree program in forestry**.

Subordinators of Adverb Clauses

An adverb clause always begins with a **subordinator**. The subordinator is a connecting word which explains the relationship between the adverb clause and the main clause; it tells the reader what kind of information is added by the adverb clause. In the preceding complex sentence about Carla, the subordinator is *because*; *because* tells the reader that the adverb clause will provide **why** information.

The following subordinators are often used to begin adverb clauses:

COMMON SUBORDINATORS

after	as if	because	so	till	whenever
although	as long as	before	so that	unless	where
as	as soon as	if	than	until	wherever
as far as	as well as	since	though	when	while

Because the subordinator is always the **first** word of an adverb clause, you can identify an adverb clause very easily.

- First, find the subordinator.
- Second, identify the words that provide the kind of information signaled by the subordinator.
- Remember, as previously noted, the whole adverb clause may often be placed before or after the main clause.
- After you identify the adverb clause or clauses, what remains in the complex sentence will be the **main** clause.

Study the following examples, in which each subordinator is in italics and the whole adverb clause is underlined.

1. Barbara required many money-management skills *when* she served as treasurer of her senior class.

2. *As* Ken worked on his research project for his English class, he learned to gather information to answer a specific question.

In the first example, the subordinator *when* begins the adverb clause: *when she served as treasurer of her senior class.* The main clause states the main idea of the sentence: *Barbara acquired many money-management skills.* In the second example, the adverb clause begins with the subordinator *as* and is set off by a comma. The main idea, that *he learned to gather information to answer a specific question,* is presented in the main clause.

```
Do exercise 11-a
```

Choosing an Appropriate Subordinator

To use the subordinators correctly, you must understand their meanings. Because adverb clauses provide five kinds of information, the subordinators can be placed in five groups according to whether they indicate (1) when, (2) where, (3) how, (4) why, or (5) to what degree. Some of the most common subordinators are grouped in the following chart. (Those subordinators that are seldom misused by beginning writers—*after, as soon as, before, until, because, as long as, as far as*—are illustrated in the chart, but no special explanation is given.)

Subordinators of Adverb Clauses

Group 1: When

after	*After* I finish my English assignment, I will go for a swim.
as soon as	*As soon as* the baby-sitter arrives, we can leave for the movies.
before	*Before* Tom goes camping, he needs to buy a new sleeping bag.
since	Sharon has not had a Saturday off *since* she started her new job. [*Since* points to a particular time when an action described in the main clause began occurring. Because the action of the main clause began at this point and continued over time, the verb in the main clause is usually written in the present perfect tense, that is, *has* or *have* plus a past participle.]
until, till	I will wait in the library *until* [or *till*] you finish your exam.
when	*When* Norma finished high school, she began working part-time as a lifeguard. [*When* points to a **specific time**; in this sentence, the specific time was marked by Norma's finishing high school.]
whenever	*Whenever* it rains, my dog hides under the couch. [*Whenever* means **every time**; this sentence means that my dog hides under the couch every time it rains.]
while, as	I listened *while* [*as*] my daughter practiced the piano. [*While* and *as* indicate that the action in the main clause and the action in the subordinate clause occur at the same time.]

171

where   The search party gathered *where* the child had been last seen. [*Where* points to a **specific place**: in this sentence, the specific place is the spot where the child had last been seen.]

wherever   I will live *wherever* I can find a job. [*Wherever* means **any place**; this sentence means that I will live any place that I can find a job.]

Group 3: How (under what conditions)

as   The students punctuated the sentences *as* they had been taught. [*As* means **in the same way**. This sentence means that the students were taught to punctuate sentences in a specific way; they then punctuated them in that way.]

as if   Donna looked *as if* she had seen a ghost. [*As if* creates a **comparison** between two events or things. In this sentence, the way Donna looks is compared to the way she might look if she saw a ghost.]

if   *If* you pass this test, you will pass the course. [*If* indicates that after one event occurs, the second may be expected to follow.]

unless   *Unless* you pass this test, you will fail the course. [*Unless* means that the second event will happen if the first does not occur.]

although, though   *Although* [*Though*] Ralph does not have much money saved, he still plans to buy a new car. [*Although* or *though* means that an event will occur but **one might expect the opposite** to happen. Because Ralph does not have much money saved, one would probably not expect him to buy a new car; under the conditions given in the adverb clause, the main clause surprises us.]

Group 4: Why

because   I missed the quiz *because* I was ill.

so, so that   Ted worked as a waiter *so* [*so that*] he could save money for college. [In Chapter 10, you learned that *so* can be used as a **coordinator** between the two clauses of a compound sentence to show that one event happened as a result of another (see page 149). Here *so* or *so that* is used as a **subordinator** showing **purpose**: Ted's purpose in working as a waiter was to save money for college. Note also that, although most adverb clauses can be placed either before or after the main clause, those formed by *so* or *so that* are almost always placed after the main clause.]

Group 5: To what degree

as long as   I will wait *as long as* I have to for an interview.

as far as   The plains extended *as far as* we could see.

as well as   The other contestants did not perform *as well as* Jack did.

As you write sentences using the subordinators in these five groups, remember that the same word may have different meanings and different uses in a sentence. Some of the words listed as subordinators—such as *before, after, since, as*—can also be used as prepositions. Thus a word such as *after* might be followed by an object and its modifiers or by a subject and verb:

Prepositional phrase: *After* his arrival, Jack wasted no time introducing himself to everyone at the party.

Adverb clause: *After* Jack arrived, he wasted no time introducing himself to everyone at the party.

Do exercise 11-b

BUILDING SENTENCES WITH ADVERB CLAUSES

You can often build a complex sentence with an adverb clause by combining two simple sentences. When you use an adverb clause to combine two simple sentences into one complex sentence, you must set up a logical relationship between the main clause and the adverb clause.

Look at these two simple sentences:

1. Brenda spent a summer working as a clerk in an appliance store.
2. Brenda decided not to make sales her career.

Clearly, these sentences are related. They are related in time: Brenda made her decision either **after** or **when** she worked as a clerk. We can combine the sentences into one complex sentence by turning the first into an adverb clause:

after   *After* Brenda spent summer working as a clerk in an appliance store, she decided not to make sales her career.
or
Brenda decided not to make sales her career *after* she spent the summer working as a clerk in an appliance store.

when   *When* Brenda spent a summer working as a clerk in an appliance store, she decided not to make sales her career.
or
Brenda decided not to make sales her career *when* she spent the summer working as a clerk in an appliance store.

Note that these adverb clauses can come before or after the main clause. Also note that, while we use the noun *Brenda* in the first clause, we avoid repeating it in the second by using a pronoun.

Here is another pair of simple sentences that can be combined into one complex sentence:

1. Students trying to select a career should take a careful look at their hobbies.
2. They can identify their interests.

These two sentences are related by purpose: the second sentence tells **why** the first action should occur. In the following complex sentence, the subordinator *so that* establishes a logical relationship between the ideas:

Complex sentence: Students trying to select a career should take a careful look at their hobbies *so that* they can identify their interests.

PLACING AND PUNCTUATING ADVERB CLAUSES

An adverb clause can often be placed before or after the main clause. Your decision will depend on the relationship of the complex sentence to the sentences that precede or follow it. In isolated sentences, it often does not matter in which position you place the adverb clause:

> After Ned had worked as a hospital volunteer, he decided to go to nursing school.
> Ned decided to go to nursing school after he had worked as a hospital volunteer.

In these examples, both placements of the adverb clause make sense.

As you place the adverb clause before or after the main clause, you should keep in mind two rules for punctuating adverb clauses.

1. When the adverb clause comes first, it is usually separated from the main clause by a comma. When the adverb clause comes after the main clause, it is usually **not** set off by a comma.
2. Never use a semicolon between the main clause and an adverb clause in a complex sentence.

Study the following examples of correct and incorrect applications of these two rules. (The adverb clauses are in italics.)

Incorrect Punctuation: Joe was hired as a waiter at a new restaurant downtown, *although he had had no experience.*
Although Joe had had no experience he was hired as a waiter at a new restaurant downtown.
Although Joe had had no experience; he was hired as a waiter at a new restaurant downtown.

Correct Punctuation: Joe was hired as a waiter at a new restaurant downtown *although he had had no experience.*
Although Joe had had no experience, he was hired as a waiter at a new restaurant downtown.

Do exercise 11-c, 11-d, 11-e, 11-f, and 11-g

SUGGESTIONS FOR WRITING

Now that you have had some experience building paragraphs, try building a paragraph about the best boss or teacher that you have ever had. Consult your journal to see if you can find an idea for this paragraph.

When you **plan** your paragraph, you will need to state your main idea in a topic sentence: for example, *Laverne Jones, my employer at Federal Savings and Loan, is the best boss I have ever had*. This time you will develop your paragraph with **reasons** as subtopics. Think of three reasons for your positive evaluation of this boss or teacher: for instance, you may want to write about three policies or rules that made this person easy to work with. Then make sure you jot down specific details for each of these reasons. Remember that planning your paragraph ahead of time keeps your paragraph organized.

Now **write** the sentences for your paragraph, being careful to include as many details as possible. If, for example, you decide to discuss your boss's liberal policy on lateness, you might want to explain the fair manner in which she treated you when you were an hour late last Friday because of a flat tire. You may not necessarily need two examples if one example involves more than one sentence and is very convincing. However, do make sure that you include only positive information about this person in your paragraph and that each example follows its own reason. Try to end your paragraph with a closing sentence.

When you **edit** you paragraph, make sure that you have built your sentences according to the rules that you have learned in the first eleven chapters of this book.

NAME _____ **DATE** _____

> In each of the following complex sentences, *underline* the whole adverb clause and *circle* the subordinator.

EXAMPLE

Some students are taking classes on Saturday (so that) they can go skiing on Wednesday afternoons.

==

1. While William was finishing an internship at the applied physics lab, Helen was completing a master's degree in biology.

2. The other children did not play their instruments as well as Bart did.

3. Because Margaret wanted to establish her own accounting firm, she took business and management classes.

4. Although many of the booths had closed as early as seven, Pamela kept hers open until eight.

5. Peggy missed the first two acts of the play because she was in a minor automobile accident.

6. After Henry worked as a volunteer firefighter for five years, he decided to return to school to study fire prevention.

7. If you bring the paper to the secretary in the History Department before four this afternoon, you will not receive a penalty.

8. My oldest brother has always given me help whenever I needed it.

9. The children looked as if they had been playing in a sooty fireplace.

10. James will not pass the geography exam unless he studies all weekend.

11. Melvin has not seen his brothers and sisters since he left home in 1987.

12. Whenever Franklin comes to visit his parents, his father tries to put him to work in the garden.

13. My grandmother listened quietly as my cousin explained the reasons for his divorce.

14. Betty went shopping while Barbara was working.

15. Before you register, be sure to send your high school transcript to the college.

16. Although Dan did not usually enjoy watching football on television, he became very excited during last year's Super Bowl.

17. Gerald swam as if he had a shark right behind him.

18. After he had tried every other way to raise his grades, Jerry decided to study.

19. The audience had become silent as soon as the movie starlet had begun to speak.

20. The two little dogs had been noisy and wild since Bill entered the room.

NAME _____ **DATE** _____

In each blank space, write a subordinator that will connect the main clause and the adverb clause in a meaningful way. (Note that some adverb clauses are before and others after the main clause.)

EXAMPLES

The coach will not leave _____*until*_____ the team arrives.

Dr. Watson had pursued his investigation _____*as far as*_____ he could.

1. The supervisor stopped work early _____ we could clean up our work areas.

2. Brent and Dolly celebrated _____ they had both been nominated to the honor society.

3. _____ the children could clean their room, they had to gather up their books and sort their toys.

4. Benjamin ironed his shirt _____ Betty hemmed her scarf.

5. Sadie will never finish on time _____ she begins painting her room this afternoon.

6. Francine had not visited Uncle Bob _____ he went to the hospital.

7. _____ Palmer goes to the movie, he must collect the garbage and put it in plastic bags.

8. _____ Janice began playing tennis, she had been having trouble sleeping.

9. Please return my lawn mower _____ you are finished with it.

10. My sister acted _____ she had never before taken a two-hour exam.

11. He will practice _____ it takes to perfect his skills.

12. No one else plays bridge _____ he does.

13. Elizabeth is much shorter_____ I am.

14. The small boy refused to go with the security guard _____ he spoke to his mother on the phone.

15. Barbara was hired to be a receptionist for the entire floor_____ she had no prior experience.

16. _____Philip returned for a second interview, he was much more confident.

NAME _____ **DATE** _____

Build a paragraph by combining each of the pairs of simple sentences into one complex sentence with an adverb clause. Think of the combination in the example as the main idea (topic sentence) of the paragraph.

- Decide how the two sentences relate to each other.
- Place a check by the sentence that you wish to use as the main clause.
- Use an appropriate subordinator to change the other sentence into an adverb clause.
- Write your combination. Check your punctuation carefully.

EXAMPLE: TOPIC SENTENCE

✓ My cousin Sarah learned a valuable lesson in her first year at Cate State. She did not realize it at first.

Combination: _**Although she did not realize it at first, my cousin Sarah**_

**learned a valuable lesson in her first year at Cate State.**

1. Sarah had enrolled in six classes.
   Sarah still tried to play field hockey and date two young men at least once a week.

   Combination: _____

   _____

2. Sarah's friends encouraged her to limit her activities or take fewer classes.
   Sarah would not listen.

   Combination: _____

   _____

3. By the fourth week of school, she was missing at least three classes a week.
   She was just too tired to go.

   Combination: _____

   _____

4. Her coach advised her to give up one of her courses or limit her dating.
   She laughed.

   Combination: _____

   _____

5. She promised to study every night.
   She would pass all her midterm exams.

   Combination: _____

   _____

6. Her boyfriends warned her against doing too much.
   She told them to mind their own business.

   Combination: _____

   _____

7. She failed three midterm exams.
   She was too tired and unprepared.

   Combination: _____

   _____

8. The coach suspended her from sports for the rest of the year.
   Sarah recognized the errors of her ways.

   Combination: _____

   _____

9. She immediately withdrew from two courses.
   This way, she could concentrate on the four remaining.

   Combination: _____

   _____

10. Since her suspension, she sometimes feels her activities are overwhelming her studies.
    She then works out and follows a realistic weekly schedule.

    Combination: _____

    _____

NAME_____ **DATE** _____

Build a paragraph by combining each of the following groups of simple sentences into **one** complex sentence. Think of the sentence in the example as the main idea (topic sentence).

- Decide how the sentences relate to each other.
- Place a check by the sentence you wish to use as the main clause in your combination.
- Then subordinate the other two sentences by using one as an **adverb clause** and changing the other to a **possessive** or **a prepositional phrase**.
- Write your combination. Check your punctuation.

EXAMPLE: TOPIC SENTENCE

Around 9:30, my parents and I returned to the house from an evening of shopping.
The house belongs to my parents.
We were shocked by the mess inside the house.

Complex sentence: _Around 9:30, when my parents and I returned to their house from an evening of shopping, we were shocked by the mess inside the house._

1. We turned into the front driveway.
   The outside of the house showed no sign.
   There was a shambles within.

   Complex sentence: _____

   _____

2. My father had opened the car door for my mother.
   My father walked jauntily up the steps.
   He walked to the front porch.

   Complex sentence: _____

   _____

3. My father had set the packages down, turned the key in the lock, and opened the door.
   The packages and the key belonged to my father.
   At that moment, he gasped and took a step backwards.

   Complex sentence: _____

   _____

4. I pushed past my father.
    I wanted to be able to see the problem.
    The problem was in the entrance hall.

    Complex sentence: _____

    _____

5. My mother and father stood still.
    They had a look of terror on their faces.
    I ran bravely into the house.

    Complex sentence: _____

    _____

6. I walked into the hall.
    I heard the back door slam and began to run swiftly toward it.
    My father was not far behind me.

    Complex sentence: _____

    _____

7. We were too late to see anyone.
    We still walked outside.
    We went into the garden.

    Complex sentence: _____

    _____

8. We heard my mother crying.
    We hurried quickly.
    We came into the kitchen.

    Complex sentence: _____

    _____

9. We looked around the kitchen.
    We saw broken dishes and glasses everywhere.
    Broken dishes and glasses were on the floor and work surfaces.

    Complex sentence: _____

    _____

10. Ever since that terrible incident, I have felt anxious.
    I approach the front door.
    The front door belongs to my parents' house.

    Complex sentence: _____

    _____

NAME _____ **DATE** _____

I. Build a complex sentence by adding an adverb clause to each main clause.

- Use the subordinator before the number to connect the two clauses.
- Write the adverb clause **after** the main clause, and **do not** separate the two clauses with a comma.
- Write the whole complex sentence on the lines.

EXAMPLE

as soon as   Patsy left the office

Patsy left the office as soon as Jean entered. _____

---

after   1. We will leave for Tucson

_____

_____

because   2. We cannot attend the lecture today

_____

_____

if   3. Maggie has to catch the 11:00 o'clock train

_____

_____

as long as   4. Frankie may stay in Colorado

_____

_____

whenever   5. Diana attends the basketball games

_____

_____

before   6. Gary must pay his telephone bill

_____

_____

when   7. I became very dizzy

_____

_____

while   8. Althea washed and waxed the car

_____

_____

even though   9. We decided to wait until the weekend

_____

_____

unless   10. My cousin Frank will not graduate this spring

_____

_____

II. On a sheet of paper, rewrite each of the complex sentences, placing the adverb clause at the beginning of the sentence and making any other changes that will make each sentence clear and economical. Be sure to punctuate your new sentences correctly.

NAME _____ **DATE** _____

Write complex sentences about your responsibilities at home, at school, or at work using the subordinators listed below. In each sentence, underline the whole adverb clause.

I. In the first six sentences, place the main clause first and the adverb clause second. Do not separate the clauses with a comma.

EXAMPLE

because _____*During my first month in the freight office, I had to learn three*_

_____*jobs because so many workers were ill with the flu.*_____

as if   1. _____

_____

_____

as soon as   2. _____

_____

_____

so that   3. _____

_____

_____

until   4. _____

_____

_____

when   5. _____

_____

_____

as well as   6. _____

_____

_____

II. In this second group, place the adverb clause first and the main clause second. Use a comma to separate the two clauses.

EXAMPLE

when _When the claims agent was on vacation, I had to inspect two cases of damaged alcoholic beverages._

whenever 1. _____

_____

_____

because 2. _____

_____

_____

unless 3. _____

_____

_____

while 4. _____

_____

_____

although 5. _____

_____

_____

after 6. _____

_____

_____

NAME _____ **DATE** _____

Some of the following sentences are incorrectly punctuated.

- If a sentence is correctly punctuated, write a *C* after its number.
- If a sentence is incorrectly punctuated, correct the error.

EXAMPLES

_____ When the babysitter arrived*/* Mr. and Mrs. Badger left for the party.   *comma*

_____ Mr. and Mrs. Badger left for the party*/* when the babysitter arrived.   *no comma*

__*C*__ When the babysitter arrived, Mr. and Mrs. Badger left for the party.

1._____ As soon as the new gym is open, I will begin my exercise program.

2._____ I must stop by the registrar's office before I leave this afternoon.

3._____ Before I leave my grandmother's house, she always gives me bags of cookies and jars of preserves.

4._____ I feel weary, whenever my cousin begins one of his monologues.

5._____ Although Jesse did not answer the phone it suddenly stopped ringing.

6._____ His life changed, when he moved from Oregon to Maine.

7._____ Even though it was 3:00 o'clock on a Sunday afternoon, the streets of Kowloon were swarming with shoppers.

8._____ As the sun sank and the sky darkened; the ferry slowly returned them to the island of Hong Kong.

9. _____ Although Lucy had cleaned the kitchen for five hours; her mother was still dissatisfied.

10._____ Bob and Karen had been married for five years, when Karen decided to return to school.

11._____ Unless you can explain why you and Herb have the same wrong answers on this midterm examination; you will fail the course.

12._____ Janice worked as a railroad engineer; when she was only twenty-two years old.

13._____ The decorations for the Halloween party will be finished by six o'clock this evening, because we started at six this morning.

14._____ If you need to review the questions at the end of each chapter should help.

15._____ Because Bill was late leaving and became ensnarled in a traffic jam; he and Diane missed the first half of the game.

Using Subordination

Adjective Clauses

12

Earlier in this book, you studied the use of single words and prepositional phrases as adjectives. In Chapter 11, you used subordinate clauses as adverbs. In this chapter, you will study **subordinate clauses used as adjectives**.

Adjectives modify nouns and pronouns; that is, they either add to or make more specific **whose, which, what kind of**, or **how many** things or persons. Like adverbs, adjective modifiers can be single words or phrases or subordinate clauses.

Look at the following simple sentence:

The supervisor hired the applicants.

This sentence has no adjectives other than the article *the*. It does not tell **which** or **what kind of** supervisor or **which, what kind of**, or **how many** applicants. We might, of course, add other simple sentences to supply this information:

1. The supervisor is new.
2. He is the supervisor of the gym.
3. These applicants had the most experience.

However, this method of adding information is wordy and requires the reader to make connections that the writer should make. Moreover, the string of simple sentences fails to indicate which information is most important. We can give the same information much more effectively by combining all four sentences into one sentence with three modifiers:

> *Combination*: The **new** supervisor **of the gym** hired the applicants **who had the most experience**.

This new sentence contains three adjective modifiers:

- *New*, which describes *supervisor*, is a single-word adjective.
- *Of the gym*, which describes *supervisor*, is a prepositional phrase.
- The third adjective modifier, *who had the most experience*, which describes *applicants*, is an **adjective clause**.

In the combination, we have built a **complex sentence** because it has two clauses that have different functions: one states the main idea, and the other functions as an adjective to add information about one word in the main clause, *applicants*.

SUBORDINATORS OF ADJECTIVE CLAUSES

An adjective clause, like an adverb clause, begins with a **subordinator**. The subordinator connects the adjective clause to the word in the main clause it modifies; it stands for this word. Study the following list of subordinators and meanings:

who, whose, whom	stand for people
that	stands for people or things, ideas, and places
which	stands for things, ideas, and places

As this list shows, the three forms *who, whom,* and *whose* can all stand for people. Like the personal pronouns—such as *he, him, his*—which you studied in Chapter 2, the three forms of *who* indicate how the subordinator is used in its clause:

who	is used as a subject
whom	is used as an object of a verb or a preposition
whose	is used as a possessive

In addition to the meaning and use of these subordinators, note the spelling of *whose*. It has no apostrophe. The contraction *who's* for *who is* is not usually used in standard written English.

Be careful as you select a subordinator to identify the word it stands for.

- The subordinator can stand for one (singular) or more than one (plural).
- The subordinator is placed as closely as possible after the word it stands for.
- If that word is singular, the subordinator has a singular meaning; if it is plural, the subordinator has a plural meaning.

Look at the following examples in which subordinators stand for first singular and then plural nouns. Note especially the use of singular and plural verbs. (An arrow is drawn from the noun to the subordinator that stands for it in the adjective clause. Each adjective clause is underlined, and verbs are in italics.)

1. The woman who *is working* with me on the project *has* not yet *found* a full-time job.

   The women who *are working* with me on the project *have* not yet *found* full-time jobs.

2. A city that *wishes* to grow *must work* to eliminate street crime.

   Cities that *wish* to grow *must work* to eliminate street crime.

3. The magic act which *is scheduled* to follow the intermission *has* not *been* well rehearsed.

   The magic acts which *are scheduled* to follow the intermission *have* not *been* well rehearsed.

Look back at the three examples. Notice that the words in each adjective clause form a unit of thought that modifies the word the subordinator stands for. The adjective clause could not be used as a simple sentence; it must function as a part of a main clause.

Do exercises 12-a and 12-b

BUILDING SENTENCES WITH ADJECTIVE CLAUSES

Adjective clauses are an important tool for adding information within a **sentence** and for maintaining appropriate focus and emphasis within a **paragraph**. As you study the examples of complex sentences, pay special attention to the various ways you can convey the same information. Each way gives a different focus to the sentence. Remember that the choice of what to emphasize and what to subordinate depends on the topic sentence (main idea) of a paragraph. In complex sentences, the idea that you want to emphasize belongs in the main clause; the less important idea should be subordinated in the adjective clause.

Using *Who*

We can often build a complex sentence with an adjective clause by combining two simple sentences about the same person(s), place(s), thing(s), or idea(s). For example, consider the following two simple sentences:

1. The young man is waiting in the manager's office.
2. The young man wishes to apply for the job.

If we want to combine them, we first need to decide which of the two ideas we want to emphasize. To emphasize the idea that the young man is waiting in the office, **we make the first sentence the main clause**. We may then rewrite the second sentence as an adjective clause by substituting the subordinator *who* for the noun *man*.

- We use the subordinator *who* because the noun *man* is the subject of the second sentence and the **subject** subordinator for a person or persons is *who*.

After making this substitution, we have an adjective clause:

who **wishes to apply for the job.**

We now need to place the adjective clause as closely as possible after the noun it modifies in the main clause. Since this adjective clause describes the *man*, it should appear immediately after the word *man* in the main clause (the first sentence):

Complex sentence: The young man **who wishes to apply for the job** is waiting in the manager's office.

If, instead, we choose to emphasize that the young man wishes to apply for the job, we will use the second sentence as the main clause. We can then rewrite the first simple sentence as an adjective clause and combine the sentences to reflect this emphasis:

Complex sentence: The young man **who is waiting in the manager's office** wishes to apply for the job.

Practice

Practice constructing adjective clauses by combining the following simple sentences using *who* as the subordinator:

1. The data processors have learned the new programs.
2. The data processors are able to complete their assignments on time.

First combine the sentences to emphasize the idea that the data processors have learned the new programs (sentence 1):

1. *Complex sentence*: _____

_____

Now combine the sentences to emphasize that the data processors are able to complete their work on time (sentence 2):

2. *Complex sentence*: _____

_____

Compare your combinations with the following complex sentences:

1. The data processors *who are able to complete their assignments on time* have learned the new programs.
2. The data processors *who have learned the new programs* are able to complete their assignments on time.

Using *Whom*

Next let's use *whom* to combine two simple sentences about the same person.

1. The young man is waiting in the manager's office.
2. We chose **him** for the job.

Suppose that we want to emphasize the first sentence—that the young man is waiting in the office. We need to rewrite the second sentence as an adjective clause.

- Since the pronoun *him* (young man) is used as a direct object in the second sentence, the subordinator that can stand for it is *whom*.
- The adjective clause will begin with the subordinator and read, *whom we chose for the job*.
- We now place this adjective clause immediately after the word *man*, the noun it modifies:

  Complex sentence: The young man **whom we chose for the job** is waiting in the manager's office.

Practice

Combine the following two simple sentences into one complex sentence. Make the second sentence the main clause; use *whom* to turn the first sentence into an adjective clause by substituting it for the direct object (*data processors*) of *hired*.

1. We hired the data processors.
2. The data processors can begin work on Monday.

Complex sentence: _____

_____

Compare your combinaton with this one:

Complex sentence: The data processors **whom we hired** can begin work on Monday.

Using *Whose*

When we use the subordinator *whose* to combine sentences, we substitute it for a possessive. Look at the following pair of sentences:

1. The young man is waiting in the manager's office.
2. We received the young **man's** job application.

We can use the first sentence as the main clause. The second sentence can be turned into an adjective clause by substituting *whose* for *man's* and moving *whose job application* so that the clause begins with the subordinator:

whose job application we received

In the complex sentence the adjective clause goes immediately after the word it modifies, *man*:

Complex sentence: The young man **whose job application we received** is waiting in the manager's office.

Using *Which* or *That*

So far, we have been combining pairs of sentences about people. Of course, we often want to combine information about things or ideas. When we do, we use the subordinator *which* or *that*. Consider the following sentences:

1. The supervisor is considering the changes.
2. The changes were recommended by our committee.

Either of these simple sentences can be used as the main clause, but the choice will determine the emphasis in the complex sentence. Let's emphasize the first sentence.

1. *Which* [*that*] can be substituted for *changes* in the second sentence to make an adjective clause: *which* [*that*] *were recommended by our committee*.
2. This clause can be placed in the main clause after *changes*, the word it modifies:

Complex sentence: The supervisor is considering the changes *which* [*that*] *were recommended by our committee*.

We may just as easily place the emphasis on the second sentence. Notice that the subordinator still goes at the beginning of the adjective clause:

Complex sentence: The changes *which* [*that*] *the supervisor is considering* were recommended by our committee.

193

Practice

Combine the following pair of sentences into one complex sentence using *which* or *that* as the subordinator.

> a. Two years ago, Kraft and Kristen planted the apple tree.
> b. The apple tree was the first in our orchard to blossom this year.

Use sentence *a* as the main clause:

> 1. *Complex sentence*: _____

Now use sentence *b* as the main clause:

> 2. *Complex sentence*: _____

Compare your combinations with these:

> 1. Two years ago, Kraft and Kristen planted the apple tree which [that] was the first to blossom in our orchard this year.
> 2. The apple tree which [that] Kraft and Kristen planted two years ago was the first to blossom in our orchard this year.

PUNCTUATING ADJECTIVE CLAUSES

An adjective clause may be **restrictive** or **nonrestrictive**. A **restrictive** clause is **necessary** to identify (restrict) the noun or pronoun it modifies. A **nonrestrictive** clause is **not necessary** for the identification of the noun or pronoun it modifies.

All the adjective clauses used in the examples in the preceding sections of this chapter are restrictive. Study the following additional examples of complex sentences with **restrictive adjective clauses**.

> 1. The **student** *who was reading in the library last period* left her magazine on the couch.
> 2. Any club **member** *who is interested in taking the bus trip to Yellowstone National Park* should speak to Sharon Marshall.
> 3. The **child** *who was sitting next to me in the movies* ate three boxes of popcorn.
> 4. The **car** *which was parked in the loading zone* has been towed away.

The italicized adjective clauses are restrictive because they are necessary to identify the nouns they modify. Without the adjective clauses, we would not know which student, which club member, which child, or which car. Because restrictive clauses are necessary to restrict a noun or pronoun to a particular one or a particular kind, they are not set off by commas.

The following sentences contain **nonrestrictive adjective clauses**.

> 1. **Anne Robbins**, *who was reading in the library lounge last period*, left her magazine on the couch.
> 2. **The club president**, *who is interested in taking the bus trip to Yellowstone National Park*, has already spoken to Sharon Marshall.

3. **My nephew Billy**, *who was sitting next to me in the movies*, ate three boxes of popcorn.
4. **Mr. Hayden's blue Corvette**, *which was parked in the loading zone*, has been towed away.

The italicized adjective clauses are nonrestrictive. They are not necessary to identify the nouns they modify: the nouns have already been identified as *Anne Robbins, the club president, my nephew Billy,* and *Mr. Hayden's blue Corvette*. Because nonrestrictive clauses add information but do not restrict the nouns they modify, they are set off by commas. Notice the two commas in each of the examples: one before the subordinator and one at the end of the adjective clause. (The subordinator *that* is not used in nonrestrictive clauses.)

Do exercises 12-c, 12-d, 12-e, 12-f, and 12-g

SUGGESTIONS FOR WRITING

Try writing a paragraph about the best trip that you have ever taken.

Perhaps you have already made some notes about a special trip in your journal; if so, you may be able to find ideas here for a **plan**. Start with a topic sentence that identifies the trip: for example, *The best trip I have ever taken was my trip to San Francisco two summers ago*. Next decide on **three** reasons that you enjoyed the trip—perhaps the person who went with you, the sight-seeing, and the restaurants that you visited. Make sure that you also jot down two specific examples for each subtopic: for example, two specific positive qualities of the person who accompanied you, two specific places that you visited, and two specific restaurants where you ate.

Now **write** sentences to develop your topic sentence idea, including as many specific details as possible. Follow your plan and stick to your main idea. Make sure to add a closing sentence: for example, *The next time I have an opportunity to take a trip, I hope I am able to return to San Francisco*.

Edit your paragraph carefully. Make sure that your verbs are in the *past* tense and make sure that you have followed the punctuation rules that you have been studying.

NAME _____ **DATE** _____

Underline the adjective clause in each of the following complex sentences. Draw an arrow from the adjective clause to the noun or pronoun which it modifies. The first sentence gives the topic for the sentences that follow.

EXAMPLES

Job applicants who have had no prior experience are sometimes passed over by employers.

College graduates are sometimes discouraged by job advertisements that require previous experience.

1. Students who wish to begin their careers right after graduation should seek work-related experience during their college years.

2. Students should begin early to plan the course of study which they wish to follow.

3. They should collect information about curricula that include on-the-job training in their requirements.

4. Many curricula, such as physical therapy, occupational therapy, recreation, and medical technology, include internships which provide work experience.

5. The curricula which offer these supervised work opportunities are often very time consuming, and students must plan their schedules carefully.

6. However, the graduates of the programs and the employers who hire them agree on the value of such internships.

7. During college, students may also select part-time or summer jobs that provide experience in their chosen fields.

8. Students who have little work experience might also consider doing volunteer work.

9. Volunteer work that directly relates to an applicant's chosen career or occupation often counts as experience.

10. The League of Women Voters, the YMCA, and the Boy Scouts of America are among the hundreds of organizations that offer educational, social, and recreational services to their communities.

11. These nonprofit organizations use volunteers whom they train to work in a wide variety of areas.

12. Applicants should include on their resumes all part-time, intern, or volunteer jobs which they have held for three months or longer.

NAME _____ **DATE** _____

Some of the following sentences contain errors in agreement.

- Underline each adjective clause.
- Draw an arrow from the subordinator to the word or words it stands for.
- Then correct any errors in agreement by drawing a line through each incorrect verb or pronoun and writing the correction above it.
- Write a *C* in the left margin by the numbers of correct sentences.

EXAMPLES

_____ A parent who ~~return~~ *returns* to school often leaves ~~their~~ *his or her* their children with relatives

for part of the day.

_____ The instructions which ~~comes~~ with the computer ~~is~~ *are* not clear.

__*C*__ He wrote three answers on the board that were completely wrong.

1. _____ Many of the students who graduates in human services are employed by the

   state health agencies.

2. _____ Each student who graduated in human services last year are employed by state

   health agencies.

3. _____ Altoona Steel is selecting applications only from persons who have had prior

   experience.

4. _____ The two companies in our area that lost money last year are laying off

   employees.

5. _____ The tutor who can help you with your biology programs have gone out for lunch.

6. _____ The tutors who are out to lunch are the only ones who know biology.

7. _____ Many of Gayle's relatives who promised to help her with school expenses has

   repeatedly turned down her requests.

8. _____ Francine, who is trying to earn money for a trip to Japan, works three different

   jobs every week.

9. _____ My two nieces, who is saving money for a trip to San Diego, work every night

   after school.

10. _____ The woman who sell beauty supplies door-to-door in my neighborhood was

arrested Tuesday for breaking and entering.

11. _____ Women who sells beauty supplies door-to-door are taking chances coming into

my neighborhood.

12. _____ The two young men who are taking their grandparents to Hawaii is my

nephews.

13. _____ My youngest brother, who is taking our grandparents to Cancun, has never

flown before.

14. _____ The computer that I used last week has been sent out for repairs.

15. _____ Gregory finally returned the library books that had been lying on the hall table

all week.

NAME _____ **DATE** _____

　　　Use an adjective clause to combine each pair of simple sentences into one complex sentence.

- Use the first sentence as your main clause.
- Rewrite the second sentence as an adjective clause beginning with the subordinator in parentheses.
- Then write the combination by placing the adjective clause after the word it modifies.

EXAMPLE

Students should make an appointment with a counselor to discuss finding a part-time job related to their chosen career.
These students plan to graduate next spring.

Adjective clause (who): _____ *who plan to graduate next spring* _____

Complex sentence: _____ *Students who plan to graduate next spring should*

_____ *make an appointment with a counselor to discuss finding a part-time job*

_____ *related to their chosen career.*

_____

1. The little old lady headed toward the exit.
   The little old lady had just placed two gold bracelets in her shopping bag.

   Adjective clause (who): _____

   Complex sentence: _____

   _____

   _____

   _____

2. Many of the older students must divide their time among home, school, and work.
   I met these older students in my biology class.

   Adjective clause (whom): _____

   Complex sentence: _____

   _____

   _____

   _____

3. Many of the summer jobs gave me firsthand knowledge about the world of work.
   I had these jobs during my teen years.

   Adjective clause (*which*):_____

   Complex sentence: _____

   _____

   _____

   _____

4. The company has never changed the construction of the baseball.
   The company's balls are used by all the major league teams.

   Adjective clause (*whose*):_____

   Complex sentence: _____

   _____

   _____

   _____

5. The April day dawned cold and foggy.
   Douglas had chosen the day for his wedding.

   Adjective clause (*which*):_____

   Complex sentence: _____

   _____

   _____

   _____

6. Each season the Rawlings Sporting Goods Company sells over 750,000 baseballs to
   major league teams in the United States.
   The Rawlings Sporting Goods Company makes the balls in Costa Rica.

   Adjective clause (*which*):_____

   Complex sentence: _____

   _____

   _____

   _____

NAME _____ **DATE** _____

    Write an adjective clause in each of the blank spaces to form a complex sentence. Be sure your clause is appropriate to the sense of the main clause you are given. Check the agreement of pronouns and verbs carefully, and add commas where they are necessary.

EXAMPLE

The first graders _____*who had perfect attendance*_____ have received coupons from a local fast-food restaurant.

1. My cousin _____
   will be attending a convention in Dallas next week.

2. The old men _____
   did not hear the police whistles or the sirens.

3. I handed in my term paper to Dr. Haskell _____

   _____

4. Where is the librarian _____

   _____

5. She turned to her husband _____

   _____ and politely asked him to leave the party.

6. My interview for a job at Karen's Kitchen _____

   _____ has been postponed.

7. Any student _____
   should first discuss it with the instructor.

8. Women _____
   should investigate careers in criminal justice or fire protection.

9. My oldest sister _____
   wants to go back into teaching.

10. The football stadium _____
    will not be finished for five years.

NAME _____ **DATE** _____

Label the adjective clause in each of the following sentences *R* for restrictive and *N* for nonrestrictive. Set off each nonrestrictive clause with commas.

EXAMPLES

N My cousin Olga, who has worked as a nurse for fifteen years, has enrolled in a physician's assistant program.

R The snow tires that I bought five years ago will probably last one more season.

1. _____ The man whom I met at the advisory board meeting last night is not a college graduate.

2. _____ Jonathan Seagull whom I met last night at the advisory board meeting is on the school board.

3. _____ The trip which Ethel is planning with her husband will take her around the world.

4. _____ Ethel who is planning a trip around the world has never been out of the United States.

5. _____ Ethel's trip which will include stops in Thailand and India will take six weeks.

6. _____ The firewood that we bought last summer is still not seasoned enough to burn well.

7. _____ The fish which is served every Friday in the school cafeteria tastes like cardboard cod.

8. _____ Angry at his rude behavior, Margaret who had tried to remain silent ordered her son to leave the restaurant.

9. _____ My friend Mary Lou who has been a dietician for thirty years is retiring this June.

10. _____ The paper which I am typing for my sister has five charts and four graphs.

11. _____ The person whom we saw in the tavern looked very much like Michael Douglas.

12. _____ The person whose car I borrowed reported it stolen.

13. _____ By the end of the week, Marilyn was ready to sell all the stocks which she had inherited from her mother.

14. _____ The triathlete whose goggles had fallen off during the swim came out of the water and ran off in the wrong direction.

15. _____ Bill Jones who has twice run in the Bud Light Triathalon in Bethany Beach will not participate this year.

NAME _____ **DATE** _____

Use an adjective clause to combine each pair of sentences.

- Read through the example and all the sentences to understand the topic.
- Select the sentence you wish to use as the main clause, and place a check by it.
- Turn the other sentence into an adjective clause and place it correctly in the main clause.
- Use commas to set off nonrestrictive clauses.

EXAMPLE: TOPIC SENTENCE

The chili is now grown in over a hundred and fifty varieties around the world.

The chili originally grew wild on vines under the rain forests of the Amazon River in South America.

The chili, which is now grown in over a hundred and fifty varieties around the world, originally grew wild on vines under the rain forests of the Amazon River in South America.

1. At least 8,000 years ago, the Incas domesticated and cultivated the chili along with their corn, squash, and beans.
   The Incas inhabited Peru.

   Complex sentence: _____

   _____

   _____

2. In Peru, archaeologists have found traces of chilies in burial sites.
   The burial sites date as far back as 6200 B.C.

   Complex sentence: _____

   _____

   _____

3. Evidently, the Incas considered the chili essential to their well-being in the next world.
   The Incas used chilies to add spiciness and flavor to their food.

   Complex sentence: _____

   _____

   _____

4. By the time Columbus arrived at the end of the fifteenth century, chilies were cultivated and used by all the people.
   The people lived in South America and Mesoamerica.

   Complex sentence: _____

   _____

   _____

5. The Mayans of Mesoamerica used the chili as medicine as well as food.
   The Mayans had developed at least thirty varieties.

   Complex sentence: _____
   _____
   _____

6. Columbus mistook the chili plant for a very valuable plant.
   The valuable plant produces black pepper.

   Complex sentence: _____
   _____
   _____

7. Consequently, he called the chili plant "pepper," a mistaken name.
   The mistaken name is still widely used in Europe and the United States.

   Complex sentence: _____
   _____
   _____

8. However, the fruit of the chili seeds became a very popular ingredient to add heat
   and spice to meats, sauces, and vegetables.
   He and his crew took the seeds back to Spain.

   Complex sentence: _____
   _____
   _____

9. Spanish and Portuguese explorers came after Columbus.
   The Spanish and Portuguese explorers carried chili seeds all over the world.

   Complex sentence: _____
   _____
   _____

10. The chili found congenial growing conditions in Europe, Africa, India, and Asia.
    The chili is returning to America in fiery new varieties and exotic recipes.

    Complex sentence: _____
    _____
    _____

NAME _____ **DATE** _____

    In this exercise, you will first write a pair of original sentences about the same person or thing. Then you will combine them into a complex sentence with an adjective clause.

I. Using *Who* as a Subordinator

    In each of the three parts of this section, write a pair of original simple sentences using the name of the same person as the subject of both. Place a check by the idea that you want to emphasize. Then combine the two sentences into a complex sentence using the less important sentence as an adjective clause beginning with *who*.

EXAMPLE

(a) *Alex moved from Maryland to Arizona last year.* _____

(b) *Alex is teaching at Maricopa Community College.* _____

Complex sentence: _____ *Alex, who moved from Maryland to Arizona last year, is*

teaching at Maricopa Community College. _____

═══

1. (a) _____

    (b) _____

_____

Complex sentence: _____

_____

_____

2. (a) _____

    (b) _____

_____

Complex sentence: _____

_____

_____

3. (a) _____

    (b) _____

_____

Complex sentence: _____

_____

_____

II. Using *Which* as a Subordinator

In each of the three parts of this section, write a pair of simple sentences about the same thing. Place a check by the sentence you wish to emphasize, and use it as the main clause. Then combine the two sentences into one complex sentence, using the less important as an adjective clause beginning with the subordinator *which*.

EXAMPLE

(a) *Sadie had carefully planned the New Year's Eve party for three weeks.*

(b) *The New Year's Eve party was a success.*

Complex sentence: The New Year's Eve party which Sadie had carefully planned

for three weeks was a success.

---

1. (a) _____

   (b) _____

   Complex sentence: _____

   _____

   _____

2. (a) _____

   (b) _____

   Complex sentence: _____

   _____

   _____

3. (a) _____

   (b) _____

   Complex sentence: _____

   _____

   _____

Using Subordination

Participial Phrases and Appositive Phrases

13

In Chapters 11 and 12, you learned how to build sentences by using the adverb clause and the adjective clause. In this chapter, you will study the **participial phrase** and the **appositive phrase**.

RECOGNIZING PARTICIPLES AND APPOSITIVES

Earlier in this book, Chapter 3 looked at how a past participle (the *-ed* form of a regular verb) and a present participle (the *-ing* form of a verb) can be used as single-word adjectives. Here are two examples of such participles. (An arrow is drawn from the participle to the noun it modifies.)

1. The waxed floor looked brand new.

2. The janitor used a polishing wax in the scrub water.

The past participle *waxed* describes what has been **done to** the noun it modifies (*floor*); the present participle *polishing* describes what the noun it modifies (*wax*) **does or is capable of doing**. These single-word adjectives come before the words they modify.

Appositives can also be single words that add information to a sentence. However, an appositive is not an adjective modifier; it is a **renamer**. An **appositive** is a noun or pronoun that renames another noun or pronoun. The appositive always comes immediately after the noun or pronoun it renames. (In the following examples a double-headed arrow is drawn between each appositive and the noun it renames.)

Our postman, Mr. Williams, hates dogs.

In the New York art gallery, Georgia O'Keeffe met her future husband, Alfred Stieglitz, for the first time.

RECOGNIZING PARTICIPIAL PHRASES AND APPOSITIVE PHRASES

Often we want to add more information than a single-word participle or appositive provides; we need to construct a **phrase**, a group of related words that does not have a subject and verb. Consider the following sentence:

My uncle needs a baby-sitter for his two young children.

Imagine that you want to include another idea:

My uncle works full-time as a librarian.

You might write a complex sentence with an adjective clause:

> My uncle, *who works full-time as a librarian*, needs a baby-sitter for his two young children.

Or you might change the verb *works* to the participle *working* and use the information to form a phrase:

> My uncle, *working full-time as a librarian*, needs a baby-sitter for his two young children.

You might also use *librarian* to rename *uncle* and construct an appositive phrase:

> My uncle, *a full-time librarian*, needs a baby-sitter for his two young children.

Notice that the adjective clause and both phrases give the same information about the noun *uncle*. The words in the clause and in each phrase work together to form a single unit of thought. The adjective clause forms the unit of thought with a subject and verb; the phrases form the unit with a participle or appositive. Both the clause and the phrases include modifiers and other words necessary to complete their meaning.

PLACING AND PUNCTUATING APPOSITIVES

An appositive phrase, like an adjective clause, can be placed in only one position—right after the noun or pronoun it renames. All appositive phrases are nonrestrictive and thus set off by commas. Look at the following nonrestrictive appositive phrase:

> Melvin Jones, *the meanest boy on our block*, is studying the flute.

The subject is identified by his name, *Melvin Jones*. The italicized appositive phrase adds information about the subject, but it does not identify him. He is already identified. Therefore, the appositive phrase is nonrestrictive and is set off by commas.

In the following sentence, two appositives are italicized:

> Miss Toombs, *a very young and inexperienced teacher*, argued with the principal, *an old and very stern administrator*.

The first appositive phrase renames the subject, *Miss Toombs*, and needs two commas to enclose it. The second appositive phrase, renaming *principal*, comes at the end of the sentence and needs only one comma to set it off.

Unlike appositive phrases, single-word appositives can be restrictive or nonrestrictive. (See page 194 in Chapter 12.) In the following two examples of restrictive appositives, notice how each is necessary to identify the noun it renames. (The appositives are in italics and arrows are drawn to the words they rename.)

1. My brother *Jack* is studying law.

2. The experimental novel *Orlando* was published by Virginia Woolf in 1928.

In the first sentence, the name *Jack* restricts the brother to the one intended. Without *Jack*, *brother* would not be identified—unless, of course, the writer has only one brother. As a restrictive appositive, *Jack* is not set off by commas. In the second sentence, the title *Orlando* identifies which of Virginia Woolf's novels is the subject.

Compare the restrictive appositives in 1 and 2 above with the following non-restrictive phrases:

1. Jack, *my oldest brother*, is studying law.
2. Orlando, *an experimental novel*, was published by Virginia Woolf in 1928.

Do exercises 13-a and 13-b

PLACING AND PUNCTUATING PARTICIPIAL PHRASES

A participial phrase may also be restrictive or nonrestrictive (see page 194).

A restrictive participial phrase comes after the noun it modifies and is not set off by commas. In the following examples, the restrictive phrases are italicized and an arrow is drawn to the nouns they modify:

Restrictive Modifiers

1. The man *standing next to me* began to laugh.

2. The child *sitting with her mother* was better behaved than the child *sitting alone*.

3. The college survey *taken last spring* showed the students' support of additional services for the handicapped.

4. The rag *used to polish your shoes* may not be washed with the dish towels.

The phrases italicized in these sentences are restrictive because each is necessary to identify the noun it modifies. Without the phrase, we would not know which man, which child, which survey, or which rag.

A nonrestrictive participial phrase can be placed before or after the noun it modifies. In either place, a nonrestrictive phrase is set off by commas. (Again, an arrow is drawn from the participle to the noun the phrase modifies.)

Nonrestrictive Modifiers

1. Jerry, *swimming rapidly toward us*, looked up and grinned.

2. *Swimming rapidly toward us*, Jerry looked up and grinned.

3. Henry, *now grown over six feet tall*, no longer feared his father.

4. *Now grown over six feet tall*, Henry no longer feared his father.

The italicized verbal phrases are not necessary to identify the nouns they modify. The two persons are identified by their names, *Jerry* and *Henry*. Because the phrases are nonrestrictive, they are set off by commas and may be placed before or after the noun they modify.

Do exercise 13-c

SELECTING THE TENSE IN MODIFIERS

Both adjective clauses and participial phrases can be written in a tense (time of action) that is the same as, before, or after that of the main verb. In the following illustration, notice that in the combinations, the two actions, of *turning* and of *controlling*, occur at the same time, in the past.

1. Charles turned to the salesman and smiled.
2. Charles carefully controlled his temper.

Combination using an adjective clause:	Charles, who carefully controlled his temper, turned to the salesman and smiled.
Combinations using verbal phrase:	Carefully controlling his temper, Charles turned to the salesman and smiled.
	Charles, carefully controlling his temper, turned to the salesman and smiled.

In each combination the two actions have the same tense: Charles *controlled* and *turned* at the same time.

We might, however, want to indicate that the subordinate action occurred before that of the main verb. Charles, for instance, might have controlled his temper and **then** turned and smiled. In the complex sentence, we can indicate this difference in time by using *had* as a helper to change the verb in the adjective clause to the **past perfect tense**—*had controlled*.

Charles, who *had controlled* his temper, turned to the salesman and smiled.

In the combinations using phrases, we can indicate this difference in time by using *having* plus the past participle—*having controlled*:

Having controlled his temper, Charles turned to the salesman and smiled.
Charles, *having controlled* his temper, turned to the salesman and smiled.

Consider the time relationship between the following two sentences:

1. Mary Jane Smith won five races.
2. Mary Jane Smith returned proudly to her parents.

We can assume that the action of the first sentence occurred before that of the second: first she won; then she returned. If we combine the sentences using the first as an adjective clause, we use *had* as a helper to create a past perfect:

Mary Jane Smith, who *had won* five races, returned proudly to her parents.

If we combine the sentence using a verbal, we must use *having* plus the past participle (*won*) to indicate that the winning occurred before the returning:

Having won five races, Mary Jane Smith returned proudly to her parents.
Mary Jane Smith, *having won* five races, returned proudly to her parents.

The following two sentences can also be combined using either an adjective clause or a verbal phrase based on a two-word verbal (*having* plus a past participle).

1. Willis lost his job as a social worker.
2. Willis decided to go to nursing school.

Which action should be emphasized? Which action occurred first? Notice how the following combinations clarify the relationship between the two ideas.

Combination using an adjective clause: Willis, who had lost his job as a social worker, decided to go to nursing school.

Combinations using a verbal phrase: Having lost his job as a social worker, Willis decided to go to nursing school.
Willis, having lost his job as a social worker, decided to go to nursing school.

Practice

Combine the following two sentences using an adjective clause and a verbal phrase placed in two positions. Assume that the action in the first sentence occurred first and that the second sentence states the more important idea.

Jim took notes on three books and five articles.
Jim was ready to write an outline for his paper.

Combination using an adjective clause:

1. _____

_____

Combinations using a verbal phrase:

2. _____

_____

3. _____

_____

Check your combinations with these. (The order of 2 and 3 may, of course, be reversed.)

1. Jim, *who had taken notes on three books and five articles*, was ready to write an outline for his paper.
2. *Having taken notes on three books and five articles*, Jim was ready to write an outline for his paper.
3. Jim, *having taken notes on three books and five articles*, was ready to write an outline for his paper.

Do exercise 13-d

215

CHOOSING PHRASES OR CLAUSES

As the examples in this chapter show, you may often choose to add information by using an adjective clause, a participial phrase, or an appositive phrase. Each of the three constructions gives different emphasis and sometimes slightly different meaning to the same information. As you write paragraphs, the choice will depend upon the main idea (topic sentence) of the paragraph and upon the other sentences that precede and follow. You will want to keep your focus on the idea in the topic sentence, to move smoothly from sentence to sentence, and to offer your reader variety in sentence construction.

Here is another illustration that shows how the same information can be combined in a variety of ways. Consider the relationship of ideas in the following sentences:

1. Bertha Steele studied the Civil War.
2. Bertha Steele learned to respect Robert E. Lee.

Using the second sentence as the main clause, we emphasize that Ms. Steele learned to respect Lee. We might then change the first into an **adjective clause**.

> *Combination using an adjective clause:* Bertha Steele, who studied the Civil War, learned to respect Robert E. Lee.

Or, by changing the first sentence to a **participial phrase**, we might combine them into a sentence with only one clause:

> *Combination using a verbal phrase:* Bertha Steel, studying the Civil War, learned to respect Robert E. Lee.
> Studying the Civil War, Bertha Steele learned to respect Robert E. Lee.

Both the adjective clause in the complex sentence and the verbal phrase in the simple sentence modify the noun *Bertha Steele*, and both convey the same information. However, because verbal phrases may be placed before or after the noun they modify, two versions are possible.

We can also change the verb *studied* to the noun *student* and use it to form an appositive phrase—*a student of the Civil War*. This phrase can be placed in the second sentence after *Bertha Steele*, which it renames:

> *Combination using an appositive:* Bertha Steele, a student of the Civil War, learned to respect Robert E. Lee.

Do exercises 13-e and 13-f

SUGGESTIONS FOR WRITING

Now take an opportunity to explore an unpleasant experience, one which you may or may not have recorded in your journal. Write a paragraph about the worst job that you have ever had.

Before you write, **plan** your paragraph by deciding on a topic sentence idea: _____ is the worst job I have ever had. Once again, you will be developing your idea with reasons as subtopics. Choose three reasons for disliking this particular job, such as your employer, your co-workers, and your low pay. Or discuss three of the responsibilities which made this job particularly unpleasant. Then decide on the specific details that you will use to make each of your three points. Jot down your topic sentence, your three subtopics, and your one or two specific examples for each reason.

Follow your plan as you **write** a paragraph. When you have finished supporting the topic sentence, add a closing sentence which states the topic sentence idea in a new way: for example, *I have never regretted quitting my job at* _____.

Do not consider your job finished until you have **edited** your paragraph. Make sure that you have followed the punctuation rules for compound and complex sentences.

NAME _____ DATE _____

Identify each appositive in the following sentences, underline it, and draw an arrow from the appositive to the noun or pronoun it renames. Some sentences will have more than one appositive. Label each appositive *R* for restrictive or *N* for nonrestrictive.

EXAMPLE

_*N*_ Aaron Burr, vice-president of the United States under Thomas Jefferson,

killed Alexander Hamilton in a duel.

1. _____ *Shogun*, a popular epic set in Japan, starred Richard Chamberlain.

2. _____ Jane's answer, surely one of her rudest, was greeted with gasps.

3. _____ My supervisor refused to read the report, a three-page complaint prepared by

the employee committee.

4. _____ *Biochemistry*, my son's favorite book, was compiled and edited by Geoffrey

Zubay.

5. _____ In 1987, Gary Hart, an unsuccessful candidate in 1983, withdrew from the

presidential race and then reentered.

6. __ The horse, a four gaited American saddler, moved smoothly under Liz's careful

control.

7. _____ My cousin Anabelle is a famous trial lawyer.

8. _____ We were told to wait in the principal's office, a small room just off the entrance hall.

9. _____ Locating the security guard, a small man in a grey uniform, was hopeless in the

crowded halls.

10. _____ Dr. Maine, usually a very serious young man, walked toward my grandparents

with a big grin on his face.

11. _____ Gretchen, the best figure skater in Arizona, placed only twentieth in the world

contests.

12. _____ However, she and her partner, a young man from Arkansas, placed tenth in ice

dancing.

13._____ The crowd booed the sudden appearance of the judge, a tall man with an arrogant face.

14._____ Marilyn took one look at her new dentist's watch, a very expensive Rolex, stood up, and left the office.

15._____ James invited all of his co-workers, six women and eight men, to the open house.

16._____ My old friend Howard was the only one from Pocatello to become famous.

NAME _____ **DATE** _____

Each of the following pairs of sentences can be combined into one sentence by using an appositive phrase. Together the combinations will make a **paragraph** that develops this topic sentence:

Many of the students in my evening psychology class have unusual outside jobs or interests.

Think about the main idea expressed in the topic sentence as you select which idea to emphasize and which to turn into an appositive phrase. Write your combinations on the blank lines.

EXAMPLE

Hadley Mason is a retired elementary school janitor.
He raises earthworms to sell to farmers.

Combination: *Hadley Mason, a retired elementary shcool janitor, raises earthworms to sell to farmers.*

1. The smallest student is an athletic young woman.
   She spends her weekends at a training camp for baseball umpires.

   Combination: _____

   _____

   _____

   _____

2. Wallace Farnes is studying for the ministry but earns a living making silver and turquoise jewelry.
   He is a former used car salesman.

   Combination: _____

   _____

   _____

   _____

3. Barton Henderson is a young elementary school aide in the winter.
   He works in the summer as a dance instructor on luxury liners sailing the Caribbean.

   Combination: _____

   _____

   _____

   _____

4. Two women spend their vacations working as guides on bicycle tours in Canada or Mexico.
   Both are file clerks for the Social Security Administration.

   Combination: _____

   _____

   _____

   _____

5. The oldest female student is a sixty-year-old postal service employee.
   She attends acting classes two nights a week and plans to try out for a part in the next community play.

   Combination: _____

   _____

   _____

   _____

6. Even though I am young and a full-time student, I, too, pursue an unusual interest.
   I am interested in the cultivation of prize orchids.

   Combination: _____

   _____

   _____

   _____

NAME _____ **DATE** _____

Label each sentence that contains a restrictive participial modifier *R* and each that contains a nonrestrictive participial modifier *N*. Then correct any errors in punctuation by adding or crossing out commas.

EXAMPLES

R   The man sitting in the middle of the front row is my father-in-law.

N   Worrying about her job interview, Esther was unable to sleep.

1. _____ The little dog ran away, dragging the old blanket.

2. _____ Laughing and gossiping with her friends Darla did not notice that Andy had come into the gym.

3. _____ Quickly hiding the note in his jeans, the delivery boy turned and went down the stairs.

4. _____ The tiny child, tightly closing his eyes cried for help.

5. _____ Finding no one at home, Peter returned to his car and wrote a note.

6. _____ Adele, having failed every exam during the semester did not bother to take the final exam.

7. _____ The woman sitting behind me in the large theatre, began to munch her popcorn.

8. _____ Drinking the milk in one gulp, little Billy smiled and left for school.

9. _____ Janice, screaming with all her might ran the two blocks to her home.

10. _____ The child standing in the middle of the aisle seemed to be looking for her mother.

11. _____ The contestant singing her final solo was unaware of the fire.

12. _____ The essay submitted by Eloise, was not the one that was lost.

13. _____ The man reading the *Daily Globe* paid no attention to the noisy teenagers.

14. _____ Jamming the stick shift into high gear, Hank passed the yellow Mercedes.

15. _____ The rock music played in the elevator offended the residents.

16. _____ Skimming across the ice in perfect unison the ice dancers suddenly fell.

17. _____ Detective Rossi, leaving no clue unexplored pursued the thief for two years.

18. _____ The broker managing my stocks has just been arrested.

19. _____ Gathering all her records in January, Beth had time to take her income tax materials to an accountant.

20. _____ No one watching the game, blamed the goalie for the loss.

NAME _____ **DATE** _____

Combine each pair of sentences in two ways: first, by using an adjective clause and, second, by using a participial phrase.

- Emphasize the topic sentence; that is, in each pair, emphasize the interest that the the person cannot pursue.
- Subordinate the other sentence about the person's job by making it an adjective clause.
- Then subordinate the job sentence by making it a participial phrase and placing it before or after the word it modifies.

Topic Sentence: Many of my friends are unhappy because their work makes it impossible for them to enjoy a social life.

EXAMPLE

Kathy works the evening shift at the nursing home.
Kathy rarely sees her friends.

Combination using an adjective clause: *Kathy, who works the evening shift at the nursing home, rarely sees her friends.*

Combination using a participial phrase: *Working the evening shift at the nursing home, Kathy rarely sees her friends.*

or *Kathy, working the evening shift at the nursing home, rarely sees her friends.*

---

1. Tom works as a sports editor for the morning edition of the local newspaper.
   Tom can never join his friends for an evening baseball game.

   Combination using an adjective clause: _____

   _____

   Combination using a participial phrase: _____

   _____

2. Sharon dances six nights a week at a downtown club.
   Sharon can rarely go out to dinner with her boyfriend.

   Combination using an adjective clause: _____

   _____

   Combination using a participial phrase: _____

   _____

3. Gary spends twelve hours a day at his parents' shoe store.
   Gary rarely has time to go shopping with his girlfriend.

   Combination using an adjective clause: _____

   _____

   Combination using a participial phrase: _____

   _____

4. Jenny works as a pool lifeguard from noon until nine P.M.
   Jenny is seldom able to go to the beach with her friends.

   Combination using an adjective clause: _____

   _____

   Combination using a participial phrase: _____

   _____

5. Robert teaches adult education classes in reading five nights a week.
   Robert cannot attend his children's school functions.

   Combination using an adjective clause: _____

   _____

   Combination using a participial phrase: _____

   _____

NAME _____ **DATE** _____

For each of the five parts of this exercise, write a pair of sentences about one of your friends. Use a different friend for each pair of sentences.

- Write one sentence about your friend's interesting hobby and one sentence about your friend's job.
- Then combine the sentences, using either an adjective clause or a participial phrase to describe the job. Emphasize the information about the interesting hobby.
- Each combination should support this **topic sentence**:

> Each of my close friends has an interesting hobby that is very different from his or her job.

EXAMPLE

(a) *Gloria manages a neighborhood day care center.*

(b) *Gloria has her evenings free to train German shephards.*

Combination: *Gloria, who manages a neighborhood day care center, has her evenings free to train German sheperds.*

or *Managing a day care center, Gloria has her evenings free to train German sheperds.*

1. (a) _____

_____

(b) _____

_____

Combination: _____

_____

_____

_____

_____

2. (a) _____
_____

(b) _____
_____

Combination: _____
_____
_____
_____
_____

3. (a) _____
_____

(b) _____
_____

Combination: _____
_____
_____
_____
_____

4. (a) _____
_____

(b) _____
_____

Combination: _____
_____
_____
_____
_____

5. (a) _____
_____

(b) _____
_____

Combination: _____
_____
_____
_____

NAME _____ DATE _____

This exercise is a review of the sentence-combining exercises in Chapters 3 through 13. You are given groups of simple sentences that can be combined into one sentence using single-word modifiers; prepositional phrases, verbal phrases, or appositive phrases; or adverb and adjective clauses.

Combine each group of sentences to build a sentence that develops the following **topic sentence:**

Last week, all five members of my family traveled from Ohio to New York City to say good-bye to my sister Abbie.

- Decide on the main idea for the subject–verb base of your combination.
- Reduce or change the other sentences to single-word modifiers, phrases, or subordinate clauses.
- Place these modifiers, phrases, and clauses in appropriate positions around the base.
- Check your punctuation and spelling carefully.

EXAMPLE

Abbie sailed for England last Wednesday.
She is going to begin an internship in political science.
The internship will last six months.
She will work with three members of Parliament.
The members are from Scotland.

Combination: *Abbie sailed for England last Wednesday to begin a six-month*

intership with three Scottish members of Parliament.

_____

_____

1. We left Marion.
   It was 6:00 A.M.
   We traveled in our VW bus.
   We arrived in New York City.
   It was the worst time to arrive.
   It was the middle of the evening rush hour.

   Combination: _____

   _____

   _____

   _____

2. My father remained calm.
   My fathcr pretended he knew where we were.
   He pretended he knew where we were going.
   He soon found the hotel.
   We were going to stay there.
   The hotel was small.
   The hotel was in midtown.

   Combination: _____

   _____

   _____

   _____

3. We spent the three days sightseeing.
   Abbie left after these three days.
   We rode the subways.
   We walked through the Museum of Natural History.
   We went to the World Trade Center.
   We took an elevator to the top of the Center.
   We ate supper in Chinatown.

   Combination: _____

   _____

   _____

   _____

4. We miss Abbie already.
   Her return will be doubly exciting.
   We will have a second trip to New York City.
   Abbie will be home.
   She will bring stories.
   The stories will tell of her many adventures.

   Combination: _____

   _____

   _____

   _____

Using Subordination

14

Noun Clauses and Verbal Phrases as Nouns

RECOGNIZING NOUN CLAUSES

You have learned that subordinate clauses can be used as adverbs or as adjectives. Some subordinate clauses are also used as nouns. These noun clauses function as nouns do in a sentence; for instance, they might be a subject or a direct object. Like an adverb clause or an adjective clause, a noun clause begins with a subordinator that connects the clause to the main clause.

Subordinators of Noun Clauses

how	where	what, whatever	whose, whosever
that	whether, if	who, whoever	which, whichever
when	why	whom, whomever	

Look at the following examples of complex sentences. The subordinator is in italics, and a slash (/) separates the noun clause from the rest of the sentence. Within each noun clause, the subject is underlined once and the verb twice.

1. The laboratory aide reported / *that* all the students had completed the experiment.

2. The students asked / *when* the biology reports were due.

3. The secretary asked / *where* the make-up examination will be given.

4. The instructor did not know / *whether* all of the students had received a syllabus.

5. The professor had not considered / *why* the students wished to see their lab reports.

In each of these examples, the noun clause functions as a direct object. In the first example, the noun clause tells what the laboratory aide reported; in the second example, the noun clause tells what the students asked.

In this chapter, you will be looking at the most common use of the noun clause, as a direct object. As you work through the chapter, you will learn how to form noun clauses and how to use them as direct objects.

BUILDING NOUN CLAUSES

As you build noun clauses, you need to follow two rules:

1. The noun clause begins with an appropriate subordinator.
2. Within the noun clause, the subject and the verb (including any helping verbs) must be in the regular order—the subject first and then the verb.

See how these rules are applied or violated in the following examples. (The noun clauses are separated from the rest of the sentence by a slash (/); within the noun clauses, subordinators are in italics, subjects are underlined once, and verbs are underlined twice.)

Correct:	The chief clerk asked / *whether* the packages had arrived yet.
Incorrect:	The chief clerk asked / had the packages arrived yet.
Correct:	Jack's teacher wondered / *how* well he works at home.
Incorrect:	Jack's teacher wondered / does he work well at home.
Correct:	The team asked / *when* the next practice would be held.
Incorrect:	The team asked / *when* would the next practice be held.

> **Do exercises 14-a, 14-b, and 14-c**

USING NOUN CLAUSES TO RESTATE QUESTIONS AND QUOTATIONS

One of the most common uses of noun clauses is to restate what someone asked or said in print or in a speech or conversation.

Changing Questions to Noun Clauses

Sometimes we want to report a question asked by someone else. When we want to report what someone has asked, we have two choices: we may use a direct quotation or we may use a noun clause. For example, the following question is written as a direct quotation:

Question: Mrs. Wilson asked, "When will the inventory be finished?"

In this sentence, we are told exactly what Mrs. Wilson asked. She said the exact words reported in the quotation, "When will the inventory be finished?"

However, we do not have to use a direct quotation to communicate this information. Instead of reporting Mrs. Wilson's exact words in a direct quotation, we can use a noun clause.

Noun clause: Mrs. Wilson asked when the inventory will be finished.

In this sentence, we are not reporting exactly what Mrs. Wilson said; she did not say the words *when the inventory will be finished*. Instead, her exact words have been rewritten as a noun clause. Notice that the noun clause follows the two noun clause rules:

1. The noun clause begins with a subordinator, *when*.

2. In the noun clause, the subject comes before the verb: *inventory will be finished*

   (In the question, part of the helping verb, *will*, comes before the subject, *inventory*.)

Now let's look at another pair of sentences. Again, the first sentence contains a question in the form of a direct quotation, and the second restates the question using a noun clause.

Question:	This morning, my supervisor asked, "How does Mike like his new job?"
Noun clause:	This morning, my supervisor asked how Mike likes his new job.

Note once again that, while the first sentence states the supervisor's exact words, the second sentence does not. The second sentence follows the two rules for noun clauses: the noun clause begins with a subordinator, *how*, and the subject *Mike* comes before the verb *likes*.

Usually, when we rewrite questions as noun clauses, we are able to find the subordinator in the question. For example, in the previous noun clause sentences, the question words *when* and *how* are used as subordinators. Here are two more examples in which the question word and the subordinator are the same.

Question:	Bill asked, "*Where* is next week's work schedule?"
Noun clause:	Bill asked *where* next week's work schedule is.
Question:	The manager asked, "*Why* weren't the paychecks ready at noon?"
Noun clause:	The manager asked *why* the paychecks weren't ready at noon.

Practice

Practice reporting questions by changing the following quoted questions to noun clauses. Use the question word as a subordinator and write the subject and verb in the normal order.

Question:	The secretary asked, "When did Mr. Ryan arrive?"
Noun clause:	The secretary asked _____
	_____

Question:	Lydia asked, "Where will the meeting be held?"
Noun clause:	Lydia asked _____
	_____

Question:	Gary asked, "Why hasn't Fran applied for a promotion yet?"
Noun clause:	Gary asked _____
	_____

Practice answers:

1. The secretary asked when Mr. Ryan arrived.
2. Lydia asked where the meeting will be held.
3. Gary asked why Fran hasn't applied for a promotion yet.

Adding a Subordinator

Sometimes, however, the question does not begin with a question word like *when, how, where, why,* or *who.* Sometimes, a question begins with a helping verb. Look at the following examples:

Question: Mrs. Petersen asked, "Have the secretaries ordered the office supplies?"

Question: Paul asked, "Are the applications for promotion ready to be typed?"

Questions like these are usually answered with a "yes" or a "no." These "yes" or "no" questions begin with helping verbs such as *have, did,* and *are*; they do not contain a question word that can be used as a subordinator in a noun clause. When we rewrite these questions as noun clauses, we add a subordinator, either **if** or **whether**. Study the correct sentences below in which each of the two questions has been rewritten twice.

Noun clause: Mrs. Petersen asked *if* the secretaries have ordered the office supplies yet.

Noun clause: Mrs. Petersen asked *whether* the secretaries have ordered the office supplies yet.

Noun clause: Paul asked *if* the applications for promotion are ready to be typed.

Noun clause: Paul asked *whether* the applications for promotion are ready to be typed.

Practice

Practice reporting questions by changing the following quoted questions to noun clauses. Add *if* or *whether* as a subordinator and write the subject and verb in the normal order.

Question: Charlene asked, "Did Marlene type the book order?"

Noun clause: Charlene asked _____

_____

Question: The custodian asked, "Has anyone found the supply room key?"

Noun clause: The custodian asked _____

_____

Question: The customer asked, "Will the store be open on Sunday?"

Noun clause: The customer asked _____

_____

Practice answers:

1. Charlene asked if [or whether] Marlene typed [or had typed] the book order.
2. The custodian asked if [or whether] anyone has found the supply room key.
3. The customer asked if [or whether] the store will be open on Sunday.

Changing Pronouns

You have learned that sometimes you must add a subordinator when you rewrite a question as a noun clause. Sometimes you must also change one or more pronouns. Study the following examples:

Question: The young man asked, "What benefits can the company offer me?"

Noun clause: The young man asked what benefits the company can offer him.

Question: Mr. Mellerson asked Sue, "When will you interview the applicants?"

Noun clause: Mr. Mellerson asked Sue when she will interview the applicants.

Question: Our boss asked us, "Have you signed up for the new dental plan?"

Noun clause: My boss asked us if we have signed up for the new dental plan.

Noun clause: My boss asked us whether we have signed up for the new dental plan.

Punctuating Quoted Questions and Noun Clauses

You have probably noticed differences in the way that the questions and noun clauses are punctuated.

The previous examples of direct quotations, all questions, follow three punctuation rules:

1. The quoted question is enclosed in quotation marks.
2. The question ends with a question mark followed by quotation marks.
3. A comma separates the quotation from the words that introduce the quotation. However, if the speaker is identified after the quoted question, no comma is necessary. See these examples:

Frank asked, "Did Alan work yesterday?"
"Did Alan work yesterday?" Frank asked.

Unlike the quoted questions, the sentences with noun clauses do not contain quotation marks or a question mark or a comma. Consider the following example:

Frank asked if Alan worked yesterday.

- We do not need quotation marks here because the sentence does not contain Frank's exact words.
- We do not need a question mark because *if Alan worked yesterday* is not a question.
- Finally, we do not separate the noun clause from the rest of the sentence with a comma.

Practice

Rewrite the following questions as noun clause sentences:

1. Nancy asked me, "When will you be working next week?"

_____

_____

2. Brad asked Tanya, "Are you going to New York tomorrow?"

_____

_____

3. Mrs. Hudson asked Robert, "Can you work for me on Saturday afternoon?"

_____

_____

Compare your sentences with these answers:

1. Nancy asked me when I will be working next week. (Notice the pronoun changes.)
2. Brad asked Tanya if [or _whether_] she is going to New York tomorrow. (Here we added a subordinator, _if_ or _whether_, and changed the pronouns.)
3. Mrs. Hudson asked Robert _if_ [or _whether_] he can work for her on Saturday afternoon. (Again, we added a subordinator and changed the pronouns.)

Changing Quoted Statements to Noun Clauses

We can also use noun clauses to report statements. When we do, we usually begin the noun clauses with the subordinator _that_. (The word _that_ does not begin the direct quotations; we add it.)

Look at the pair of sentences that follow:

Quoted statement: The manager said, "This inventory must be finished by noon."

Noun clause: The manager said that this inventory must be finished by noon.

While the two sentences present the same information, they do the job in two different ways. The quotation presents the exact words of the manager. The noun clause in the second sentence reports what the manager said without giving the exact words; the manager did not say _that the inventory must be finished_. Notice that the second sentence follows the two noun clause rules:

1. The noun clause begins with a subordinator, _that_. (Sometimes, in informal speech and writing, we omit the subordinator _that_.)
2. The word order in the noun clause is subject, then verb: _inventory must be finished_.

Changing quoted statements to noun clauses sometimes requires pronoun changes. Study the following pairs of sentences, noticing the pronouns:

Quotation: Mr. Taylor told Ms. Henson, "You will receive medical and dental insurance."

Noun clause: Mr. Taylor told Ms. Henson that she will receive medical and dental insurance.

Quotation: Ned replied, "I will interview the applicants on Thursday."

Noun clause: Ned replied that he will interview the applicants on Thursday.

Quotation: The union members answered, "We have all signed up for the new dental plan."

Noun clause: The union members answered that they have all signed up for the new dental plan.

Punctuating Quoted Statements and Noun Clauses

The punctuation rules for quotations are similar to the rules for punctuating questions. The important difference is that whereas the question ended with a question mark, the statement ends with a period.

1. The statement is enclosed in quotation marks.
2. The statement ends with a period. (The period is placed inside the quotation marks.)
3. A comma separates the statement from the words that introduce the statement.

Bill stated, "Alan worked a double shift yesterday."
"Alan worked a double shift yesterday," stated Bill.

Practice

Rewrite the following quotations as noun clause sentences. Then compare your sentences with the answers that follow.

1. The personnel manager stated, "The starting salary is $5.00 per hour."

_____

_____

2. Ms. Franklin replied, "I can start work on Monday."

_____

_____

3. Ben told Mrs. Connors, "I will be late for work on Tuesday morning."

_____

_____

Here are the answers:

1. The personnel manager stated that the starting salary is $5.00 per hour.
2. Ms. Franklin replied that she can start work on Monday.
3. Ben told Mrs. Connors that he will be late for work on Tuesday.

> **Do exercises 14-d and 14-e**

RECOGNIZING VERBALS AS NOUN SUBSTITUTES

Like a noun clause, a **verbal phrase** can be substituted for a noun. You have seen how all the words in a noun clause work together to build a single idea that does the job of a noun. The words of a verbal phrase perform the same function: they name an action that can be used in place of a noun or pronoun. Two kinds of verbals are used to name actions and thus can be used as we use nouns.

One kind of verbal noun is the *infinitive*. An infinitive can be constructed by adding the word *to* in front of the main form of the verb as in the following examples:

to go	to tell	to sell	to move
to swim	to vote	to stay	to creep
to study	to walk	to practice	to answer

The second kind of verbal noun is called a *gerund*. A gerund is the present participle (*-ing* form) of a verb as in the following examples:

going	telling	selling	moving
swimming	voting	staying	creeping
studying	walking	practicing	answering

Look at these examples of verbals used as nouns:

1. *Subject*:   *To swim* was his ambition.
2. *Subject complement*:   His ambition was *to swim*.
3. *Direct object*:   He liked *to swim*.
4. *Subject*:   *Swimming* was his goal.
5. *Subject complement*:   His goal was *swimming*.
6. *Direct object*:   She enjoys *swimming*.
7. *Object of a preposition*: After *swimming*, she walked to the beach house.

Each of these verbals can be expanded into a phrase. These verbal phrases still have single functions as subjects, as direct objects, or as complements.

1. *Subject*:   *To swim across Lake Hiawatha in thirty minutes* was his ambition.
2. *Subject complement*:   His ambition was *to swim across Lake Hiawatha in thirty minutes*.
3. *Direct object*:   He liked *to swim alone in the early morning*.
4. *Subject*:   *Swimming well* was his goal.
5. *Subject complement*:   His goal was *swimming well*.
6. *Direct object*:   She enjoys *swimming alone in the early morning*.
7. *Object of a preposition*: After *swimming in the lake*, she walked to the beach house.

Do exercises 14-f and 14-g

SUGGESTIONS FOR WRITING

Use your journal to write about an argument or disagreement that you recently had with another person.

As you **plan** your paragraph, first make notes by writing sentences about what you and the other person said. Try to vary your sentences by using both direct quotations and noun clauses as you report the dispute. Now that you have made some notes about what happened, write a topic sentence in which you introduce the argument and your reaction to it: for example, *I was very upset by my argument with my mother last night about my curfew.* Review your notes to determine three specific things that upset you about the argument and then support each of your three ideas with specific ideas. When you have decided on your subtopics and examples, you are ready to build your paragraph.

Write sentences to develop your topic sentence idea, making sure that you include specific information, that you stick to your topic sentence idea, and that you follow your plan.

Finally, **edit** your sentences, paying particular attention to the punctuation and capitalization of sentences with direct quotations and with noun clauses.

NAME _____ **DATE** _____

I. In the following sentences, underline the whole noun clause and draw a circle around the subordinator.

EXAMPLES

Yesterday, my math instructor said (that) she would give a quiz on Wednesday.

I asked (if) I could take the quiz a day early.

═══

1. She then asked why I would miss Wednesday's class.

2. I explained that I had to work all day Wednesday.

3. I said that I work at a sporting goods store in the mall four nights a week.

4. She wondered why I would be missing her afternoon class.

5. I told her that my manager was going on vacation on Wednesday.

6. My manager had promised a raise to whoever would work his shift on

   Wednesday.

7. He said that he works from 9:00 A.M. to 5:00 P.M.

8. I decided that I needed that raise too badly to turn down the offer.

9. I told my instructor that I was sorry about missing the class.

10. Fortunately, she said that I could take the quiz on Thursday.

═══

II. Complete each noun clause by writing an appropriate subordinator in each of the blank spaces.

EXAMPLES

Yesterday, my supervisor asked me _____*whether*_____ I would like to learn to use the new word processor.

I told her ___*that*_____ I was very interested in computers.

═══

1. She asked _____ I could attend training sessions.

2. I replied _____ I had free time on Thursday afternoons.

3. She then asked _____ I would like a computer at my desk.

4. I answered _____ a computer would make my secretarial job much easier.

5. I wondered _____ I had been chosen to receive the new equipment.

NAME _____ DATE _____

Correct any of the sentences that are incorrect. Each error can be corrected in one of two ways:

- Change the order of the subject and verb in the noun clause.

  or

- Add a subordinator and then change the subject–verb order.

Write *C* by the number of any correct sentence.

EXAMPLES

_____ Richard asked Kim ~~would~~ she *if* like *would* to go out to dinner on Friday evening.

__*C*__ Kim told Richard that she had already made plans.

1. _____ Kelly wondered should she apply for the promotion.

2. _____ Her supervisor assured her that she had an excellent chance of being promoted.

3. _____ Ron asked his sister how many courses she planned to take in the spring.

4. _____ His sister wondered why was he interested in her college program.

5. _____ Last night, my mother asked me when was I going to start looking for a job.

6. _____ I told her that I had already found a job at the college.

7. _____ My grandmother always says whatever is on her mind.

8. _____ My grandfather once asked her why does she talk so much.

9. _____ Karen forgot that her sister Mary Ellen was arriving this morning.

10. _____ Mary Ellen wondered why wasn't Karen at the airport.

11. _____ Darryl wondered where was the newspaper.

12. _____ He wanted to find out did his girlfriend's basketball team win the championship.

13. _____ Christy will help whoever is having difficulty with the math problems.

14. _____ She says that she enjoys explaining the problems to other students.

15. _____ Mr. Jones wonders how did he ever manage without his assistant.

NAME _____ **DATE** _____

In each blank space, write a noun clause to complete the sentence. Be sure that your noun clause is correctly constructed and that it makes sense.

EXAMPLES

The salesperson asked me   *if I needed any help.* _____

I told her   *that I was doing very well on my own.* _____

---

1. I asked my mechanic _____

2. My mechanic told me _____

3. During the history lecture, Sarah wondered _____
   _____

4. Sarah's instructor explained that _____
   _____

5. After the movie, the twins asked their father _____
   _____

6. Their father told them _____

7. My son's teacher wanted to know _____
   _____

8. I said _____

9. I asked Uncle Henry _____

10. Uncle Henry stated _____

11. Evelyn asked her brother _____

12. Evelyn's brother replied _____

13. The customer asked the waitress _____
    _____

14. The waitress answered _____

15. The customer wondered _____

NAME _____ DATE _____

Change each direct quotation in the following conversation into a noun clause that explains what was said.

EXAMPLES

I asked my cousin Linda, "Do you still work in your father's office?"

_____*I asked my cousin Linda if she still works in her father's office.*_____

She replied, "I quit my office job in 1987."

_____*She had replied that she quit her office job in 1987.*_____

1. I asked Linda, "Did you find another job?"

   _____

2. She answered, "Now I make doll house furniture and sell it in my own shop."

   _____

   _____

3. I asked her, "Where is your shop located?"

   _____

   _____

4. She told me, "I have one shop in New York City, and I am planning to open another shop in White Plains."

   _____

   _____

5. She explained, "I have become so busy that my father and mother are now working for me."

   _____

   _____

6. She added, "I have begun to send my furniture to stores in Pennsylvania and New Jersey."

   _____

   _____

NAME _____ **DATE** _____

In each of the eight parts of this exercise, you will write a pair of sentences: first a sentence with a noun clause and then a direct quotation.

- First, report what someone asked or said using the given verb and subordinator.
- Second, communicate the same information using a direct quotation. Punctuate the direct quotation correctly.

EXAMPLES

asked when

Noun clause: _The teacher asked when we will finish the assignment._

Direct quotation: _The teacher asked, "When will you finish the assignment?"_

stated that

Noun clause: _Bill Baxter stated that he will be finished on Monday._

Direct quotation: _Bill Baxter stated "I will be finished on Monday."_

1. asked when

   Noun clause: _____

   _____

   Direct quotation: _____

   _____

2. asked where

   Noun clause: _____

   _____

   Direct quotation: _____

   _____

3. asked who

   Noun clause: _____

   _____

Direct quotation: _____

_____

4. asked why

Noun clause: _____

_____

Direct quotation: _____

_____

5. asked how

Noun clause: _____

_____

Direct quotation: _____

_____

6. asked if

Noun clause: _____

_____

Direct quotation: _____

_____

7. said that

Noun clause: _____

_____

Direct quotation: _____

_____

8. stated that

Noun clause: _____

_____

Direct quotation: _____

_____

NAME _____ **DATE** _____

In each sentence, underline the verbal phrase used as a noun.

EXAMPLES

After losing their fifth game, the baseball team was extremely discouraged.

The team was determined to win the next home game.

1. David hates to walk the dog in the rain.

2. Delivering pizzas was Helen's first job.

3. Before leaving the party, Ron drank three cups of coffee.

4. My nephew has decided to quit his job at the music store.

5. Ellen offered to drive her brother to the movies.

6. Justin enjoys throwing his baby brother's toys out the window.

7. My aunt lost twenty pounds by swimming a half mile three times a week.

8. Spending our vacation at home was an excellent idea.

9. Tina wants to visit her cousins in Norway.

10. The twins are responsible for vacuuming the living room.

11. Larry is excited about moving to California.

12. Dr. Russell's ambition is to establish an animal hospital in her hometown.

13. Washing his father's truck is Billy's favorite job.

14. After reading for three hours, Shannon needed a break.

15. Brian enjoys selling flowers at the market.

16. My greatest accomplishment was graduating from high school.

17. Inviting Gary to the party was a mistake.

18. The reporter wanted to interview my manager after the robbery.

19. After riding the exercise bike, Sue watched the news on television.

20. The candidate refused to explain her position on abortion.

21. Taking care of the triplets is a tremendous job.

22. My daughter wants to babysit for her five-year-old cousin.

23. I couldn't help laughing at the teacher's answer.

24. My parents' plan is to move to a larger apartment next summer.

25. Kim learned French by living in Paris for a year.

NAME _____ DATE _____

Complete each sentence by writing an appropriate verbal noun in each blank space. Be sure that your sentence makes sense.

EXAMPLES

The nurse tried *to entertain* the little boy.

Walking is Margie's favorite exercise.

1. After _____ her paper, Anna proofread it carefully.

2. Nick decided _____ his motorcycle to his sister.

3. My grandmother's most difficult decision was to stop _____.

4. My father is tired of _____ the house every summer.

5. After _____ our apartment, the landlord raised the rent.

6. The plumber tried _____ the leaking faucet.

7. _____ was too difficult for Janet.

8. By _____ , Claudia passed her math course.

9. _____ dishes is my little brother's responsibility.

10. The student aide enjoys _____ quizzes for the instructors.

11. The teacher's decision was _____ the test.

12. My sister is teaching her second grade students _____ a computer.

13. The kitten's favorite game is _____ with string.

14. Kelly's goal is _____ college next year.

15. Before _____ the essay question, Virginia wrote an outline.

16. After _____ the chicken, my brother made the gravy.

17. Walter is nervous about _____ to the dentist.

18. _____ as a waitress can be very profitable.

19. My neighbor hates _____ his lawn.

20. The students in my biology class always postpone _____ their lab reports.

Maintaining Continuity

Verbs in Sequence

15

In Chapters 9 through 14, you have worked on coordinating and subordinating ideas. That is, you have combined ideas of equal importance and ideas of unequal importance to form single sentences and groups of sentences which support a topic sentence.

Now that you are beginning to write paragraphs, you need to learn to edit them, to read them over carefully and correct your mistakes. In particular, you need to pay attention to your **verb sequence**—the verb forms that you use one after another—to make sure that the sequence makes sense and establishes clear relationships among your ideas. These relationships are important to the **continuity** of your thought; they help the reader understand how one idea relates to another.

In this chapter, you will learn to pay attention to the relationships among ideas so you can make correct decisions about tense. If you need to review the verb forms or tenses, return to Chapters 5, 6, and 7.

USING COORDINATE VERBS

When you write sentences with compounds of two verbs or a series, all the verbs should usually be in the same tense. That is, the tense should be **consistent**. Shifting from tense to tense within compounded verbs confuses the reader. Compare the following examples of consistent and inconsistent verb tense.

Consistent verb tense (correct):	The new students *completed* their registration forms, *met* their advisers, and *took* pretests in math and English.
Inconsistent verb tense (incorrect):	The new students *completed* their registration forms, *met* their advisors, and *take* pretests in math and English.
Consistent verb tense (correct):	Charles *filled* out his application, *updated* his resume, and *scheduled* an interview with the personnel manager.
Inconsistent verb tense (incorrect):	Charles *fills* out his application, *updated* his resume, and *scheduled* an interview with the personnel manager.

In each of the correct sentences, the verbs are in the same tense, and the sequence is logical. In each of the incorrect sentences, one verb is written in a different tense, and this inconsistency is confusing.

Remember that, when you write several coordinate verbs in a tense that requires a helping verb, you do not have to repeat the helper. However, you must be consistent: use the helper only with the first verb, or use it with each verb. Repeating it before each verb emphasizes the helper.

Correct:	Before we leave tomorrow, I *will cancel* the newspaper, *ask* the neighbor to pick up our mail, and *take* the dog to the kennel.
	or
	Before we leave tomorrow, I *will cancel* the newspaper, *will ask* the neighbor to pick up our mail, and *will take* the dog to the kennel.
Incorrect:	Before we leave tomorrow, I *will cancel* the newspaper, *will ask* the neighbor to pick up our mail, and *take* the dog to the kennel.
Correct:	In the past five years, I *have worked* as a cashier in a super-market, *painted* houses, and *sold* vacuum cleaners.
	or
	In the past five years, I *have worked* as a cashier in a super-market, *have painted* houses, and *have sold* vacuum cleaners.
Incorrect:	In the past five years, I *have worked* as a cashier in a super-market, *painted* houses, and *have sold* vacuum cleaners.

Do exercise 15-a

USING VERBS IN COMPOUND SENTENCES

When you write a compound sentence, you use at least two verbs. You must be sure that the verb sequence in the clauses is logical.

When, as in the following examples, the actions in the clauses occur at the same time, the verbs are written in the same tense.

1. Tom's new hobby, making stained glass decorations, *is* very profitable; he *earns* from five to ten dollars on each finished product.
2. The Jordans *wanted* to go to the movies last night, but Mr. Jordan *had* to work.

However, the verbs in a compound sentence are not always written in the same tense. When one action happens (or happened) before another, the tenses should change to indicate this change to the reader. In each of the following compound sentences, the action in the first clause took place before the action in the second clause. The change in tense is necessary to indicate this change in time.

1. Rose and Wanda *had* never *gone* horseback riding before, but they *had* no problems with the two horses.
2. I *have* never *pulled* a trailer before, but I *will rent* a U-Haul to move my be-longings to my new apartment.

The reader is often alerted to the shift in tense by adverbs—words, phrases, or subordinate clauses—that indicate when the action takes place. In the two pre-vious sentences, the word *before* alerts the reader. Which adverbs indicate time in the following sentences?

1. I *caulked* the bathtub this morning; tomorrow, I *will tile* the floor.
2. Yesterday afternoon, my sister *arrived* in town for the reunion, but my brother *will* not *arrive* until late tomorrow night.

Do exercise 15-b

USING VERBS IN COMPLEX SENTENCES

Verb sequence is particularly important in complex sentences. When the sequence is logical, it helps to establish the relationship of the clauses; when the sequence is not logical, it confuses the reader.

Complex Sentences with Adverb Clauses

Sometimes the sense of a complex sentence with an adverb clause requires that the verbs in the clauses be written in the same tense. When, as in the next two examples, both clauses describe actions that occurred at the same time or one after the other in the past, both verbs are written in the past tense.

1. I *missed* a week of work when I *served* on a jury.
2. Stanley *missed* the exam in his 8:50 class on Friday because he *had* a flat tire.

When both clauses describe actions that happen regularly, they are both written in the present tense:

1. After the students *complete* a quiz, the teacher *corrects* it in class.
2. Whenever my secretary *answers* the phone, he *leaves* a message on my desk.

Often, however, the actions described in the main and in the subordinate clauses happen at different times, and a change of tenses is necessary. Consider **why** the tense changes in each of the following complex sentences:

1. Because Joe *had* not *turned* in his research paper on time, he *received* an incomplete for the course.
2. Nora *has seen* her brother twice since he *moved* to New Mexico three years ago.

In sentence 1, Joe failed to turn in the paper before he received the incomplete. In sentence 2, Nora's brother moved at a particular time in the past, but her visits with him have occurred over a three-year period.

Practice

In each of the complex sentences that follow, the actions described in the two clauses take (or took) place at different times. Pay attention to the time indicators, and fill in an appropriate form of the verb given in parentheses.

1. (take)   After I *had finished* painting the living room, I _____ a break.

2. (hide)   I *stayed* home from school yesterday because my little brother _____ my car keys.

3. (move)   Carson *has been working* at the bike shop since he _____ to Greenlawn in 1982.

4. (leave)   Every afternoon as soon as Barbara *finishes* her last class she _____ for work.

5. (arrive) If you _____ late, you *are* not *permitted* to enter the classroom.

251

Check your verbs:

    1. took   2. had hidden   3. moved   4. leaves   5. arrive

Complex Sentences with Adjective Clauses

An adjective clause, like an adverb clause, is written in the same tense as the main clause when the two actions happen (or happened) at the same time. When both actions took place in the past, the verbs are both written in the past tense.

1. Marcia, who *graduated* from Western High School, *was* proud of her high honors.
2. Kevin *borrowed* the book that you *wanted* to read.

Sometimes both clauses describe actions that happen regularly. In complex sentences of this type, both verbs are written in the present tense.

1. Dr. Brown, who *covers* for Dr. Hall on Fridays, *sees* patients at the professional building on Cedar Street.
2. Every summer, my cousin Claire, who *works* as a social worker in Philadelphia, *spends* three weeks in Oregon.

On many occasions, however, you will find it necessary to change to another tense for your second clause. Consider the meaning of the following sentences:

1. Mrs. Clark, who *had* never *held* a job outside her home, *was* not aware of her many talents.
2. Dr. Ripple, who *has taught* speech at Jefferson High School for thirty-five years, *will retire* in June.
3. The dress that I *will wear* to the party *is hanging* in the hall closet.

Practice

In each complex sentence that follows, a change in tense is necessary to establish a logical relationship between the main clause and the adjective clause. Pay attention to the time indicators, and fill in the blanks with an appropriate form of the verbs given in parentheses. Add helping verbs where necessary.

1. (need)   The bookstore *has run* out of the book that I _____ for my English course this semester.
2. (stay)   The strikers, who _____ off the job for the past two weeks, *are demanding* better retirement benefits.
3. (order) Sam, who *had been driving* for three hours, _____ a cup of coffee and a sandwich.
4. (found) Ed, who *quit* his job at the bakery in March, _____ still not _____ a new job.
5. (return)The reference librarian, who *can help* you with your research, _____ in fifteen minutes.

Now check your verbs:

1 need *or* will need   2. have stayed   3. ordered   4. has . . . found
5. will return

Complex Sentences with Noun Clauses

Since a complex sentence with a noun clause is often used to report something that was said or thought, the verb in the main clause is often written in the past tense. However, the verb in the noun clause may be in the present tense to indicate that an action takes place regularly or in the present, as in these examples:

1. She *said* that she *is* usually free on Fridays.
2. The child *would* not *believe* that the earth *is* round.
3. He *asked* whether the country *is experiencing* an economic recovery.

The verb in the noun clause may also be written in the past tense if both actions occurred in the past:

1. The supervisor *asked* why the typists *were* not at their desks.
2. Gail *wondered* if her notebook *was* in the lab.

More often, a noun clause describes a situation in which a person reports or questions something that has already happened. The clauses are then written in different tenses.

1. The instructor *asked* if the students *had* already *finished* their exercises.
2. Gail *wondered* if the check *had bounced*.

In each case, someone questioned something that had already taken place. The change in tense makes the time relationship clear to the reader.

Sometimes a noun clause is used to report what a person said or asked about something that has not yet happened. In complex sentences of this type, we use *will* or *would* as a helper with the verb in the noun clause.

1. Mr. Chase *asked* where the committee *will meet*.
2. Catherine *wondered* when she *would find* a job.

Do exercise 15-c

SEQUENCING VERBS IN PARAGRAPHS

When you write paragraphs, you need to use a verb sequence that will allow your reader to understand what you mean. In some paragraphs, all the verbs should be in the same tense. For instance, you may write a description of an event that occurred in the past and use the past tense for all of your verbs. Or you may describe an event that occurs regularly and use the present tense for all of your verbs.

Past Events in the Past Tense

I *spent* most of today in my car. This morning, I *gave* my neighbor a ride to work. I then *stopped* at the library, the hardware store, and the supermarket. At noon, I *picked* up my daughter at a friend's house and *took* her to the dentist. When I *returned* home, I *received* a phone call from my son, who *needed* a ride home from school. When my wife *arrived* home and *asked* me if I *wanted* to go out for a drive, I *laughed*.

All of the actions in this paragraph happened in the past, on the same day, and in the order in which they are given; therefore, all the verbs are in the past tense.

253

Sunday morning *is* the most relaxing time of my week. When I *awake* at nine A.M., I *brew* a full pot of coffee. I then *walk* five blocks to the bakery, where I *buy* a half dozen doughnuts, and, on my way home, I *stop* at the drug store for a newspaper. When I *return* home, the smell of the coffee *welcomes* me to the kitchen, where I *read*, *relax*, and *eat* until noon.

In other passages, you may find it necessary to change tense several times. In the following series of sentences, the writer used several different tenses because the actions occurred at different times. Notice what time indicators prepare the reader for changes of tense.

Events at Different Times

My friend Mary *runs* more than anyone I know. She often *runs* twenty miles in one day. So far this week, she *has run* fifty miles. When I *phoned* her yesterday, her husband *said* that she *was running* around Wilde Lake. I *wonder* if she *will run* in the Boston Marathon next year.

Practice

Pay attention to the time indicators in the following passage. Fill in each blank with an appropriate form of the verb *drink*, using helpers when necessary.

Marvin _____ only vegetable or fruit juices. He _____

never _____ an alcoholic beverage. Last night, he _____

a pint of orange juice and a pint of grape juice. When he goes out with his

brothers, they _____ beer, but he _____ carrot juice.

These are the verbs in order:

drinks   has . . . drunk   drank   drink   drinks

> **Do exercises 15-d and 15-e**

SUGGESTIONS FOR WRITING

Now **plan** a paragraph about one particularly busy day. You might write a paragraph for the topic sentence *Last Monday was the busiest day I have had in many months*. As you consider this day, decide on the three activities that made it especially hectic. Then develop each of these three ideas with sentences which explain exactly what you did. Jot down these subtopics and examples.

Write a paragraph which supports your topic sentence. As you follow your plan, be as specific as possible about what you did and make sure that you always support the idea that you were extremely busy. End your paragraph with a closing sentence such as *I am very glad that every Wednesday is not as hectic as last Wednesday was*.

Now **edit** your sentences. Because you are writing about a specific day in the past, all of your sentences should be written in the *past* tense.

NAME _____ **DATE** _____

I. To each sentence, add a coordinate verb and its complements and modifiers. Make sure that your verb is in the same tense as the two other verbs.

EXAMPLE

The work crew cut down the trees, sawed off the branches, and *removed*

the debris. _____

1. Every morning, Randy wakes up, puts on his slippers, lets the dog out, and _____

_____.

2. Before school, Georgette cooks breakfast, cleans the kitchen, and _____

_____.

3. The three children rushed in the door, threw off their coats, and _____

_____.

4. Grant went to the garden shed, set out the rake and mower, and _____

_____.

5. Before starting to write the paper, Hank cleaned off his desk, set his notes near at

hand, and _____

_____.

II. Write three sentences of your own, each containing three coordinate verbs. Make sure that the verbs in each sentence are written in the same tense.

1. _____

_____

_____

2. _____

_____

_____

3. _____

_____

NAME _____ **DATE** _____

I. Complete each of the following compound sentences by adding a verb. Make sure that the verb sequence is logical and that you have paid attention to the time indicators.

EXAMPLE

Esther is a vegetarian, but her sister _____*eats*_____ meat twice a day.

1. The train left, but Debbie's mother _____ not _____ crying.

2. Three voters were waiting in line, but none of them _____ to each other.

3. Either Sidney broke the vase and hid the pieces, or someone _____ it during the night.

4. The neighborhood garage sale had been over for an hour; however, none of the participants _____ to clean up.

5. Eric was thrilled to see his cousins after all these years, and he _____ almost unable to speak.

6. Jan enjoys a large party, but Paul _____ to spend time at home with his wife and children.

II. Complete each of the following compound sentences by adding a second coordinate clause. Make sure that your verb sequence is logical.

EXAMPLE

Kevin left work an hour early, but *he was delayed by the storm.*_____

1. Ben usually leaves for work before 7:30 in the morning, but _____

_____.

2. Gail cleans her kitchen very slowly and carefully, but _____

_____.

3. Three members of the audience stood up at the same time, and _____

_____.

4. Melvin had never visited New Orleans, and _____

_____.

5. Jack's new stereo system did not have the sound quality he wanted; therefore, _____

_____.

NAME _____ **DATE** _____

I. In each of the complex sentences below, use an appropriate form of the verb
next to the number to fill in the blank. The verb form should help clarify a logical
relationship between the main clause and the subordinate clause. (The verb you
add may include helpers to provide tense or condition of the action.)

EXAMPLE

take   Robert had studied for three years before he ___*took*___ the entrance
            exam.

---

ring   1. Before we arrived, the last bell _____ already _____ .

drink   2. Although my sister has been to many college parties, she _____

               never _____ any alcoholic beverage.

lose   3. Charolene left the room as if she _____ her best friend.

become   4. Eddie _____ angry at his aunt long before he left home.

hurt   5. Steven _____ his foot when he fell from the window.

II. Complete each of the following complex sentences by adding a clause. Each
sentence should be about your experiences at work or at school. Pay close attention to the tense of the verbs.

EXAMPLE

I wonder if _*I will ever find a satisfying job.*_____

---

1. Before I began, I had decided that _____

   _____ .

2. After I had been there for a few weeks, my work became easier because _____

   _____

3. I would be happier if _____

   _____

4. I would enjoy working for someone who _____

   _____ .

NAME _____ **DATE** _____

The following short passages require verbs in different tenses because the actions happen (or happened) at different times.

- Read through each passage, paying close attention to time indicators.
- In the blank spaces, write the correct forms of the verb whose principal parts are given at the top of the passage.
- Use helping verbs whenever necessary. Be sure the verbs agree with the subjects.

EXAMPLE

Principal parts: *see, saw, seen, seeing*

Last week, Bill ____*saw*____ a red-headed woodpecker. It was the first one he

____*had*____ ever ____*seen*____. He ____*saw*____ it in his aunt's back yard.

1. Principal parts: *see, saw, seen, seeing*

   When Sadie and David went to Yellowstone National Park last year, they

   _____ not _____ a single grizzly bear. However, they

   _____ several small herds of buffalo. They also _____

   several moose and a few elk. They remained disappointed that they _____

   not _____ a bear.

2. Principal parts: *drive, drove, driven, driving*

   Marilyn's father often _____ to Salt Lake City to hear the Utah

   symphony. He _____ _____ there every month for the

   past year. He first _____ there in 1980. He _____

   _____ there again next week.

3. Principal parts: *buy, bought, bought, buying*

   How often _____ you _____ expensive clothes on impulse?

   My friend Bonnie _____ at least two pieces of clothing every time

   she goes out. Last week, she _____ a pair of running shoes and a

   blouse. She_____ probably _____ something right now.

4. Principal parts: *run, ran, run, running*

Hugh and Bill _____ now_____ twice a week. They

_____ not _____ enough last year and lost time in the

running part of the Bud Light Triathlon. They usually_____ through

my neighborhood. When I saw them Tuesday evening, they _____

_____ _____ for over an hour.

5. Principal parts: *choose, chose, chosen, choosing*

Next Tuesday, the students in my dorm _____ _____a new

representative to the student council. For the past two years, we _____

_____ the wrong person; each one attended only two out of six

meetings of the council. These representatives _____ _____

by a small number of the dorm residents. I hope we have a good turnout next

week and that someone reliable _____ _____ _____ .

6. Principal parts: *give, gave, given, giving*

My friend Jack always _____ generous gifts. Last year, he_____

a new suit to his brother for a high school graduation gift. When his sister

graduates from college next spring, he _____ _____ her a set

of luggage. He never _____ a gift which did not surprise his family.

7. Principal parts: *bring, brought, brought, bringing*

I never_____ the right clothes with me when I go on vacation. Last

summer, when I went to England, I _____ jeans and sweaters. When

the temperature hit 95 degrees, I wished that I _____ _____

shorts and tee shirts. Last Christmas, when I went to Florida, I _____

light slacks and a light jacket; I had to buy sweatshirts and jeans because the

temperature dipped below freezing. Now that I am packing for a summer

vacation in Maine, I am sure that I_____ _____ the right

clothes because I have packed four suitcases.

NAME _____ **DATE** _____

    Read through the following passages so that you understand the sequence of events. Then correct each misused verb by drawing a line through it and writing your correction above it or by adding a helping verb.

EXAMPLE

    My mother ~~has~~ once advised me never to shop on an empty stomach. She

warned
~~warns~~ me that if I ~~was~~ hungry when I go to buy clothes, I ~~might~~ be in a hurry to
             am   *may*

can   *may*
make choices so that I ~~could~~ return home to eat. Some of these choices ~~might have~~

be
~~been~~ wrong, so I may have to return later to exchange them. Shopping for gro-

is   *said*
ceries ~~has been~~, she ~~says~~, particularly dangerous. To someone with an empty stom-

looks
ach, everything ~~looked~~ good. Not only do hungry shoppers buy too much; they

buy
also ~~bought~~ unusual and often expensive foods.

═══

    Last week, I remembered my mother's warnings. I am later than usual leaving work and decide to stop at a supermarket to buy something fresh for supper. As I pull into the parking lot, the window of a discount clothing store catches my eye. "Savings up to 60%," the sign read. I quickly decided to stop in to see these bargains. I am becoming hungrier by the minute, but I pushed on. I had grabbed two cotton sports sweaters and am looking around for a dressing room when a red suit catches my eye. It was beautifully tailored. It cost more even with the discount than I had ever paid for a suit before. I pick it off the rack anyway. It was grand, a true power suit. I leave the sweaters, bought the suit, and hurry toward the grocery store, but not fast enough. Hunger and vague feelings of guilt for spending so much on myself instead of my children were soon to take their toll. I fill a large basket with exotic fresh fruit, cookies, unusual juices, sugared cereals, dainty sweet rolls, three kinds of chips, a six-pack of Classic Coke, and one ready-to-eat barbecued chicken.

As I lift these purchases onto the cashier's counter, I realized that, except for the chicken, I had not bought any healthy food. Suddenly, I recalled my mother's warning. With a blushing face, I apologize to the cashier, puts my groceries back into the cart, and return the foods that were too expensive for my budget or that have little food value.

As I exchange my selections, I pondered my mother's advice. I certainly have made a mistake in the grocery store, but that does not mean I should return the red suit, too. So I kept it.

Maintaining Continuity

Pronoun Reference and Agreement

16

In Chapter 15, you practiced using the correct forms of verbs to maintain continuity in a paragraph. Using pronouns correctly is also important for establishing clear relationships. You have been using a variety of pronouns in the writing exercises in this book. (See Chapter 2.) As you write groups of sentences about one topic, you will probably find yourself using pronouns frequently. As you do so, you can maintain continuity by clear pronoun reference and consistent pronoun agreement.

UNDERSTANDING PRONOUN REFERENCE

A personal pronoun must refer to a particular person or thing. The **reference** of a pronoun is to the noun it stands for. You are aware that pronouns such as *he* or *she* must refer to a particular noun. You know that you cannot just walk up to someone and announce, "He needs help"—not unless you are pointing at the "him" with your finger. The pronoun *he* has no meaning unless it is in a sequence that clearly identifies who "he" is. You know that you cannot point in your writing; you must name the person you mean. Usually, the name of the person should come before the pronoun that refers to it.

Naming the Noun

As you use personal pronouns, be sure that you have actually used the noun to which the pronoun must refer. Study the following examples. In the first sentence of each pair, the italicized pronoun is used incorrectly because it does not refer to a particular noun. In the second sentence, the noun is named; the error in pronoun reference is corrected. (There are many possible corrections for this kind of error; the ones given here show some of the possibilities.)

Incorrect:	After the yellow Buick had changed lanes too quickly and caused an accident, *he* claimed that *he* had not seen a signal light on my grandmother's car.
Correct:	After the driver of the yellow Buick had changed lanes too quickly and caused an accident, he claimed he had not seen a signal light on my grandmother's car.
Incorrect:	In Poland, *they* had been under martial law since December 1981.
Correct:	Poland had been under martial law since December 1981.
Incorrect:	In the evening *Tribune, it* says that fifty steel workers have been laid off.
Correct:	The evening *Tribune* says that fifty steel workers have been laid off.
Correct:	In the evening *Tribune*, a reporter says that fifty steel workers have been laid off.

Using *It*, *This*, and *Which*

The three pronouns *it*, *this*, and *which* are sometimes carelessly used to refer to a whole preceding idea rather than to stand for a particular noun. When you look over your writing, you should watch for these pronouns; be sure that you have already used the noun for which they stand. If the pronouns do not refer to a specific noun, you may have to rebuild the sentence to eliminate the reference problem.

Study the following examples. In the first sentence of each pair, *it* or *this* or *which* does not refer to a particular noun. In the second, this reference error is corrected.

Incorrect: When sixty instead of six part-time openings were mistakenly announced in the school paper, *it* caused much confusion in the student personnel office.

Correct: The mistaken announcement in the school paper of sixty instead of six part-time openings caused much confusion in the student personnel office.

Correct: When sixty instead of six part-time openings were mistakenly announced in the school paper, the student personnel office was thrown into confusion.

Incorrect: Jack rarely repays his debts to friends, and *this* makes them distrust him.

Correct: Because Jack rarely repays his debts to friends, they distrust him.

Incorrect: No dates were given on the reports, *which* made them impossible to trace.

Correct: Because no dates were given on the reports, they were impossible to trace.

Do exercise 16-a

Referring to a Single Noun

In the following sentence, *he* clearly refers to the noun *Tom*:

Mary suggested to Tom that *he* needs help.

At times, however, you may find that you have used a pronoun which could refer to more than one noun. The **reference** of the pronoun is not clear. In the examples that follow, each pronoun could refer to either of two nouns:

1. Jason told Ted that *he* needed a vacation.
2. Margaret told Betty that *her* report had been hurriedly written.

In the first example, the reader does not know who needed the vacation, Jason or Ted; in the second, the reader does not know whose report had been hurriedly written, Margaret's or Betty's. These errors in pronoun reference can be eliminated by completely rewriting the sentences, or they can be corrected in one of two ways:

- By repeating the name of the person intended.
- By using a direct quotation.

1. (a) Jason told Ted that Jason needed a vacation.
   or
   Jason told Ted that Ted needed a vacation.
   (b) Jason told Ted, "I need a vacation."
   or
   Jason told Ted, "You need a vacation."
2. (a) Margaret told Betty that Margaret's report had been hurriedly written.
   or
   Margaret told Betty that Betty's report had been hurriedly written.
   (b) Margaret told Betty, "My report was hurriedly written."
   or
   Margaret told Betty, "Your report was hurriedly written."

Do exercise 16-b

Using First Person Plural Pronouns

The forms of the first person plural are *we, us, our,* and *ours.* These pronouns refer to the person speaking (I) plus some **specific other people.** When you use these forms to stand for yourself and others, be sure you identify exactly who those others are.

1. *My roommate and I* lost the keys to *our* apartment. *We* reported the loss to the caretaker, but he would not give *us* another set.
2. *Two other members of the class and I* were late for the examination. After *we* apologized to the instructor, he allowed *us* to stay and finish.

In these sentences, the reader knows exactly who "we" are. Failure to identify the others will make your writing unclear. In the following sentences, we are not told who the writer means by *we, us* and *our.*

Last Thursday, I learned the importance of using safety belts in automobiles. We had been visiting Aunt Rose in the hospital and decided to drive downtown for supper. As we got settled in Tom's car, two of us fastened our seat belts. However, my cousin Janet, who was the only passenger in the back seat, did not.

The situation is unclear. How many passengers were there? Who were they? Where were they sitting? By adding the answers to these questions, we specify the meanings of the pronouns and make the passage clear to the reader:

Last Thursday, I learned the importance of using safety belts in automobiles. My brother Tom, my cousin Janet, and I had been visiting Aunt Rose in the hospital and decided to drive downtown for supper. As we got settled in Tom's car, Tom and I fastened our seat belts. However, Janet, who was the only passenger in the back seat, did not.

UNDERSTANDING AGREEMENT

As you check your writing to make sure that each of your pronouns refers to a particular noun, you should also check for consistency among nouns and pronouns. You should make sure that all the nouns and pronouns that refer to the

265

same person or thing **agree** with each other; that is, you should make sure that you have not unnecessarily shifted from a singular to a plural or from one person to another.

Selecting Third Person Pronouns

In Chapter 2, you studied these forms of the third person pronouns and possessives:

	Subject	Object	Possessives
Masculine singular	he	him	his, his
Feminine singular	she	her	her, hers
Neuter singular	it	it	its
Plural	they	them	their, theirs

The third person is the one used most often in writing; we usually write **about** another person or persons or **about** places, things, or ideas.

We often use the third person singular to mean a kind of person, not a particular one. A noun that means a kind of person—a *student*, an *instructor*, a *boss*, an *employee*—does not have gender; that is, it can mean a male, a female, or both, as in the following sentence:

Each student should register before August 15.

A sentence such as this presents a special problem when we need a pronoun to refer back to *student*. English has no common pronoun that can stand for either male or female. Should we use *he, him, his* or *she, her, hers* to stand for *student*? Until recently, writers used the masculine forms as the common pronoun in sentences that form generalizations about a kind or type of person:

1. By August 15, each new *student* should submit the registration form *he* has completed.
2. A *person* who recognizes *his* weaknesses can begin to eliminate them.
3. An *employee* who wants to advance *himself* should become familiar with the company's personnel policies.

However, the women's movement has made most writers conscious of a sexual bias in this use of the masculine. Consequently, many writers now use double pronouns—"he or she," "his or her," and "himself or herself"—instead of the masculine alone:

1. By August 15, each new *student* should submit the registration form *he or she* has completed.
2. A *person* who recognizes *his or her* weaknesses can begin to eliminate them.
3. An *employee* who wants to advance *himself or herself* should become familiar with the company's personnel policies.

Double pronouns often make sentences sound awkward, especially if the double pronouns are repeated throughout a long passage. Consequently, writers often try to avoid them. In the first example above, for instance, we might avoid using a pronoun:

Each new student should submit a completed registration form by August 15.

The other two sentences might use the plural forms for both the nouns and the pronouns:

> *Persons* who recognize *their* weaknesses can begin to eliminate them.
> *Employees* who want to advance *themselves* should become familiar with the company's personnel policies.

Avoiding Shifts in the Third Person

Once you decide to generalize in the singular or the plural, you must be consistent. Be careful to avoid sentences that begin in the singular and shift to the plural. Shifts within a sentence can confuse the reader.

1. *Shifted pronoun*: A *person* who recognizes *their* weaknesses can begin to eliminate them.
2. *Shifted pronoun*: An *employee* who wants to advance *themselves* should become familiar with the company's personnel policies.

Shifts in a series of sentences can be even more confusing. Look at the example that follows, in which the writer has shifted from singular (*a student*) to plural (*their* and *they*), back to singular (*a late student*), and, finally, to plural (*they*) again. The nouns and pronouns in these sentences do not agree with each other.

Shifted pronouns

A *student* who registers late must pay *their* fees in person in the business office. *They* must also give each class card to *their* instructor at the beginning of the first class *they* attend. A *late student* is responsible for making up any work *they* may have missed.

We can correct the errors in agreement by writing all the nouns and pronouns either (1) in the third person singular or (2) in the third person plural.

Corrected: Singular

A *student* who registers late must pay *his or her* fees in person in the business office. *He or she* must also give each class card to *his or her* [or *the*] instructor at the beginning of the first class *he or she* attends. A *late student* is responsible for making up any work *he or she* may have missed.

Corrected: Plural

Students who register late must pay *their* fees in person in the business office. *They* must also give each class card *to their* instructor at the beginning of the first class *they* attend. *Late students* are responsible for making up any work *they* may have missed.

Do exercise 16-c

Avoiding Shifts to the Second Person

The forms of the second person—*you, your, yours*—should be used in writing to address the reader directly. The second person is used to give directions or instructions to the reader. Cookbooks or instructional texts such as this one frequently use the second person.

Because the word *you* occurs so frequently in speech, it can creep into your writing in inappropriate usages. As you check over your sentences, make sure that you have not shifted from third person pronouns such as *he, she, they* to second person pronouns. Study the shifts that occur in the following passage.

A *job seeker* often spends too little time on the cover letters that accompany *their* resumes. These letters are *your* first introduction to those who are screening applications. A *job seeker* should try to make the letters represent *their* best writing. *You* should be sure that *your* letters are clear and grammatically correct and that *your* letters reflect *your* abilities and interest in a particular position.

The shifts in this passage, highlighted by italics, can be eliminated by changing all the nouns and pronouns referring to them to the same number and person—to the third person singular ("a job seeker") or to the third person plural ("job seekers"). See the following revisions, first in the singular, then in the plural. (Note that the passage is repetitious and awkward in the singular because of all the double pronouns. If you choose to use the singular, you should eliminate the pronouns whenever possible.)

Corrected: Singular

A *job seeker* often spends too little time on the cover letters that accompany *his or her* resumes. These letters are *his or her* first introduction to those who are screening applications. A *job seeker* should try to make the letters represent *his or her* best writing. *He or she* should be sure that *his or her* [or *the*] letters are clear and grammatically correct and that they reflect *his or her* abilities and interest in a particular position.

Corrected: Plural

Job seekers often spend too little time on the cover letters that accompany *their* resumes. These letters are *their* first introduction to those who are screening applications. *Job seekers* should try to make the letters represent *their* best writing. *They* should be sure that *their* [or *the*] letters are clear and grammatically correct and that *their* [or *the*] letters reflect *their* abilities and interest in a particular position.

Do exercises 16-d and 16-e

SUGGESTIONS FOR WRITING

Throughout this book, we have suggested that you might use your journal to record experiences that you found especially pleasant or difficult.

Just as most people have endured interruptions to their studying or an unpleasant job, most people have suffered through an embarrassing experience. **Plan** a paragraph in which you describe an experience that embarrassed you. For example, you might begin with a topic sentence such as *I felt very embarrassed when my younger brother read my diary.* Now decide on your subtopics, perhaps the three aspects of the diary that embarrassed you, and develop each of these aspects in preliminary notes.

Use your plan as you **write** a paragraph to support your topic sentence. Include as many specific details as you can recall to make the point that you were very embarrassed.

Once you have written your paragraph, be sure that you **edit** it carefully, paying special attention to your verb sequence and your pronouns. Make sure that the reader always knows when an event happened and who was involved.

NAME _____ **DATE** _____

In each of the following sentences, the italicized pronoun has no noun to which it can refer. In the space provided, rewrite each sentence to eliminate the error in pronoun reference.

EXAMPLES

Della was an hour late on her first day at work, and *this* angered her boss.

Della was an hour late on her first day at work, and her lateness angered her boss.

or

When Della was an hour late on her first day at work, her boss was angry.

If your union representative does not call a meeting, *it* does not prevent you from calling one.

You can call a meeting even if your union representative does not call one.

or

If your union representative does not call a meeting, you can call one.

1. Uncle Randolph would not stop smoking, *which* resulted in his developing emphysema.

_____

_____

_____

2. As the driver turned left onto Center Street, *it* skidded on the ice and went up over the curb.

_____

_____

_____

3. Vida's parents are both teachers, but she does not want to study *it*.

_____

_____

4. Saul has worked in a biology lab for the past two summers, but he does not want to study *it* in school.

_____

_____

_____

5. When Paula returned at 2:00 A.M. with five noisy friends, *it* made her roommate very angry.

_____

_____

_____

6. In Tokyo, *they* celebrate Christmas with more parties and presents than the Americans do.

_____

_____

_____

7. The lab assistant could not find my lab report, *which* made the professor suspicious of me.

_____

_____

8. In my history book, *it* says that World War II, not Franklin D. Roosevelt, stopped the Great Depression.

_____

_____

_____

9. Thelda has collected stamps since she was five years old, but none of her children are interested in *it*.

_____

_____

_____

10. The math instructor had the students make up questions of their own, and *this* helped them learn the formulas.

_____

_____

_____

11. Margaret studies every night for six hours, *which* helps her learn the material and prepare questions for the next class.

_____

_____

_____

12. In Switzerland, *they* have many banks.

_____

_____

NAME _____ **DATE** _____

      Each of the sentences that follow contains an error in pronoun reference. The italicized pronoun could refer to more than one noun. Rewrite each sentence so that the reference of the pronoun is to one particular noun.

EXAMPLE

Leslie told Anna that *her* typewriter needed a new ribbon.

Leslie told Anna that Leslie's typewriter needed a new ribbon.

or

Leslie told Anna that Anna's typewriter needed a new ribbon.

or

Leslie told Anna, "My typewriter needs a new ribbon."

or

Leslie told Anna, "Your typewriter needs a new ribbon."

1. Alice reminded Shirley that *she* was to meet the visiting Russians at seven that evening.

   _____

   _____

2. Sid smiled at Walt, left the room, and returned *his* rented cap and gown.

   _____

   _____

3. Sally, who had left the steak and the hamburger on the kitchen counter to thaw, was shocked to come home and find that her dog had eaten *it*.

   _____

   _____

   _____

4. James told Frank that *his* stereo was broken.

   _____

   _____

5. The student aide suggested to Mary Ellen that *she* should be paid time and a half.

   _____

   _____

6. Sandra asked Sylvia if *she* should take the cat to the vet.

_____

_____

7. When the cat jumped on the dog, *it* was terrified.

_____

_____

8. Susan had left the computer and the printer running all morning, and *it* had become overheated.

_____

_____

9. Marilyn told Joan that *she* would never be able to pay her dentist's bill if she had all her teeth capped.

_____

_____

_____

10. After Daisy prepared her annual report, she explained to Ms. Hillsworth why *her* work had not improved.

_____

_____

_____

11. When Betty opened her purse to look for her address book, she noticed immediately that *it* was torn.

_____

_____

_____

NAME _____ **DATE** _____

In the following groups of sentences, nouns are repeated instead of being replaced by pronouns. Combine each group of sentences into one sentence, substituting appropriate subordinators and **third person singular** pronouns where necessary. Circle all the pronouns in your combinations.

As you combine the sentences, you will be building a paragraph to support the following topic sentence:

Topic Sentence: A college student who wants to learn should carefully collect and study the material for each class.

EXAMPLE

The student should prepare for each class.
The student should read the assigned text thoughtfully.
The student should underline important passages.
The student should prepare questions on any parts the student does not understand.

Combination: _The student should prepare for each class by reading the assigned_

text thoughtfully, underlining important passages, and preparing questions on

any parts he or she does not understand.

---

1. In class, the student should listen attentively.
   In class, the student should ask questions. The questions occur during the instructor's lecture.

   Combination: _____

   _____

   _____

   _____

2. In class, the student should also take orderly notes.
   The notes should be in an outline form.
   The outline form should reveal the relationships among ideas and information.

   Combination: _____

   _____

   _____

   _____

3. A new idea is presented in class.
   The student does not understand the new idea.
   The student writes down the idea.
   The student leaves empty lines after the new idea.

   Combination: _____

   _____

   _____

   _____

4. The empty space may be filled with an explanation.
   The explanation may be found in the textbook or other readings.
   The explanation may be given later in the class hour by the instructor.
   The later explanation may be in answer to the student's question.

   Combination: _____

   _____

   _____

   _____

5. After class, the student should carefully review the notes.
   The student took the notes in class.
   The student should also refer to the textbook for explanations of the difficult lecture material.
   The student did not understand this material.

   Combination: _____

   _____

   _____

   _____

NAME _____ **DATE** _____

I. The following paragraph is confusing because it contains several pronoun shifts. Correct the paragraph by using the **third person singular** throughout. Cross out the nouns, pronouns, and verbs you wish to change and write your correction above. The topic sentence is correct; the second sentence in the Paragraph has been corrected as an example.

═══

A single parent has many responsibilities. ~~They~~ *He or she* generally ~~have~~ *has* to work to

support ~~themselves~~ *himself or herself* and ~~their~~ *the* children. Before the single parent can leave for work

in the morning, ~~they~~ *he or she* may have to pick up a baby-sitter or deliver the children to a

day care center or school. After working a full day, the single parent has to return

home to a routine of cooking, cleaning, and caring for ~~their~~ *his or her* children. The single

parent may even be required to attend classes in the evening to improve ~~their~~ *his or her* job

skills. It is not surprising that a single parent often appears exhausted.

═══

II. Rewrite the paragraph using the **third person plural** throughout. The topic sentence has been written for you.

Single parents have many responsibilities. _____

_____

_____

_____

_____

_____

_____

_____

_____

_____

_____

NAME _____ **DATE** _____

I. Write three sentences of ten or more words each about things that are expected of a student. Write your sentences in the third person singular, carefully avoiding any shifts in person or number. Check subject–verb agreement.

EXAMPLE

   A student is expected to turn in his or her assignments on time.

1. _____

_____

2. _____

_____

3. _____

_____

II. Rewrite each of your sentences in the third person plural, carefully avoiding pronoun shifts. Check subject–verb agreement.

EXAMPLE

   Students are expected to turn in their assignments on time.

1. _____

_____

2. _____

_____

3. _____

_____

Avoiding Common Sentence Errors

17

Fragments, Comma Splices, and Run-on Sentences

As you have acquired more writing skills, you have learned to write longer, more complicated sentences which help to form a paragraph. You have also learned the importance of checking your writing for errors and correcting them. In Chapters 15 and 16, for instance, you learned how to recognize and correct errors involving verbs and pronouns. In this chapter, you will learn to recognize and correct **fragments**, and you will review two other common sentence errors, the **comma splice** and the **run-on sentence**.

RECOGNIZING FRAGMENTS

As you worked through the earlier chapters of this book, you studied simple, compound, and complex sentences. You learned that all sentences are made up of clauses: main clauses, which can stand alone, and subordinate clauses, which must be linked to a main clause.

A sentence should be one complete, unified thought. A group of words that lacks a subject or a verb or both is not a complete clause. A subordinate clause or a phrase by itself is not complete. Neither of these should be written alone as a sentence. When one of these parts of sentences is written as a sentence—that is, with a capital letter at the beginning and with a period or question mark at the end—the part is called a **fragment**. Fragments such as these are not acceptable in written work.

Fragments come in many varieties. Here are a few examples:

1. With a neatly typed resume and letters of recommendation from former employers.
2. Having just spent two months in Alaska.
3. The most demanding instructor in the school.

Each group of words, when written by itself, is clearly recognizable as a fragment. The first is simply a long prepositional phrase, the second is a verbal phrase, and the third is a noun with modifiers.

Fragments, however, are rarely written in isolation. Furthermore, they are more difficult to find when they are surrounded by complete sentences in a paragraph. Consider each of the italicized fragments in the passage that follows. Can you explain why each is only a part of a sentence?

(1) Last Friday, my husband and I drove to the shore. (2) Several weeks ago, we had been invited to spend the weekend with the Laurences. (3) *Our neighbors who spend most weekends at their house on the beach.* (4) We had loaded our car on Thursday evening. (5) *With food, clothes, beach chairs, and rubber rafts.* (6) *No tents or sleeping bags.* (7) *Because we had been invited to stay in their house.* (8) When we arrived, we found the beach house

empty. (9) The Laurences had forgotten about us. (10) *And gone back to the city.* (11) We realized that we were not prepared to camp out. (12) So we went for a swim. (13) *And then returned home.* (14) *Disappointed and a little angry.*

Do exercise 17-a

CORRECTING FRAGMENTS

After you recognize a fragment, you need to correct it. There are usually two ways to correct a fragment:

1. You can combine the idea expressed in the fragment with a related sentence, usually one that immediately precedes or follows the fragment.
2. You can add the words necessary to construct a sentence.

The first method is usually better because it is more economical and because it reveals a specific relationship between ideas. Your choice, however, will depend on the type of fragment and on how much you want to emphasize the idea presented in the fragment.

Let us take another look at the three fragments listed at the beginning of this chapter and pair each with a related sentence. Each fragment can then be corrected in both ways—by combining it with the related sentence or by adding the words necessary to make it a sentence. Notice how the emphasis changes with the method of correction.

> **Incorrect** fragment with a related sentence:
> Mrs. Howard entered the manager's office. With a neatly typed resume and letters of recommendation from former employers.
>
> **Corrected** by linking the fragment to a related sentence:
> Mrs. Howard entered the manager's office with a neatly typed resume and letters of recommendation from former employers.
>
> **Corrected** by adding words to the fragment:
> Mrs. Howard entered the manager's office. She brought a neatly typed resume and letters of recommendation from former employers.

Both revisions are correct. The main difference is in the emphasis placed on the resume and the letters. In the first correction, the prepositional phrase is added on to the related sentence. The main idea of the new sentence is in its subject–verb base, *Mrs. Howard entered.* If you wanted to emphasize this idea more than the resume and the letters, you would choose the easy and economical method of placing the prepositional phrase in this other sentence. In contrast, in the second correction, the fragment is rewritten as a separate sentence. In this version, the idea that she had a neatly typed resume and letters of recommendation receives as much emphasis as the idea that she entered the manager's office. If you wanted to emphasize the resume and the letters, you would choose this method.

Now look at the second fragment in the context of a related sentence.

> **Incorrect** fragment with a related sentence:
> Having just spent two months in Alaska. David and Donna were ready to return to their apartment in New York.

This fragment can be corrected in these ways:

> **Corrected** by linking the fragment to a related sentence:
> Having just spent two months in Alaska, David and Donna were ready to return to their apartment in New York.
>
> **Corrected** by adding words to the fragment:
> David and Donna had just spent two months in Alaska. Now they were ready to return to their apartment in New York.

Again, your choice depends on whether you want to give the idea expressed in the fragment as much emphasis as the idea in the related sentence. The first correction subordinates the idea of the two months in Alaska; the second correction gives it importance equal to the idea of returning to their apartment in New York.

Look at the third fragment in the context of a related sentence.

> **Incorrect** fragment with a related sentence:
> My sister's biology teacher is Mr. Hammond. The most demanding instructor in the school.
>
> **Corrected** by linking the fragment to a related sentence:
> My sister's biology teacher is Mr. Hammond, the most demanding instructor in the school.
>
> **Corrected** by adding words to the fragment:
> My sister's biology teacher is Mr. Hammond. He is the most demanding instructor in the school.

In the first correction, the fragment becomes an appositive phrase renaming *Mr. Hammond*. Consider the two corrected versions and answer these questions:

1. Which version is more economical?
2. Which version emphasizes the idea that the sister's biology teacher is Mr. Hammond?
3. Which version gives equal emphasis to both ideas—that Mr. Hammond is the sister's teacher and that Mr. Hammond is the most demanding instructor?

Four Common Types of Fragments

Because any incomplete group of words or subordinate clause written by itself is a fragment, you should be alert for many different types of fragments. You will probably find, however, that most fragments fall into four groups:

1. Verbal phrase fragments
2. Prepositional phrase fragments
3. Noun plus adjective clause fragments
4. Subordinate clause fragments

Verbal Phrases as Fragments

In Chapters 13 and 14 you learned about verbals—participles, gerunds, or infinitives—that may be used as noun substitutes or as modifiers. Sometimes student writers mistake verbals for verbs and write verbal phrases as fragments.

Study the following examples of verbal phrase fragments and their corrections. Some of the fragments are corrected in two ways. In other cases, however, it seems unnecessarily wordy to change the fragment into a separate sentence; these fragments are corrected by adding them to the related sentence.

Fragment with a Related Sentence	Correction
Jack is trying very hard to find a job. Reading the want ads every morning and sending his resume to local businesses.	Reading the want ads every morning and sending his resume to local businesses, Jack is trying very hard to find a job.
	or
	Jack is trying very hard to find a job. He is reading the want ads every morning and sending his resume to local businesses.
Worried about her mother's hospital bills. Jill finally called her uncle to ask for help.	Worried about her mother's hospital bills, Jill finally called her uncle to ask for help.
	or
	Jill was worried about her mother's hospital bills. She finally called her uncle to ask for help.
My cousin Sharon has one goal. To find a satisfying and well-paying job in the San Francisco area.	My cousin Sharon has one goal, to find a satisfying and well-paying job in the San Francisco area.
I have to stop at the post office on my way home from work. To mail a wedding present to my cousin in Minnesota.	I have to stop at the post office on my way home from work to mail a wedding present to my cousin in Minnesota.

Prepositional Phrases As Fragments

A prepositional phrase fragment is usually corrected by adding it on to a related sentence. Occasionally, as in the previous example of Mrs. Howard and her resume and letters of recommendation, you may want to rewrite this type of fragment as a separate sentence for emphasis. In general, however, the combining method is better.

Fragment with a Related Sentence	Correction
1. We plan to spend all next summer traveling across the United States. From New York to Oregon.	We plan to spend all next summer traveling across the United States from New York to Oregon.
2. No one remembered Ralph's birthday. Except his brother.	No one remembered Ralph's birthday except his brother.
3. Karen sent me a memo. About the meeting on Tuesday morning.	Karen sent me a memo about the meeting on Tuesday morning.

Nouns Plus Adjective Clauses As Fragments

Sometimes a student writes a noun and an adjective clause modifying the noun but fails to complete the subject–verb base of the main clause. This kind of fragment is corrected by adding whatever words are necessary to complete the main clause.

Fragment	Correction
The bus that arrives at the college at 8:50 A.M.	The bus that arrives at the college at 8:50 A.M. does not stop near my house.

Fragment	Correction
The refrigerator that is on sale at Sears this week.	I would like to buy the refrigerator that is on sale at Sears this week.
The job applicant who was viewed just before me.	The job applicant who was interviewed just before me was asked to return at the end of the week.

Subordinate Clauses as Fragments

Any subordinate clause—adverb, adjective, or noun—written by itself is a fragment. Fragments like these are usually combined with a related sentence, which is the main clause of the combination.

Fragment with a Related Sentence	Correction
I will take you out to dinner. If I get a new job.	I will take you out to dinner if I get a new job. *or* If I get a new job, I will take you out to dinner.
After my sister finds a job. She look for an apartment.	After my sister finds a job, she will look for an apartment. *or* My sister will look for an apartment after she finds a job.
Tom cleaned his desk and found the book. Which belongs to Jan.	Tom cleaned his desk and found the book which belongs to Jan.
Yesterday in the business office I met the woman. Who is president of the food co-op.	Yesterday in the business office I met the woman who is president of the food co-op.
He asked us a question. Whether men had been fired.	He asked us whether the men had been fired.
He was curious about it. When I would be home.	He was curious about when I would be home.

Note in the last two examples that the words *question* and *it* have been eliminated in the corrections. Once the fragment becomes a noun clause in the sentences, these words are not necessary.

Do exercises 17-b and 17-c

CORRECTING COMMA SPLICES AND RUN-ON SENTENCES

Now that you have learned how to identify and correct the parts of sentences called fragments, you should review two other common sentence errors, the comma splice and the run-on sentence. A **comma splice** consists of two main clauses separated by a comma; a **run-on sentence** consists of two main clauses with no punctuation between the clauses.

Two complete, coordinate clauses can be joined in only two ways:

1. By a comma and a coordinator
2. By a semicolon

Look at the following examples of run-on sentences and comma splices. In each case, the focus is not clear because the clauses have simply been strung together.

Run-on sentences:

1. He came we left.
2. Bart left camp early with the guide Mary was gone when he returned.
3. The solution is a simple one the secretary needs to take more accurate phone messages.

Comma splices:

1. He came, we left.
2. Bart left camp early with the guide, Mary was gone when he returned.
3. The solution is a simple one, the secretary needs to take more accurate phone messages.

Of course, each can be corrected by placing a semicolon or a comma and co-ordinator between the two clauses or by rewriting the clauses as separate sentences. We might, for instance, correct the first examples in these three ways:

He came, and we left.
He came; we left.
He came. We left.

However, the relationship between the two ideas is still not clear. By subordinating one of the ideas, we can specify the relationship between them and show which of the two ideas is the more important. As you check over and correct your writing, you should continue to apply the principles of subordination that you have been studying.

In the preceding section, we asked whether a fragment was best corrected by turning it into a simple sentence or by adding it, as a subordinate part, to another sentence. In correcting comma splices and run-on sentences, you should consider the same kinds of possibilities. Ask yourself these questions:

1. Do the two ideas belong in a single sentence?
2. Should both ideas be given equal importance, or should one be subordinated to the other?

Look back at the three examples of run-ons and comma splices. The first example might be a better sentence if we provide a more precise relationship between the two ideas by subordinating one of the clauses:

As soon as he came, we left.
After he came, we left.

The second example might just as well be written as two sentences:

Bart left the camp early with the guide. Mary was gone when he returned.

Only the third example seems to work best as a compound sentence; the second clause is equal to the first because the second restates the first.

The solution is a simple one; the secretary needs to take more accurate phone messages.

Practice

Read over the following paragraph. Underline all the fragments, run-ons, and comma splices, and decide how you would correct each error. Mark your corrections on the sentences.

(1) This spring my sister Janet graduated from our local community college with an A.A. degree. (2) Although she had decided to attend the state university in the fall. (3) She had not made any career decisions that would direct her studies. (4) She made an appointment with Dr. Brown. (5) A counselor who had helped several of her friends. (6) Dr. Brown pointed out that Janet needed to assess her interests, her abilities, and her goals, (7) she needed to determine what she could do and what she wanted to do. (8) He questioned her about her previous jobs. (9) About the responsibilities she had fulfilled. (10) He asked about her hobbies (11) he suggested that determining what she chooses to do in her leisure time could help her determine what kind of job she might enjoy. (12) He advised her to write an essay about her accomplishments, (13) this essay would make her more aware of her abilities. (14) Finally, he urged her to identify her goals. (15) Where did she hope to be living in ten years and how much money did she hope to be earning? (16) As she continues to see Dr. Brown, Janet is making important decisions. (17) Decisions which will give her the direction she will need in college and in the job market.

Now check your changes against these corrections:

Fragments	Corrections
2	Although she had decided to attend the state university in the fall, she had not made any career decisions that would direct her studies.
5	She made an appointment with Dr. Brown, a counselor who had helped several of her friends.
9	He questioned her about her previous jobs and about the responsibilities she had fulfilled.
17	As she continues to see Dr. Brown, Janet is making important decisions which will give her the direction she will need in college and in the job market.

Comma splices	*Corrections*
6/7	Dr. Brown pointed out that Janet needed to assess her interests, her abilities, and her goals; she needed to determine what she could do and what she wanted to do.

Comma splices	*Corrections*
12/13	He advised her to write an essay about her accomplishments so that she would become more aware of her abilities.

Run-on	*Correction*
10/11	He asked her about her hobbies, suggesting that determining what she chooses to do in her leisure time could help her determine what kind of job she might enjoy.

Do exercise 17-d

SUGGESTIONS FOR WRITING

Have you used your journal to record your thoughts about your friends? Read over any notes you may have made about one of your friends earlier in the semester. Do you still feel the same way about this person?

Try to identify one person about whom you feel differently now than you did earlier in the semester. Use these ideas as the basis of a paragraph.

As you **plan** your paragraph, you will need to identify the change of heart in a topic sentence. You might, for example, state *I do not trust my friend Joey as much as I did three months ago.* This paragraph should consist of three sections built to develop three subtopics: how you felt about the person initially, the experience that caused you to change your mind, and the way you feel about this same person now. Jot down specific details for each of the three parts of your new paragraph.

Write sentences for each of the three parts, making it clear to the reader how and why your feelings have changed. Be sure to stick to your one topic sentence idea.

When you **edit** your paragraph, you will need to make sure that the tense for the sentences in each section is correct. The first two sections, which explain how you felt in the past and what happened to change your mind, must be written in the *past* tense; the final section, which explains how you feel now, must be in the *present* tense. As you edit, also make sure that you have no fragments, run-ons, or comma splices.

NAME _____ **DATE** _____

I. Some of the items below contain fragments. If an item contains a fragment, underline the fragment. If it does not contain a fragment, write a *C* before the number.

EXAMPLES

_____ I will not be able to attend the choir rehearsal tonight. <u>Because my brother is using my car.</u>

C The officer explained that the road was closed because of an accident. He pointed out an alternate route to the store.

1. _____ My son Jerry works all night as a short order cook in a diner. And goes to school every morning from 7:45 until noon.

2. _____ After the rain had stopped and we had once again begun to cook breakfast. Suddenly, a black bear came trudging out of the woods.

3. _____ The baby, who was frightened by the loud fire alarm sounding in her bedroom. She began to bawl.

4. _____ We never did see Grandmother last Friday. Although we had all been in the same department store for three hours that afternoon.

5. _____ Having tried for three years to get a job as an assistant gardener for the city. Harry decided to build a greenhouse and start his own garden store.

II. Underline each fragment in the following paragraph.

In January, my brother and sister-in-law bought a sixty-year-old farm house in Connecticut. A "do-it-yourself special" which needs extensive repairs. They need to install a new wood stove in the living room and several vents. So that the heat can circulate throughout the two-story house. The house needs rewiring. Only six outlets in the entire house and only one outlet in the kitchen. The plumbing also needs work. Leaking pipes in the basement. Not enough water pressure for a shower or dishwasher. In addition to these major repairs, the house also needs to be painted. Inside and outside. It will take years for my brother and his wife to make this house comfortable. Years of very hard work.

NAME _____ **DATE** _____

Some of the items that follow contain a fragment. Underline each fragment and correct it, either by adding the idea in the fragment to a related sentence or by changing the fragment to a sentence.

As you correct the fragments, you will be building support sentences for the following topic sentence:

Topic sentence: My friend Mary has always wanted to teach deaf children in an elementary school for hearing children.

EXAMPLE

She is aware of the problems of deaf children. Having a deaf son.

Having a deaf son, she is aware of the problems of deaf children.

1. Soon after her son Steve was born, Mary began to learn sign language. To enable her to communicate with her child.

   _____

   _____

   _____

2. When Steve turned five, he was not allowed to attend the local elementary school. Which was not equipped to handle handicapped children.

   _____

   _____

   _____

3. He began spending his weekdays at the residential school for the deaf. Located 150 miles from home.

   _____

   _____

   _____

4. On Friday evenings, he would arrive home exhausted. After a three-hour bus ride.

   _____

   _____

   _____

5. Mary and her husband missed their son during the week. They wanted him at home with them and their other two children.

_____

_____

_____

6. Mary felt that deaf children such as Steve should be educated in their home towns. So that they could live with their families as hearing children do.

_____

_____

_____

7. Mary made two career decisions. To go back to college to become a teacher of the deaf and to try to convince the local school board to provide an education for deaf children.

_____

_____

_____

_____

8. Four years later, Mary graduated from college. With a degree in special education.

_____

_____

9. By this time, local school districts were required to offer special education to special students. In the public schools.

_____

_____

_____

10. Her local school board offered her a job as a teacher of deaf children. In the elementary school that her son had not been able to attend.

_____

_____

_____

NAME _____ **DATE** _____

     Some of the items below contain a fragment. Underline each fragment and correct it, either by adding the idea in the fragment to a related sentence or by rewriting the fragment as a sentence. If an item does not contain a fragment, write *C* on the first line.

     As you correct the fragments, you will be building support sentences for this topic sentence.

     Topic Sentence: Last night, my cousin Nancy told me about her difficulties as a new resident of New York City.

EXAMPLE

Nancy moved to New York because she wanted to be a public health nurse in a large city. After graduating from nursing school.

After graduating from nursing school, Nancy moved to New York because she wanted to be a public health nurse in a large city.

1. After finding a job, she learned about two problems of city life. Finding an apartment and finding a parking space.

_____

_____

_____

2. She had a very difficult time finding an apartment. One that she could afford.

_____

_____

_____

3. While staying with friends for a week, she looked at twenty-five apartments. Which were all too small or too expensive.

_____

_____

_____

_____

_____

_____

4. Finally, a real estate agent showed her a three-room apartment in Greenwich Village. It suited her need for space and her budget.

_____

_____

_____

5. Having found a place to live. She realized that she could not find a place to park her Volkswagen.

_____

_____

_____

6. The local parking garage charged over $100 a month. Which was much more than she could afford to pay.

_____

_____

_____

7. Then one of her neighbors told her something. That she could park her car in Queens and take a subway to her apartment.

_____

_____

_____

8. She made a decision. To use the subways and buses in the city and to use the car only for weekend trips.

_____

_____

_____

9. She was then able to enjoy the city's museums, restaurants, and concerts. Without always worrying about finding a parking space.

_____

_____

_____

_____

NAME _____ **DATE** _____

Each of the four paragraphs below contains fragments, comma splices, and run-on sentences. Underline each of these errors. Then, on a separate sheet of paper, rewrite the paragraphs, correcting the errors so that all the sentences are complete and unified.

People in my rural county still know each other and take a personal interest in each other's lives. One good example is Mr. Gibbons, he is seventy-nine years old. Early every morning, Mr. Gibbons meets his friends at Sadie's diner for coffee. Around ten, they go their separate ways. Some to work at part-time jobs. Others to do the rounds of neighbors, farms, and country stores. Mr. Gibbons is one of those who do not work, he retired ten years ago. From a local chain of convenience stores called Big Slim's. Mr. Gibbons likes to know all the employees at Big Slim's. And visits at least one store nearly every week. Few people know that Mr. Gibbons is on a quest. Looking for someone who deserves to be helped.

Five years ago, Mr. Gibbons started to spend a lot of time with my brother Pete. Who had graduated from high school. And then had become a full-time cashier in the Big Slim's in Meridian. Mr. Gibbons coaxed and teased Pete. About Pete's being smart but never able to get ahead. Unless, of course, he enrolled in the community college and took business accounting. When my brother finally admitted he needed more education. Mr. Gibbons told Pete what he was prepared to do. He would pay Pete's tuition and other fees. Even buy all Pete's textbooks and other materials.

Pete wondered. What he would have to do in return. Mr. Gibbons did have his terms, Pete would have to graduate with an A.A. degree. Or pass the Certified Public Accountant exam. Pete did both. It took him three years of night school and summer classes. To complete the curriculum and prepare for the exam. Since then Pete has been moving steadily up the management ladder. Becoming assistant manager two years ago and manager last spring. Two weeks ago, Pete received an offer. To become a district manager for a chain of large home improvement warehouse stores. He is thinking it over.

Last night, I was in the Big Slim's in Snoville. And saw Mr. Gibbons. Talking to a young cashier about making the most of her life. She laughed when he suggested going to college. She was, she explained, older than she looked. To her, attending college seemed impossible. She had been working hard. Ever since she graduated from high school. She is married and has two children. I almost went over and told her to give up, Mr. Gibbons would have his way in the end, the community college would have a new student.

Reviewing the Comma **18**

As you have worked through this book, you have learned how to build sentences of increasing length and complexity which support a topic sentence idea. You have also seen the importance of reading over your own sentences, finding your own errors, and correcting them. As you check your writing, you should pay close attention to the placement of commas. In this last chapter, you will review the rules for using commas which you have been studying throughout the book.

RULE 1: COMPOUND SENTENCE

When two coordinate clauses are joined to form a compound sentence, the two clauses can be correctly connected in two ways:

1. By a comma and a coordinator:

   I would like to take a tennis course on Saturday mornings, *but* I usually work on weekends.

2. By a semicolon, with or without a conjunctive adverb:

   My older brother is a social worker in New York; my younger brother manages a ski shop in Denver.
   I have to go to work tomorrow; *otherwise*, I will not be able to pick up my paycheck.

(The comma splice and run-on sentence, two incorrect ways of joining coordinate clauses in a compound sentence, are reviewed in Chapter 17.)

RULE 2: COMMAS IN A SERIES

When we join three or more coordinate items, we construct a series. Each item in a series is separated from the next item by a comma.

1. *Nora, Jan,* and *Julie* have already registered for the spring semester.
2. Bob *filled* out the job application, *delivered* it to the personnel office, and *scheduled* an interview.

Remember that there is no comma after the last item in a series; it would be incorrect in sentence 1 to place a comma after *Julie.*

When we compound two coordinate items, we do not have a series. The two are not separated by a comma.

1. *Ruth* and *Mike* spent spring vacation in New Orleans.
2. Early in September, my mother *cans* peaches and *makes* catsup.

Do exercise 18-a

RULE 3: COORDINATE ADJECTIVES

Coordinate adjectives are separated by commas. Adjectives are coordinate (1) if they can be connected by *and* and (2) if they can be presented in any order.

1. My *nosey, friendly* cocker spaniel always answers the door with me.
2. The *talkative, aggressive* salesman convinced me that I needed a second car.

Adjectives that are not coordinate are not separated by commas:

1. The *beautiful oak* table had been covered with five coats of paint.
2. My daughter wants to use my *new black* skirt as part of her Halloween costume.

Do exercise 18-b

RULE 4: INTRODUCTORY ADVERBS

When an adverb—a single-word, a phrase, or a subordinate clause—appears at the beginning of a sentence, it is usually set off by a comma.

1. *Cautiously*, the inexperienced driver pulled over to the side of the road.
2. *In the spring of 1861*, the Union forces surrendered at Fort Sumter.
3. *To allow the defendant to compose himself*, the judge ordered a recess.
4. *When I get my first paycheck*, I will take you out to lunch.

When an adverb is placed in the middle or at the end of a sentence, it is usually not set off by a comma.

1. The inexperienced driver *cautiously* pulled over to the side of the road.
2. The Union forces surrendered at Fort Sumter *in the spring of 1861*.
3. The judge ordered a recess *to allow the defendant to compose himself*.
4. I will take you out to lunch *when I get my first paycheck*.

Do exercise 18-c

RULE 5: NONRESTRICTIVE WORDS, PHRASES, AND CLAUSES

A word or group of words is **nonrestrictive** when it is not essential to identify the noun it modifies or renames. Nonrestrictive modifiers and appositives are set off by commas.

(Remember that although adjective clauses and appositives follow the nouns they modify or rename, verbal phrases can be placed before or after the noun.)

1. *Verbal*:	The delivery man, *finding no one at home*, turned to leave.
	or
	Finding no one at home, the delivery man turned to leave.
2. *Appositive*:	Dr. John Roberts, *founder of the college's research center*, will retire in June.
3. *Adjective clause*:	Dr. Anders, *who was called to the hospital*, had to cancel all her morning appointments.

A **restrictive** modifier or appositive is one that is necessary for the identification of the noun it modifies or renames. Restrictive elements are not set off by commas.

1. *Verbal*: The young man *standing by the diving board* has won the first swimming meet.

2. *Appositive*: My cousin *Jane* is flying to San Francisco on Wednesday.

3. *Adjective clause*: The librarian *who is sitting at the information desk* can help you find the magazine.

Long complicated phrases are often set off by dashes instead of commas:

Tim read the shopping list—alfalfa sprouts, chamomile tea, carob chips, and sea salt—and decided to go to a health food store.

Do exercises 18-d and 18-e

SUGGESTIONS FOR WRITING

As we have suggested throughout this book, writing in a journal can help you evaluate your experiences at home, with friends, on the job, and at school.

Plan a final paragraph in which you consider the most interesting course that you have been taking this semester. Write a topic sentence naming the course and stating your favorable reaction: for example, _____ *is my most interesting course this semester*. Then decide on three subtopics, possibly three factors that make the course interesting, such as the instructor, the textbook, and the outside readings. Make notes about the specific details you want to include for each factor.

As you follow your plan and **write** the paragraph, try to convince your reader that your course has been interesting by including as much specific information as possible. End your paragraph with a closing sentence that restates your feeling about the class; you might make a statement such as *I wish all my courses fascinated me as much as* _____ .

As you **edit** your paragraph, pay special attention to the comma rules that you reviewed in this chapter.

NAME _____ **DATE** _____

I. Correct any punctuation errors in the following sentences. Add commas where necessary; cross out any unnecessary commas. If a sentence is punctuated correctly, write *C* before the sentence.

EXAMPLE

_____ Do not forget to add the cinnamon/and nutmeg to the pie.

1. _____ Mark said he would never lie to his parents, cheat in school, or borrow money from a friend.

2. _____ The big red dog, ran through the kitchen, onto the sun porch, and out the back door.

3. _____ My boss attended two seminars, spoke at a business luncheon, attended her son's graduation, and still finished, all her routine work last week.

4. _____ The waiter said he would recommend, the filet of flounder, the crab cake, and the linguini with shrimp.

5. _____ The March wind felt cold, and wet to the children as they trudged home from school.

6. _____ Dan always plants lilies, irises, miniature roses, and impatiens in his garden.

7. _____ Judith phoned each of her three children, told them her plans, and asked them to come by on Sunday to tell her goodbye.

8. _____ The four children had made a salad, baked bread and marinated the meat for the barbecue before their father returned from the office.

9. _____ They listened to the three compositions, by John Harbison John Rouse, and Charles Ives.

10. _____ Mary, Sharon, Bill, and Stan stopped by a Chinese restaurant for noodles, and ended the evening at Mary's making fudge.

II. Combine each group of sentences to make one simple sentence. Be sure to check your punctuation carefully.

EXAMPLE

Nancy rented a cottage at Deep Creek Lake for a week.
Mary rented a cottage at Deep Creek Lake for a week.
Cathy rented a cottage at Deep Creek Lake for a week.
Joan rented a cottage at Deep Creek Lake for a week.

Combination: *Nancy, Mary, Cathy, and Joan rented a cottage at Deep Creek Lake for a week.*

1. Marianne and Sally met on Monday.
   Marianne and Sally went for a walk.
   Marianne and Sally stopped by Barbara's for lunch.

   Combination: _____

   _____

2. The custodians searched for the children in the trash room.
   The custodians searched for the children under the stairs.
   The custodians searched for the children in the parking lot.

   Combination: _____

   _____

   _____

3. Last year in Cancun, we bought several silver bracelets.
   Last year in Cancun, we bought two bowls carved from rock.
   Last year in Cancun, we bought three polished conch shells.

   Combination: _____

   _____

   _____

4. How long has it been, she demanded, since Tom and Joe visited our cousins in San Pedro?
   How long has it been, she demanded, since Tom and Joe visited our grandparents in San Diego?

   Combination: _____

   _____

5. We skipped lunch.
   We waited impatiently in line for four hours.
   Then we were finally told there were no more tickets.

   Combination: _____

   _____

   _____

6. Gwen hummed along with the music.
   Gwen tapped her toes.
   Then Gwen jumped up to dance with Robert.

   Combination: _____

   _____

NAME _____ **DATE** _____

I. Correct any punctuation errors in the following sentences. Add commas where necessary; cross out unnecessary ones. Write *C* by the numbers of any sentences that are correctly punctuated.

EXAMPLE

*C*___ The handsome, smiling stranger approached her.

1. ——— The long thin stems of the rose bushes need to be trimmed.

2. ——— The announcer turned away from the embarrassed young contestant and asked for the curtain to be drawn.

3. ——— The little dog's matted yellow hair needed to be cut.

4. ——— Into the mall came two little boys in identical blue cotton jackets and pants.

5. ——— The love birds sang in loud shrill voices.

6. ——— The pale, weak and feverish instructor reported to the infirmary.

7. ——— The teacher walked hurriedly into the empty, smoky cafeteria.

8. ——— The strong sweet smell of apple blossoms delighted all the hikers except Sherman.

9. ——— Abigail felt ready for the biggest, longest, most challenging, competition of her life after practicing for three years.

10. ——— She looked with disgust at the faded stained kitchen curtains.

II. Combine each group of sentences to make one simple sentence. Use the sentence marked with a check (✓) as your subject–verb base. Separate coordinate adjectives with a comma.

EXAMPLE

　My aunt was desperate.
　My aunt was teary-eyed.
✓ My aunt asked to see her husband.

　Combination: ___*My desperate, teary-eyed aunt asked to see her husband.*___

_____

_____

1. Ellen's voice was high-pitched.
   Ellen's voice was thin.
   The judges could not hear Ellen's voice.

   Combination: _____

   _____

   _____

2. The daffodils were delivered in a bucket.
   The bucket was stained.
   The bucket was wooden.

   Combination: _____

   _____

   _____

3. At the end of the meeting, the moderator gave Basil a stare.
   The stare was long.
   The stare was cold.

   Combination: _____

   _____

   _____

4. The explanation given by the two children was ignored.
   The explanation was confused.
   The explanation was contradictory.

   Combination: _____

   _____

   _____

5. The immigrants took their oath of allegiance.
   The immigrants were smiling.
   The immigrants were proud.

   Combination: _____

   _____

   _____

6. Mary Ellen was startled by the irises growing in the tall green grass.
   The irises were blue.
   The irises were soft.

   Combination: _____

   _____

   _____

NAME _____ **DATE** _____

I. Correct any punctuation errors in the following sentences. Add commas where necessary; cross out any unnecessary ones. Write *C* by the number of each correct sentence.

EXAMPLES

_*C*_ After Corrine bought a new electric typewriter, she began typing all her assignments.

_____ You must complete each step/ to find the answer.

1. _____ After visiting his grandparents in Arizona Clyde drove to see his parents in Salt Lake City.

2. _____ Without seeing or hearing the snake the child ran down the path.

3. _____ Jackson and Smedley had found little time to practice, until yesterday.

4. _____ Joan cannot attend the PTA meeting this Wednesday, because she promised to take Andy to the airport.

5. _____ Before any of the children knew what was happening, Kate grabbed a broom and swooped the bat back out the open door.

6. _____ Ginny decided to wear her blue dress, instead of the green one.

7. _____ In the winter wild bison roam through Yellowstone Park in large herds.

8. _____ Early in March, Jodie had planted seed potatoes and broccoli, in her parents' garden.

9. _____ Erin spent her first year learning Japanese, from her friends and from her teachers.

10. _____ Without hesitation, she turned to the would-be muggers, slapped them with her purse, and ran, across the street and into the hotel.

II. Combine each group of sentences into one simple sentence by using adverb modifiers.

- Use the sentence marked with a check( ) as the subject–verb base of your combination.
- In some combinations, you will simply be adding a single word or a phrase to the base. In others, you will need to change one of the sentences to a phrase or a subordinate clause.
- Write two versions of your combination: (a) one in which an adverb modifier (single word, phrase, or subordinate clause) introduces the sentence and is set off by a comma, and (b) one in which the adverb modifier appears in the middle or at the end of the sentence.

EXAMPLE

John saved money for his skiing trip to Aspen.
John saved money for two years.

Combination (a): *For two years, John saved money for his skiing trip to Aspen.*

Combination: (b) *John saved money for two years for his skiing trip to Aspen.*

---

1. The children may have a Halloween party.
   The family room must be cleaned.
   It must be cleaned thoroughly from top to bottom.

   Combination (a): _____

   _____

   Combination (b): _____

   _____

2. Brian submitted his first report.
   The report was three days late.
   Brian's wife had been in an automobile accident.

   Combination (a): _____

   _____

   Combination (b): _____

   _____

3. We studied long hours.
   We studied on Saturday and Sunday, but not on Monday.
   We wanted to be rested and fresh for the exam on Tuesday.

   Combination (a): _____

   _____

   Combination (b): _____

   _____

4. Jake could not get control of his skis or his fear at first.
   Jake learned to ski before the end of his vacation.

   Combination (a): _____

   _____

   Combination (b): _____

   _____

NAME _____ DATE _____

I. Correct any punctuation errors in the following sentences. Add commas where necessary; cross out any unnecessary ones. Write *C* before each correct sentence.

EXAMPLE

_____ Ellen Jones, president of Hartsdale's neighborhood association, is in charge of the flea market/scheduled for June 4.

1. _____ Every member of the club who plans to go on the trip to Scottsdale, should take his bus money to my office.

2. _____ George who had saved for two years to attend the Los Angeles Technical Training College, enrolled full-time for the second semester.

3. _____ Durwood my brother's roommate in college, had not seen his parents in six years.

4. _____ It took my brother an hour to gather up the books, papers, shopping bags, pencils, and pens on the seats and floor of his car.

5. _____ Having never been in Arizona before, Whitney was excited about visiting her aunt in Glendale.

6. _____ Seeing an opportunity to prolong his vacation James quickly agreed to take care of the Reynolds' house.

7. _____ Mr. Jones and Ms. French, my favorite teachers were invited to the students' award banquet.

8. _____ Hidden under the cushion by my tiny cousin my sister's glasses were bent but not broken when we found them.

9. _____ Harry's house guest, who had never taken care of herself could not understand why her bed was not made or her clothes washed and ironed.

10. _____ Stranded in San Diego with no money and no friends, Mark was grateful when a stranger took him to the tourist office where an information officer was able to find help for him.

11. _____ During their spring break, Jason and Pete, neither of whom had ever been in the South, drove to South Carolina to visit their father's cousins.

12. _____ The cold, greasy dishes left sitting on the kitchen counter after the party the night before were a very unwelcome sight when Denise came down to fix coffee.

13. _____ The strange message on the answering machine terrified Marcy who had been living alone for only one week.

14. _____ Amy, always surrounded by family and friends, had never thought about being alone.

15. _____ Once elected secretary-treasurer, Emily began keeping careful records of every transaction.

16. _____ The answers so quickly given by Andrew, were all correct.

NAME _____ **DATE** _____

Correct any punctuation errors in the following paragraph. Add commas where necessary; cross out unnecessary ones. The example is the topic sentence for the paragraph.

EXAMPLE

My neighbors' son Josh/ spent most of his middle school years playing, thinking about, or discussing computer games.

At home, his Super Nintendo Entertainment System which he called the SNES, was permanently connected through an RF switch to the television monitor, in his bedroom. When he traveled to visit family or for a vacation at the beach, his Game Boy, and at least six power packs went with him. Josh longed to possess, Sega Genesis, Turbo Graphix, and Game Gear, a competitor of Game Boy with a colored monitor. His conversations with his father consisted of attempts to convince him to buy one or all of these systems; his conversations with his friends were intricate analyses of how to master complicated, new games. Josh was not competitive; he seemed uninterested in winning and always played alone. The tension of playing, and the private pleasure of mastering the games seemed to be the main incentives for his constant, compulsive play. Josh's gratification came from learning to manipulate the controls precisely to make his figure jump, lunge run, roll, and sometimes even swim to dodge, or destroy the enemy. Throughout those years, the thin pure tones of electronic music and sound effects emanated hour after hour from his room as the silent immobile Josh sat completely absorbed in the movements, and explosions on the screen.

Using Singular and Plural Nouns

Although the spelling of plural nouns is often given in the dictionary, knowing the common rules for forming plurals will make your writing easier. Use your dictionary whenever you are not sure how to form a plural.

RULE 1: ADDING –S

Most nouns are made plural by adding -s to the singular form:

Singular	Plural
tree	trees
building	buildings
reason	reasons
worker	workers

RULE 2: ADDING –ES:

Nouns that end in **sounds** of s, x, ch, sh, j (dg), or z would be difficult to pronounce if we added only an -s. We need a whole syllable, -es, at the ends of words such as these:

Singular	Plural
kiss	kisses
fox	foxes
church	churches
brush	brushes
buzz	buzzes

When a singular noun ends with a silent e, we need, of course, add only an -s; however, when the silent e is preceded by one of the sounds listed in rule 2, adding the -s adds a whole syllable.

Singular	Plural
phase	phases
maze	mazes
judge	judges
disease	diseases
piece	pieces
vase	vases
excuse	excuses

As an aid to your spelling, practice pronouncing these plurals.

RULE 3: CHANGING –Y TO –I

Singular words that end in the letter *y* form their plural regularly, that is, by adding an -*s*, when the *y* is preceded by a **vowel**:

Singular	Plural
key	keys
attorney	attorneys
boy	boys

When the letter before the final *y* is a **consonant**, we usually change the *y* to an *i* and add –*es*:

Singular	Plural
activity	activities
anxiety	anxieties
army	armies
emergency	emergencies
fly	flies
lady	ladies
reply	replies
sky	skies

RULE 4: WORDS THAT END IN *O*

Most singular words that end in the letter *o* form their plural regularly by adding an –*s* when the *o* is preceded by a **consonant**:

Singular	Plural
ego	egos
solo	solos
soprano	sopranos
piano	pianos

There are, however, some exceptions:

echo	echoes
hero	heroes
potato	potatoes
tomato	tomatoes

IRREGULAR PLURALS

For many irregular plurals, there are no rules. When you have a question, you should look up the word in a desk-sized dictionary. If the word is not regular, the plural will be listed after the pronunciation of the word. You should be especially alert to the kinds of words listed under the Spelling Hints that follow.

• Spelling Hint 1

A few nouns that end in the letter *f* or *fe* change the *f* to *v* and add *–es*.

Singular	Plural
leaf	leaves
life	lives
knife	knives
thief	thieves
wife	wives

However, many words ending in *f* simply add an *–s* for the plural:

chief	chiefs
cliff	cliffs

• Spelling Hint 2

Some singular nouns change in the middle of a singular to make a plural:

Singular	Plural
man	men
mouse	mice
woman	women
foot	feet
tooth	teeth

• Spelling Hint 3

Some singular nouns use special endings:

child	children

• Spelling Hint 4

Some words are the same in the singular and in the plural:

deer	deer
fish	fish

• Spelling Hint 5

Some foreign words taken into English have kept their foreign plural forms:

Singular	Plural
analysis	analyses
crisis	crises
criterion	criteria
medium	media
datum	data

Do exercise A-1

NAME _____ **DATE** _____

I. Write the plural form of the following nouns. If necessary, refer to the rules and hints in Appendix A or use your dictionary.

EXAMPLES

holiday ___*holidays*___   foot ___*feet*___

1. loaf _____   7. crisis _____

2. emergency _____   8. tooth _____

3. woman _____   9. hero _____

4. child _____   10. potato _____

5. boss _____   11. leaf _____

6. crutch _____   12. soprano _____

II. Rewrite the following sentences, changing each italicized noun to a plural form. Also change the article—*a*, *an*, or *the*—to a number word so that the sentence makes sense.

EXAMPLE

Last night, my mother hung *a shelf* in the laundry room.

___*Last night, my mother hung three shelves in the laundry room.*___

1. On Tuesday, I donated *a box* of books to the American Veterans.

_____

_____

2. Sheila brought *an adorable puppy* home from the mall yesterday.

_____

_____

3. *A man* from Glen Burnie won the seven million dollar lottery last weekend.

_____

_____

4. My brother chased *a deer* from his garden this morning.

_____

_____

Using A, An, and The

The words *a*, *an*, and *the*, called articles, are frequently used in front of nouns. We follow rules when we use these articles.

USING A AND AN

- We use *a* and *an* only in front of nouns that name people, places, things, or ideas **that can be counted**. We use *a* and *an* when we mean **any** person, place, thing, or idea, **not a particular one**.

  1. a person (We can count people.)
  2. an apple pie (We can count apple pies.)
  3. a Christmas elf (We can count elves.)

These two articles are used only in front of singular nouns.

- We use *a* in front of a word beginning with a consonant sound.

  1. a friend
  2. a couch
  3. a new teacher

- We use *an* in front of a word beginning with a vowel sound.

  1. an enemy
  2. an arm
  3. an old teacher

The article *a* does not have the long sound of *a* as in *hay* or *may*; it is pronounced like the *a* that begins *about*. Practice pronouncing *a* correctly before words that begin with consonant sounds and *an* before words that begin with vowel sounds.

1. a room	1. an orange
2. a student	2. an instructor
3. a quiz	3. an exam
4. a bus station	4. an airport
5. a sunny day	5. an extremely cold night

- We often use *a* and *an* when we mention a person, place, thing, or idea for the *first* time. If we continue to talk or write about this person, place, thing, or idea, we often use the article *the*.

  1. Maggie bought *a* new coat on Saturday. *The* coat was marked down to half price.
  2. My family adopted *a* dog from the animal shelter. *The* dog is completely trained.
  3. I ordered *an* orange chiffon cake at the bakery. *The* cake was not ready on time for my party.

Practice

Practice filling in the correct articles: *a, an,* and *the.*

1. Frank found_____umbrella in his mailbox. _____ umbrella was in perfect condition.

2. Every Monday, our instructor assigns _____ practice test in our
   textbook. He collects_____test on Wednesday.

3. My sister wrote _____ excellent paper for her history class. She
   worked on _____ paper for three weeks.

Answers:

1. an, The
2. a, the
3. an, the

USING *THE*

- We use the word *the* when we mean a particular one or ones.

  1. Betsy is *the* youngest child in *the* room.
  2. *The* reasons for his behavior are obvious.
  3. Karen hid *the* birthday presents behind *the* coats in *the* hall closet.

- *The* can be used before a singular or a plural noun.

  Singular: the table, the city, the child
  Plural: the tables, the cities, the children

Practice

In each sentence, fill in the correct article, *a, an,* or *the.*

1. _____ examples in my math book are very confusing.

2. My younger brother always leaves_____ lights on in_____
   living room.

3. Gail wrote_____essay about her experiences as _____
   foster mother. Her English teacher gave_____essay an *A*.

Now check your answers:

1. The
2. the, the
3. an, a, the

As mentioned in the preceding section, we often use *a* or *an* when we mention a noun for the first time. If we continue to talk or write about this noun, we use *the*.

```
Do exercise B-1
```

USING NO ARTICLE

We do not always use an article before a noun.

- We do not use an article before a noun that names, for the first time, something that cannot be counted, but must instead be measured.

  1. My father buys coffee at the gourmet shop.
  2. I need gas for my car.
  3. Sandra never drinks milk.

In these three examples, some of the nouns—coffee, gas, and milk—do not have articles because they cannot be counted. We can measure these things, but we cannot count them. For example, we can order a cup of coffee in a restaurant or buy a pound of coffee in the supermarket, but we cannot buy *a coffee*. Similarly, although we would not order *a gas* for the car, we might order six gallons of gas or ten dollars' worth of gas. We might buy milk by the glass or by the gallon, but we probably would not simply ask a cashier for *a milk*.

- If we continue to talk or write about a noun that names something that cannot be counted, we follow the rule for nouns that name things that can be counted. When we mention the noun again, we use the article *the*.

  1. My father buys coffee at the gourmet shop. *The coffee* is decaffeinated.
  2. I need gas for my car. *The gas* must be unleaded.

- We also do not use articles before most proper nouns. As explained in Appendix C, a proper noun is a noun that names a particular person, place, thing, or idea. A proper noun is capitalized.

Common nouns	Proper nouns
the teacher	Dr. Jones (not the Dr. Jones)
a college	Gallaudet University (not the Gallaudet University)
the city	Baltimore (not the Baltimore)

```
Do exercise B-2
```

NAME _____ **DATE** _____

I. Underline each article (*a, an, the*) in the following sentences. If an article is incorrectly used, draw a line through it and write your correction directly above it. Write *C* before each correct sentence.

EXAMPLE

         An
_____ ~~A~~ eager young man brought a tape recorder into the room.

1. _____ My brother gave a explanation for his absence.

2. _____ Ron needs to buy an uniform before the game on Friday.

3. _____ A honest employee is an asset to any company.

4. _____ Frank plans to take an economics class next semester.

5. _____ Rhoda hopes to receive a packages for her birthday.

II. Write *a, an,* or *the* in the blanks that follow. If no article is necessary, put an *x* on the line.

EXAMPLE

I took __*an*__ English exam yesterday. Fortunately, __*the*__ exam was not difficult.

Bill put __*the*__ new chair in __*the*__ living room.

1. Gabrielle is _____ oldest child in _____ Cardall family.

2. I give my dog _____ raw egg every week. _____ egg is good for his coat.

3. _____ elevator is broken. You will have to use _____ escalator.

4. Olga does not have _____ excuse for her behavior.

5. Carrie looked through her notes for _____ answer to the Mr. Thomas's question.

   She did not realize that _____ answer was on _____ blackboard.

6. Henry bought _____ azaleas for _____ front yard.

7. _____ flowers on _____ boss's desk are beautiful.

8. Kari will buy _____ new dress and _____ new pair of shoes for _____

   Valentine's dance.

9. Donald parked his truck in _____ alley behind Joe's apartment.

10. Please write _____ letter to your grandfather and _____ postcard to your

    uncle.

NAME _____ DATE _____

Write *a*, *an*, or *the* wherever necessary. If no article is necessary, put an *x* on the line.

EXAMPLES

I made ___*x*___ coffee and ___*x*___ cookies for my bridge club.

Bonny bought ___*a*___ pair of skis at the local ski shop yesterday.

===

1. Please put _____ gas in my car tonight.

2. _____ answer to _____ first question is in _____ last chapter.

3. Where do you buy _____ vegetables? I always buy my vegetables at _____

   farmers' market.

4. My grandmother never drinks _____ coffee; she always drinks _____ tea.

5. I bought _____ new car last year, but I cannot find _____ sales receipt.

6. My friend Danny has written _____ movie script and _____ novel.

7. _____ walls in my mother's study are covered with _____ photographs.

8. Whenever my brother and sister have to clean the garage, they have _____

   argument.

9. Jim bought _____ new sweater at the mall last night. This morning, his wife

   bought him _____ same sweater.

10. Do you use _____ sugar in your coffee?

11. My brother gave our parents _____ VCR for Christmas. Unfortunately,

    _____ VCR was broken.

12. Do you ever prepare your papers on _____ computer?

13. _____ school library has _____ computers for student use.

14. Please pass me _____ apple and _____ orange.

15. Pat brought bottle of wine to the party. _____ host quickly put _____ bottle in

    refrigerator.

Capitalizing Nouns

Appendix C

You learned in Chapter 1 that the first word of every sentence is capitalized. In addition, certain kinds of words are capitalized wherever they appear in a sentence. The rules that follow cover some of the most common kinds of nouns that are capitalized.

COMMON NOUNS AND PROPER NOUNS

Some nouns, called **common nouns**, name general classes of things; others, called **proper nouns**, specify particular ones. When we name a particular person, place, or thing, we use a proper noun. Proper nouns are capitalized. Note in the following examples that all the proper names are capitalized.

General (Common Nouns)	Specific (Proper Nouns)
a newspaper	the Baltimore *Evening Sun*
an airport	Dulles International Airport
a college	Miami-Dade Community College
a day	Wednesday
a high school	Pikesville Senior High School
my aunt	Aunt Marie
a mayor	Mayor Cynthia Dickinson
a general	General Mark Clark
a motel	the Holiday Corral
an actor	Burt Reynolds
a movie theater	Eastlake Cinema I
an ocean	the Atlantic Ocean
a singer	Billie Holliday
a state	North Dakota
a city	Houston
a movie	*Star Wars*

Notice that family titles are not capitalized when they do not name a specific person, as in *my aunt*; however, they are capitalized when they name a specific person, as in *Aunt Marie*. Similarly, family titles such as *mother* or *father* are not capitalized when they are preceded by possessive adjectives such as *my* or *your*; they are capitalized when they are used by themselves as names.

Correct: My mother refuses to lend me her new sports car.
Incorrect: I am afraid to tell mother that I lost her keys.

Notice also in the examples that *mayor* and *general* are capitalized when they are used before a person's name as an official title. They are not capitalized when they are used alone in a sentence or after a person's name:

William Borah, a senator from Idaho, opposed the League of Nations.
William Borah was a senator from Idaho.

Note that names of specific places, including general geographical areas, are also capitalized:

Route 66	Yellowstone National Park
the South	Main Street
the Northeast	Pike's Peak
Cook County	the Pennsylvania Turnpike
Chicago, Illinois	the Snake River
the Rocky Mountains	South Africa

However, the nouns must name a region, not give a direction:

Last summer, we drove south into North Carolina and then west to Arkansas.

Particular names of buildings, other structures, airplanes, and ships are also capitalized:

Grayson Hall	Apollo II
the Salt Palace	U.S. Constellation
Memorial Stadium	the White House

The names of nationalities and the official names of groups are capitalized:

the English
an American
a Canadian
the Congress of the United States
the old Brooklyn Dodgers
the University of Virginia
the United States Marine Corps
the Federal Reserve Bank
the Beatles
the Rolling Stones

Full, official names of academic courses are capitalized. Note the difference in *accounting* in the following sentences:

Jerry is taking an accounting course this semester.
Jerry is in Accounting 201 this semester.

Of course, names of languages are always capitalized:

Jerry is taking a French class this semester.

Do exercises C-1 and C-2

NAME _____ **DATE** _____

      Rewrite each sentence, substituting a proper noun for the italicized common noun. Be sure that you capitalize your proper noun.

EXAMPLE

I watched *an actor* filming a movie scene yesterday.

I watched William Hurt filming a movie scene yesterday.

═══

1. I have not visited *one of my aunts* for five years.

   _____

2. Janet will meet me in front of *a department store* at noon.

   _____

3. Andy has every album recorded by *his favorite rock group*.

   _____

4. *The local baseball team* will play three home games this week.

   _____

5. Last week, John visited *his hometown* for the first time in ten years.

   _____

   _____

6. Anne's parents drove her to *a college* for an interview last Friday.

   _____

   _____

7. My cousin from Nebraska has never been swimming in *an ocean*.

   _____

   _____

8. *An English teacher* encouraged me to enter the essay contest.

   _____

   _____

Correct each error in capitalization by crossing out incorrect letters and writing your correction above. Write *C* by the number of each correct sentence.

EXAMPLE

_____ Kate has registered for ~~h~~*H*istory 101 for next semester.

═══

1. _____ My parents have invited my Grandfather to live with them.

2. _____ Patapsco middle school will be closed tomorrow because of heating problems.

3. _____ The construction on the Jones Falls Expressway always annoys my husband.

4. _____ My danish cousins will be visiting the United States this summer.

5. _____ All of Paula's classes are held in kauke hall.

6. _____ My brother speaks spanish with his girlfriend's parents.

7. _____ Kevin has taken two American history courses at the University of Maryland.

8. _____ Nancy has already missed her english class twice this semester.

9. _____ Every weekend, our neighbors drive East to their cottage on the Chesapeake Bay.

10. _____ From her apartment, my niece can see the hudson river.

11. _____ My boss will begin his two-week vacation next wednesday.

12. _____ I saw Governor Schaeffer at memorial stadium on Sunday.

13. _____ Aunt Janet and uncle Frank have been married for fifty-five years.

14. _____ My brother and my cousin attended Paul smith's college for one semester.

15. _____ Karen's plane is due at kennedy Airport at noon.

16. _____ Every summer, Donald and Ken go fishing in the catskill mountains.

17. _____ I was surprised to see the Mayor at the concert.

18. _____ Gina has lived in cuyahoga county all her life.

19. _____ My daughter is learning to play the french horn.

20. _____ Mike dropped his Chemistry course last week.

Using Possessive Nouns

When we change nouns to the possessive form, we usually follow two rules.

RULE 1: POSSESSIVE FORM OF SINGULAR NOUNS

Singular nouns are made possessive by adding an apostrophe and an -s ('s).

Singular	Possessive
boy	boy's remark
girl	girl's question

Study the following additional three examples of singular possessive forms.

	Singular	Possessive
1.	family	family's car

My family's car is a Chevrolet.
(One family owns one car.)

	Singular	Possessive
2.	lady	lady's glove

Bring the lady's glove to the office.
(One lady owns one glove.)

	Singular	Possessive
3.	Chris	Chris's

Mr. Williams praised Chris's answer.
(One student had one answer.)

RULE 2: POSSESSIVE FORM OF PLURAL NOUNS

If the plural noun ends in -s, as most plurals do, we add an apostrophe after the -s to make the possessive form. If the plural noun does not end in -s, we add an apostrophe and an -s('s).

Plural	Possessive
boys	boys' remarks
children	children's questions

Be very careful not to confuse the plural form and the possessive form when you write. Although these forms sound the same, their written forms are different.

Singular possessive	Plural possessive	Plural
family's	families'	families
lady's	ladies'	ladies

USING POSSESSIVE FORMS

- Use an apostrophe when you want to show that something or someone belongs to another. Be sure to place the possessive in front of the person or thing that belongs to it.
- If you want to write about more than one person, place, thing, or idea, use the plural form and do not use an apostrophe. Look at the following examples.

Correct: a. The two boys were cruel.
              b. The two boys' remarks were cruel.
Incorrect: c. The two boys' were cruel.
              d. The two boy's remarks were cruel.

Example *a* is correct because the plural form *boys* is used to name the persons the sentence is about; the boys do not possess anything. Example *b* is correct because the remarks belong to two boys and the possessive form (*boys'*) is used. The possessive nouns in examples *c* and *d*, however, are incorrect. The possessive form should not be used in *c*, and the singular possessive should not be used in *d*.

A possessive noun is usually written in front of the word it identifies. However, once the word to be identified is clear, the possessive noun may be used alone to indicate possession and the person or thing possessed:

1. These are Brent's books.
2. The books in the car are Jane's.

In the first sentence, the possessive *Brent's* precedes the noun it identifies, *books*. In the second, the possessive noun *Jane's* indicates possession and the thing possessed, *books*.

Study the following examples. Why are examples *a*, *b*, and *c* correct and examples *d*, *e*, and *f* incorrect?

Correct: a. The students left the papers on the instructor's desk.
              b. The students' papers are on the two instructors' desks.
              c. The papers on the instructor's desk are the students'.
Incorrect: d. The students' left the papers on the instructors desk.
              e. The students papers are on the two instructor's desks.
              f. The papers' on the instructors desk are the students.

Practice

In which of the following sentences is the possessive form used correctly? Place a *C* before each correct sentence.

1. —— Both twins' medicine is on the kitchen table.

2. —— Her two sisters' left for Florida this morning.

3. —— My cousin's took me to dinner last night.

4. —— The children's toys are in the trunk of Gail's car.

5. —— Three supervisor's quit this morning.

Sentences 1 and 4 are correct. The possessives in the other sentences should be plurals:

sisters   cousins   supervisors

These nouns are **not** followed by a noun naming something or someone belonging to them.

```
Do exercises D-1 and D-2
```

NAME _____ **DATE** _____

I. Complete the following chart to show the possessive form of the singular noun given.

EXAMPLE

Singular noun	Singular possessive	Thing possessed
student	_**student's**_	quiz

Singular noun	Singular possessive	Thing possessed
brother	1. _____	farm
employee	2. _____	benefits
nephew	3. _____	tricycle
grandfather	4. _____	coin
gardener	5. _____	rakes
friend	6. _____	letter
computer	7. _____	keyboard

II. In the following chart, first change the singular noun to a plural form; then write the possessive.

EXAMPLE

Singular noun	Plural noun	Plural possessive	Thing possessed
manager	_managers_	_managers'_	meeting

Singular noun	Plural noun	Plural possessive	Thing possessed
cat	1. _____	_____	tails
governor	2. _____	_____	mansions
child	3. _____	_____	homework
actress	4. _____	_____	salaries
church	5. _____	_____	steeples
fox	6. _____	_____	tails
tutor	7. _____	_____	schedules

NAME _____ **DATE** _____

> Study the examples carefully. Rewrite each group of sentences as one sentence by using possessive forms. Copy your sentence on the line.

EXAMPLES

Gail has a new coat. The coat needs to be hemmed.

Combination: *Gail's new coat needs to be hemmed.* _____

═══

1. Sarah has a cousin. The cousin cannot come to the party.

   Combination: _____

2. Brian has a vegetable garden. The vegetable garden is bordered by lilies.

   Combination: _____

3. The employees have a work schedule. The work schedule changes on December 1.

   Combination: _____

4. My parents have a friend. The friend has a daughter. The daughter can babysit on Saturday night.

   Combination: _____

   _____

5. Dr. Charles has an office. The office is on Main Street.

   Combination: _____

6. The teachers have a meeting. The meeting is scheduled for Monday afternoon.

   Combination: _____

7. Lynn has a new job. The new job starts next week.

   Combination: _____

8. My sister has a boyfriend. The boyfriend has a collie. The collie is tied up in the backyard.

   Combination: _____

   _____

9. The Cub Scouts have a meeting. The meeting is in the gym.

   Combination: _____

10. My grandparents have a beach house. The beach house was damaged during the hurricane.

    Combination: _____

    _____

Spelling Principal Parts of Verbs

Like some nouns, some verbs change their endings before adding suffixes.

RULE 1: VERBS ENDING IN SOUNDS OF S, CH, X, SH, Z

Most verbs form the third person singular of the present tense by adding an -*s*:

walk, walks	sleep, sleeps
see, sees	appeal, appeals

However, when verbs end in the sounds *s, ch, x, sh, j(dg)*, or *z*, we must add -*es* to form a full syllable at the end of the verb:

kiss, kisses	buzz, buzzes
confess, confesses	match, matches
judge, judges	push, pushes

RULE 2: VERBS ENDING IN Y

When a verb ends in the letter *y* preceded by a **consonant**, we change the *y* to *i* before adding -*es* for the third person singular or -*ed* for the past or past participle:

Verb	First Person Singular	Past and Past Participle
try	tries	tried
cry	cries	cried
study	studies	studied
reply	replies	replied
apply	applies	applied

If the *y* at the end is preceded by a **vowel**, the *y* is not changed:

enjoy	enjoys	enjoyed
stay	stays	stayed
play	plays	played
employ	employs	employed

RULE 3: VERBS ENDING IN E

For most verbs, the past and the past participle are formed by adding -*ed* to the main verb:

walk	walked
wink	winked

However, if a verb ends in *e*, we add only the *-d*:

taste	tasted
use	used

Also, for main verbs ending in *e*, we drop the *e* before adding *-ing* for the present participle. Notice also that in the following examples the consonant at the end is **not** doubled:

write	writing	**not** writting
bite	biting	**not** bitting
drive	driving	
smoke	smoking	
hope	hoping	**not** hopping

RULE 4: VERBS ENDING IN A SINGLE CONSONANT

For some verbs, we double the final consonant before adding *-ed* to form the past or the past participle and before adding *-ing* to form the present participle. The final consonant is doubled only under these conditions:

1. The word has only one syllable, or, if it has more than one, the accent is on the last syllable.
2. The final consonant is preceded by a short vowel sound.

Look at the following chart:

One syllable, short vowel:	plan	planned, planning
One syllable, long vowel:	fail	failed, failing (the *l* is not doubled)
Two syllables, accent on second:	equip	equipped, equipping
Two syllables, accent on first:	happen	happened, happening (the *n* is not doubled)

Practice the rules by applying them to the following pairs of words. Why are some consonants doubled and others are not?

fit	fitted	fitting	mail	mailed	mailing
omit	omitted	omitting	bail	bailed	bailing

Do exercises E-1 and E-2

NAME _____ **DATE** _____

       Use the rules in Appendix E to write the principal parts of the following regular verbs.

EXAMPLES

Main verb	Past	Past participle	Present Participle
bark	*barked*	*barked*	*barking*
beg	*begged*	*begged*	*begging*
state	*stated*	*stated*	*stating*
fry	*fried*	*fried*	*frying*

Main verb	Past	Past participle	Present participle
1. try	_____	_____	_____
2. stay	_____	_____	_____
3. possess	_____	_____	_____
4. stoop	_____	_____	_____
5. study	_____	_____	_____
6. prefer	_____	_____	_____
7. erase	_____	_____	_____
8. dry	_____	_____	_____
9. omit	_____	_____	_____
10. escort	_____	_____	_____
11. trace	_____	_____	_____
12. occur	_____	_____	_____
13. open	_____	_____	_____
14. worry	_____	_____	_____
15. wish	_____	_____	_____

NAME _____ DATE _____

     Some of the sentences have an incorrectly spelled verb. Cross out each incorrectly spelled verb and write the correct spelling above it. If the sentence is correct, write *C* before it.

EXAMPLE

_____ The soccer team is ~~hopping~~ *hoping* to win the division title.

1. _____ Alex copyed Jane's class notes.

2. _____ My husband stopped smokking and started exercising.

3. _____ Ray and Gail are planing a vacation to Switzerland.

4. _____ My uncle offerred to help me with my math problems.

5. _____ Four students droped English last week.

6. _____ Alison is writing a letter to her boyfriend in the Army.

7. _____ The band is practicing for next week's concert.

8. _____ I studied my history notes for three hours last night.

9. _____ Matt married his best friend's sister.

10. _____ Edna always worryes about her daughter's grades.

11. _____ Anna and Ken are useing their new wood stove this winter.

12. _____ I pitied the victims of the flood.

13. _____ My boss orderred new furniture and a new carpet for my office.

14. _____ Fred accidentally omitted two paragraphs of his paper.

15. _____ The class listenned very carefully to the directions.

16. _____ Glen tried to replace the fan belt on his car.

17. _____ Walter is bakeing an angel food cake for the card party.

18. _____ My sister begged my parents for a kitten.

19. _____ I prefered the lasagna over the manicotti.

20. _____ The collision occurred at exactly midnight.

Index